The Planning Game

Trading information is an essential aspect of the negotiations that underpin planning practice across the globe. In this book, Alex Lord uses information economics to outline a way of thinking about these negotiations that places the strategies that actors in the planning game use at the heart of the debate.

Dialogue between economics and planning theorists has been, until now, rare. Lord argues that information economics' toolkit, game theory – including well-known examples such as the Prisoners' dilemma, the Stag hunt game and Follow the leader – offers an analytical framework ideally suited to unpacking planning processes.

This use of game theory to understand how counterparties interact draws together two distinct bodies of literature: first, the mainstream economics treatment of games in abstract form and second, accounts of actual bargaining in planning practice from a host of international empirical studies.

Providing a novel alternative to existing theories of planning, *The Planning Game* provides an explanation of how agencies interact in shaping the trajectory of development through the application of game theory to planning practice.

Alex Lord worked in the financial services industry before completing a Ph.D. at the University of Manchester's School of Environment and Development. He is currently lecturer in the Department of Civic Design at the University of Liverpool.

The Planning Game

An information economics
approach to understanding urban
and environmental management

Alex Lord

Routledge
Taylor & Francis Group

LONDON AND NEW YORK

First published 2012
by Routledge
2 Park Square, Milton Park, Abingdon, Oxon OX14 4RN

Simultaneously published in the USA and Canada
by Routledge
711 Third Avenue, New York, NY 10017

*Routledge is an imprint of the Taylor & Francis Group, an informa
business*

British Library Cataloguing in Publication Data
A catalogue record for this book is available from the British
Library

Library of Congress Cataloging in Publication Data
Lord, Alex.
The planning game : an information economics approach to
understanding urban and environmental management / Alex Lord.
p. cm.
Includes bibliographical references and index.
1. City planning – Economic aspects. 2. Regional planning –
Economic aspects. 3. Urban economics. 4. Urban policy. I. Title.
II. Title: Information economics approach to understanding urban
and environmental management.
HT166.L668 2012
307.1'216 – dc23
2011034593

ISBN: 978-0-415-59905-4 (hbk)
ISBN: 978-0-415-59906-1 (pbk)
ISBN: 978-0-203-12744-5 (ebk)

Typeset in Goudy
by Taylor & Francis Books

Contents

List of text boxes and figures   vi

Introduction   1

Part I   7

1 Planning in the 'information age'   9

2 Is there something wrong with planning theory?   20

3 Is there an alternative way of understanding planning?   40

4 The infusion of economics into planning thought   54

Part II   69

5 Introducing the planning game   71

6 Conflict, power and risk   86

7 Bargaining, negotiation and tactics   113

8 Team games, coalitions and collaboration   141

9 Putting the planning game in context   163

References   174
Index   199

Text boxes and figures

Figures

4.1 The Stag hunt game   65
5.1 The classic Prisoners' dilemma   82
6.1 Matching pennies   90
6.2 The Prisoners' dilemma (formal)   92
6.3 Follow the leader I   98
6.4 Follow the leader II   101
6.5 Follow the leader III   102
6.6 Follow the leader I with an intervention by Nature   104
6.7 Utility functions   110
6.8 Nash bargaining programme   110
7.1 Chicken in strategic form   119
7.2 Quiche when Player A is 'tough'   125
7.3 Quiche when Player A is 'weak'   125
7.4 Quiche with Nature (complete, unreduced)   126
7.5 Quiche in reduced form where Nature chooses types   128
7.6 Quiche of figure 7.5 in strategic form   128
8.1 Potential coalition formation under three-player
     cooperation   150
8.2 McCain's waste game   151

Boxes

4.1 Getting less than you bargained for: deficiencies in
     planning theory's account of 'deal making'   60
5.1 Making collaborative planning systems   75
5.2 Giving the game away? Spatial planning as a vessel for
     neoliberalism   77

6.1 Game theory, cooperation and sustainable development in the USA and Mexico 93

6.2 Tit for tat in Taipei 96

6.3 Who competes in environmental planning? Local authority competition in the USA and Britain 104

7.1 Playing a waiting game: do planners use delaying tactics? 120

7.2 Quiche and the planning gain game 135

8.1 Breaking up is hard to do: curious planning marriages and why they work ... 148

8.2 When three is not a crowd: coalitions in planning theory and practice 152

8.3 The 'essentials': are leaders needed to engineer collaboration in planning practice? 160

9.1 Is game theory any use? Planning as 'beauty contest' or auction? 167

Introduction

Information could be said to be the most valuable commodity in environmental planning. The relationship between knowledge and information has been the central concern for all schools of planning theory from the rationalists' first reification of quasi-scientific data to the communicative turn's argument that planning should seek to learn from and respond to the local knowledge of community consciousness. Objective, subjective; positive, normative; scientific, intuitive; facts, fictions: interpreting information in all its forms is the first and last step in the practice of environmental planning.

In taking this wide variety of conceptions of what information might comprise as its primary interest this book seeks to develop a connection between how planning theorists and some economists think about information. In so doing it introduces a strain of economics – information economics – to which planning theory has had only the most limited exposure. Taking a cue from this branch of economics it is argued in the chapters that follow that the ways in which information is used and interpreted by counterparties in environmental planning can be usefully thought of as a game – the planning game – in which the information to which players have access plays a significant role in determining how we manage change in the urban and natural environments.

Taking planning theory in this direction forces a confrontation with the methodological language of information economics, game theory, and the idea that often the outcome of planning games is the result of strategic behaviour – negotiation and bargaining being two examples – that is not well accounted for by existing theory. The ultimate destination is, therefore, a new way of thinking about planning. En route the volume seeks to unravel the various ways in which we have theorised urban and environmental management in the past and shows how those areas where our theories seem to lack purchase against the material world can be explained by reference to how they conceptualise information, its derivation and its relationship to a theory of knowledge.

More specifically, through an engagement with analytic philosophy this book hopes to draw an epistemological connection between the philosophy of language and information economics that might ultimately aid our understanding of urban and environmental management. Using the work of the principal figure in this movement, Ludwig Wittgenstein, information economics is put in epistemological context, as an endeavour that seeks to elucidate social interactions – to Wittgenstein, the 'language games' we play in daily life. The result is a theory of planning that seeks to explain in a value-free manner the ways in which agents relate to one another and the strategies they might employ in playing the planning game.

This forces us to go beyond the fundamental recognition that information economics demands – that information could come in many forms, have different values to different players and may be costly to transmit and/or obtain – and develop a micro-agential account of how the social interactions that these broad acknowledgements entail might be explained.

What this book seeks to achieve

To accomplish this, the first and overriding objective of this volume is to parse a wide body of literature – both theoretical and empirical – to demonstrate how it elucidates a new way of thinking about planning predicated on information economics. Several factors have prevented this exchange in the past. First, most of the theoretical work is published by, and for, a 'mainstream' economics audience, sources with which planning academics have rarely engaged, as planners and economists are said to 'travel on different tracks to different destinations' (Adams and Tiesdell, 2010: 189; see also Evans, 2003). This is not to suggest that planners are solely to blame for the lack of dialogue; for their part those working with information economics' methodological language, game theory, have 'tend[ed] to exert little effort toward making their results accessible to a less technical readership' (Landa and Meirowitz, 2009: 428).

To correct this failing this volume seeks to introduce game theory to a planning audience by presenting some standard games that have a particular relevance for urban and environmental planning. All the examples in this volume are premised on existing contributions that draw attention to the types of game we play in planning. To reinforce this point the chapters that are most concerned with setting out principles of game theory – Chapters 5, 6, 7, and 8 – include text boxes where empirical accounts of its application to issues of interest to planners, both urban and environmental, are isolated from the surrounding theoretical discussion.

A second reason inhibiting a fuller engagement between planning and information economics is that much of the empirical work is confined to specialist journals and, in some rare cases, published in a language other than English (for example, Asami, 1993; Hideshima *et al.*, 1995). The result is that considerable advances – again both in conceptual and empirical research – have gone almost totally unacknowledged by planning theorists despite the work having significant bearing on many of the questions with which the subject is most preoccupied: for example, how do coalitions form and with what effect?; and how might we account for power relations in those aspects of planning practice that rely on bargaining and negotiation?

To answer questions such as these the volume is split into two components. The first section (Chapters 1–4) seeks to articulate the rationale for a reconsideration of what a theory of planning should seek to achieve. This builds on a frustration felt by both theorists and practitioners alike that there is a mismatch between the capacity of existing planning theory to inform, or even explain, practice: the well-established 'theory–practice gap' (Alexander, 1997). The sequence of chapters in this first part of the book seeks to diagnose the problems that have been said to afflict existing planning theory and propose an alternative built from entirely different epistemological foundations. To this end the intellectual parentage of information economics is contrasted with that of other schools of planning theory such as the positivist informed 'rational' school (Chapter 1) and the phenomenology that informs post-positivist accounts such as the Habermasian strain in the more recently dominant communicative turn (Chapter 2). The final two chapters in the opening part of the volume situate information economics within its own philosophical lineage as arising from, and using a common language with, analytic philosophy (Chapter 3), before contrasting an information economics interpretation of planning with past experiments designed to marry welfare, neoclassical and institutional economics with planning (Chapter 4). Of these two chapters the first, Chapter 3, draws heavily upon the work of Ludwig Wittgenstein, in particular his 'later' philosophy as set out in *Philosophical Investigations* (1953) and in contrast to his earlier thinking captured in *Tractatus Logico-Philosophicus* (1922). Both books take the format of a numbered set of propositions.

Throughout, the convention adopted in the vast majority of the literature on Wittgenstein has been followed, using the abbreviation TLP or PI followed by the appropriate clause number to refer to elements of the *Tractatus* and *Philosophical Investigations*, respectively. The second part of the volume provides an engagement with game theory, the methodological language of information economics. Throughout, care has been taken not to use the terms interchangeably. Where a specific investigation is the objective, the expression 'game theory' has been used to establish a focus on the detail of a game-type of particular relevance to planning practice; where this illustrates a point of wider significance to the issue of how information is valued, revealed and traded, reference is made to the parent discipline, 'information economics'. With this in mind Chapter 5 sets out the traditional 'planning game' as an encounter conditioned by the 'rule book' of planning law and introduces the metaphor of a 'black box' to indicate the complex, and often hidden, workings of planning practice – the task of theory being to unpack its contents. A core distinction is drawn between existing theories of planning and one derived from information economics, which uses game theory to delve into the black box, whatever its contents might be – including the strategic behaviour of signalling and screening information and the potential duplicity of 'cheap talk'.

Chapters 6 and 7 build on the work of Chapter 5 by introducing non-cooperative game theory as a method of understanding those instances where the planning game is a competitive one. In this respect conflict is the focus of Chapter 6, whilst games of strategy that include the potential for participants to mask their real intentions are covered in Chapter 7. Examples of standard, classic games are used throughout to illustrate some of the most fundamental concepts in game theory. In the vast majority of cases these examples include 'pay-offs' expressed as integers. In many cases the formal structure of a game could have been expressed without recourse to the arbitrary assignment of values; however, the use of values makes the games easier to follow for the reader and also means the games are truer to their original articulation. To leaven the diet of game theory in these chapters, as noted above, text boxes are included that summarise the application of the theoretical topic under consideration to a specific example of urban and/or environmental management.

Whilst Chapters 6 and 7 summarise some of the most pertinent features of non-cooperative game theory, it would be odd and unrealistic to believe that all the games we play in planning are unerringly competitive. Its counterpoint, cooperative game theory, provides a powerful way of thinking about those instances where coalitions of interest emerge. But why do the coalitions that ultimately form prevail? are they durable?; why do some counter-intuitive coalitions endure? Chapter 8 uses cooperative game theory to investigate these issues before Chapter 9 serves to close the circle by providing an account of how the planning game runs on self-determined rules analogous to the way Wittgenstein understands the rules of our language games to be established by speakers themselves in the act of using their own language. The resulting research agenda has implications for both policy makers and academics. Consequently Chapter 9 ends with some suggestions for how the project of infusing planning theory with information economics might be advanced; similarly, the use of game theory to devise new and innovative ways for policy makers to redefine the planning game are proposed. Neither is exhaustive, and the development of both the intellectual project and its policy counterpart are areas that will benefit from the input of others.

As with any book that seeks to develop a connection between two or more existing schools of thought I have, throughout this volume, necessarily drawn extensively on the work of others. In the chapters on planning theory it goes without saying that the work of Allmendinger, Faludi, Forester, Friedman, Healey, Innes, Taylor and Tewdwr-Jones, together with their various collaborators, has been essential. On information economics in general the three economists who won a Nobel award for their work in the area – Akerlof, Spence and Stiglitz – have been a constant guide; and the games that comprise the bulk of the second half of the volume owe a great debt to Axelrod, Nash, Dixit and Skeath, Kreps and Cho, Rasmusen and, particularly, Binmore. Finally, on Wittgenstein's philosophy of language, Grayling's, Pears's and, especially, McGinn's books have been instrumental. The debt owed to these writers is great but, as ever, the responsibility for any omissions, errors or oversights resides with the author.

Part I

1 Planning in the 'information age'

If, as was argued in the Introduction, information is the most valuable commodity in the conduct of environmental planning, our next questions must surely be: how do we determine what information is 'legitimate' in arriving at planning decisions?; and how might that information then be gathered and subsequently converted into knowledge? The first issue – how widely we interpret what constitutes 'legitimate' information – is of critical significance for environmental planning for several reasons. First, it exposes a clear divide between the two principal academic ways of thinking about planning practice. Indeed, their varying attitude to what types of information might be appropriate with which to furnish planning practice has often been understood to be the core distinction between planning theories derived from an almost unreconstituted Comtian positivism and an inherently normative version drawn from Habermasian sociology. Second, for a discipline such as environmental planning, with a close association to a world of professional practice, the likely correspondence between the quality of policy outcomes and the quality of the information used in the decision-making process makes the question of what types of data are held to be admissible the most fundamental question. Finally, it forces us to confront epistemological questions about how we derive knowledge from information – for example, how do we translate environmental impact studies or community consultation exercises into knowledge? This prompts us to consider what sources of data might exist and how the data that is collected is used to devise an evidence base for planning practice.

In beginning to address these questions this chapter is principally concerned with setting them in historical context, considering the development of planning theory from its first modern expression in the early part of the twentieth century through to the beginning of more recent post-positivist developments such as communicative

theory, which will be the subject of Chapter 2. In taking this chronological focus the purpose is to consider the enduring influence of
the positivist rationalist school, particularly on practice, and of the
Habermasian sociologists, especially on theory, before diagnosing the
potential epistemological shortcomings with both, and proffering an
alternative, in Chapter 3.

Planning, information and evidence-based policy

The potential for public policy to be influenced by information,
particularly scientific research, stretches back to the Enlightenment
(Sanderson, 2003) and, more distantly, to the 'Philosopher Kings' of
Plato's *Republic* (Lee and Lee translation, 2003). Its more recent
history has been understood as coinciding with the early–mid-
twentieth-century heyday of modernism (for a review, see Nutley
et al., 2002; see also Lasswell, 1951; Lindblom, 1959). In environmental
planning this is perhaps best dated, following Hall and Tewdwr-Jones
(2010: 6) to, approximately, the period 1920–60 and understood as
exemplified in the work of Geddes; in particular the identification of
the 'survey-analysis-plan' approach, which has been understood as
entirely consonant with the principles of high modernism's faith in
progress through science (Faludi and Waterhout, 2006a). Such is the
standing of Geddes as the forefather of urban and environmental
planning that there now exists a vast corpus of work, both biographical and analytical, devoted to cataloguing the methods of planning advocated in his writings, all of which emphasise his role in
transforming planning into a 'scientific' endeavour, as Dehaene (2002: 48)
argues:

> Discussions about survey in urbanism introduced models of sci
> entific thinking into a profession which was still dominated by
> architects. The introduction of scientific methods was believed to
> grant the profession greater authority, and expanded the scope of
> its activities. On the surface, the introduction of scientific meth
> ods seems to constitute a radical redefinition of urbanism, turning
> it overnight from a liberal art into a positive science.

Critically this revolution, here portrayed as the transition of planning from art to science, was perhaps more complex. For Geddes the
'science' of the survey in generating fine-grained information about
the nature of the place for which a plan was being prepared was
understood to be a necessary, but preliminary, stage upon which the

subsequent art and design of planning as an outgrowth of architecture were incumbent. This idea of science first, art later can be seen in much of Geddes's work, where 'information', understood as the quasi-scientific modelling of human kind's relationship with the urban and natural environments, is constructed as precursor to imagining the possible:

> The corresponding constructive endeavour is now no mere School of traditional learning or of useful information. It is one of science in a new and reorganised sense; one of philosophy also, one of ideals above all ... The mere observations of the senses and their records in memory become transformed into the images of the poet, the imagery too of the artist, for art proper is only thus born.
>
> (Geddes, 1905: 59)

For many authors the planning that this approach spawned went on to become the dominant paradigm for both the theory and practice of urban and environmental management throughout the middle years of the twentieth century (for a review, see Muller, 1992). Moreover in the 1960s and 1970s the continued trajectory of this conception of planning, rooted in an *a priori* judgement about what types of information are of most use to the planner, can be seen in the subsequent development of the 'rational' (see Meyerson and Banfield, 1955; Faludi, 1973) and 'systems' (see McLoughlin, 1969) theories of planning. Whilst recasting the activity as a goal-orientated, problem-solving exercise, echoing the 'management by objectives' literature popular at the time, to some extent distinguishes these theories from Geddes's conception of planning as well-informed creativity, in other respects the parallels between earlier and later positivist theories are significant. For example both incarnations draw on pseudo-scientific analogy: evolutionary biology in the case of Geddes (Muller, 1992) and cybernetics in systems theory (McLoughlin, 1969) and, to a lesser extent, in the rationalist school of thought (Thomas, 1979). In the case of Faludi (1973: 25), responsible for the seminal articulation of the comprehensive/procedural-rationalist conception of planning, this supports an understanding of planning that echoes strongly that of Geddes, based upon the 'rational process of thought and action which ultimately aims (as science does) at promoting human growth'. As this notion of rationality carries with it a compulsion to base decision-making processes on reason, it follows that information is no less central to fulfilling the positivist epistemological requirements of this theory than that of the survey-before-plan approach of Geddes.

With information of this quasi-scientific nature understood to form the orthodox basis of planning in many contexts by the 1970s (or in some cases before), the subsequent years, it might be argued, have not seen a significant diminution in the reification of positivist data, particularly amongst policy makers. The emergence in the 1980s of tools such as Geographical Information Systems software has paved the way for more refined geodemographic analyses and the construction of more detailed indicators, models, forecasts, projections and geographically weighted regressions (Brunsdon and Fotheringham, 1996), the reliability of which is fundamentally dependent on the quality of the data upon which they are predicated. The result is that by the 1990s the use of quantitative indicators and metrics had become a staple part of planning practice around the globe. Indeed, as the computational tools at the disposal of the planning profession have become ever more sophisticated it is clear that, by the new century, information and communications technologies have come to play an increasingly prominent role in how planning policy is designed and implemented. The dawn of a mass-communication 'information age' makes this a role forecast to grow, not diminish (Drummond and French, 2008).

Understanding the longevity and persistence of this trend is accomplished by reference to a wider movement in public administration that emphasises the desirability for policy to be unequivocally based on ostensibly apolitical, objective evidence. This has been particularly relevant in planning where the value of impartial evidence might be twofold: first, to legitimise policy choices as consistent with an objective construction of the 'public interest' and, second, to quell the controversy that would accompany a more conspicuously political decision-making process. The resultant conception of planning as part of a public sector designed to collect and respond to information has given rise to a vast corpus of academic literature that has variously understood this type of evidence-based policy as either a progressive activity associated with the New Public Management movement (Newman, 2001; Nutley and Davies, 2000; Nutley et al., 2000; Pawson, 2002a, 2002b) or else the elision of independent research with policy activism (Bridges, 1998; Harris, 2002; Solesbury, 2001). In addition, for some, the political impulse behind this drive to connect policy with evidence has been understood as part of a 'post-ideological' (Painter and Clarence, 2001: 1215) strain in the progressive movements that dominated politics in those nation states where evidence-based policy has enjoyed most prominence since the 1990s: Clinton's Democrats, *Die Neue Mitte* in Merkel's Germany and the New

Labour project of Blair and Brown. On this account, the idea that policy could be led by evidence rather than conviction has been neatly summarised by the aphorism, 'what matters is what works' (Southern, 2001: 264; see also Davies *et al.*, 2000; Perri 6, 2002).

Extending this line of thought, others (Newman, 2001; Stoker, 1999) have seen evidence-based policy as inextricably bound up with the transition from government to governance (for instance, Rhodes, 1997). The erosion of state power by the forces of trans-national economic organisation, it is argued, necessitates organs of the state at all territorial scales to recognise the multiplicity of stakeholders with a de facto involvement in the design and delivery of policy and so forge partnerships that acknowledge and mirror this diversity (Pawson, 2006). Across the globe in areas as wide ranging as education policy (Pirrie, 2001; Simons *et al.*, 2003), healthcare (El Ansari *et al.*, 2001), social work (Humphries, 2003) and urban policy (Dobbs and Moore, 2002) the necessity for evidence to instil a shared purpose and sense of coherency by which partnership-based governance might be sustained has been identified (see Young *et al.*, 2002). For instance Nutley *et al.*, (2002: 4; see also Laycock, 2000; Nutley *et al.*, 2000) advise that:

gaining consensus or even widespread agreement will not be easy. The need to secure some common ground between diverse stakeholders does, however, point the way to more positive approaches. The traditional separation between the policy arena, practitioners communities and the research community has largely proven unhelpful. Much of the more recent thinking in this area now emphasises the need for partnerships if common ground is to be found.

This logic is easy to see: if policy – such as that in urban and environmental management – is to be made and implemented by complex networks of actors, some public, some private, some hybrid, some third sector, it follows that a binding rationale for action is essential to realise coherency and coordination. More simply, as Powell and Moon (2001: 48) argue, what is required for this style of governance to work is 'an evidence base for partnership'.

Making evidence count

In addition to the argument that evidence binds together the partnerships needed to devise and deliver joined-up policy, an alternative view has emphasised a loss of public confidence in political process, politicians and policy makers across the globe as explaining the move towards public policy supported by ostensibly impartial, objective evidence (Norris, 1999; Stoker, 2010). If decisions can be made that rely purely on hard facts, political wilfulness and bias might be nullified, so the argument goes. When added to the simultaneous austerity in public finances encountered in many states following the international financial crisis of 2007 onwards, this perhaps explains increased scrutiny of public spending on activities such as urban regeneration and regulatory practices like environmental planning and a corresponding demand to justify decisions on the grounds of being 'useful' and 'relevant' (Solesbury, 2002). But what is useful or relevant is itself an inherently subjective matter.

With respect to environmental planning this throws into sharp relief the issue of normative information. Whilst it is clear that planning might need to take into account positivist research across a whole range of areas – geodemographic change, environmental assessments of various types, transport patterns, changes in the demand for different types of housing, to name only a few – much of the daily work of a planner (Healey, 1992a) is concerned with weighing judgements. Sometimes this might be testimonies, for example, about the aesthetic value of historic built environments and the quality of life implications of access to green space; these are important issues that are not easily captured by the positivist framework. However, they might equally well be subjective *interpretations* of what is ostensibly objective data. Just as in all aspects of the social sciences where the variables under consideration are inherently complex, deciphering a coherent evidence base when confronted by information of such differing types is inevitably fraught with difficulty (Martin and Sanderson, 1999).

It is from this perspective that many have come to criticise the positivist conception of what counts as information. Specific to environmental planning, in commenting on the work of Taylor (1980), Faludi (1986: 38) describes the approach pioneered by Geddes as informed by a 'crudely positivist view of scientific method', an assessment echoed by McLoughlin's (1969: 125) critique that the rationalist approach is pregnant with the 'tendency towards collecting information for its own sake, unselective and uncritical wallowing in facts and figures'. Sharing this perspective, the first articulations of communicative planning theory in the 1980s (Forester, 1980, 1989) date the beginnings of a post-positivist wave of planning theory that has ever since urged academics and practitioners alike to take normative information seriously and ensure that plans respond effectively to the subjective aspirations and preferences of communities. For such communicative theorists the information derived from the testimonies of residents and representative groups is just as vital in framing good planning policy as that of experts. In short, the opinions of the people who have to live with planning decisions should feature at least as prominently in the policy- and decision-making processes as the bureaucrat's understanding of what constitutes the public interest, premised frequently on technical analyses conducted at city hall, remote from the site of any intervention. The effects of this agenda on practice have been profound. For example, in reflecting on these ideas Nadin (2006: 21; see also Box 5.1, Chapter 5 of this volume), using the example of the English system of planning, urges a reconsideration of the types of information that might be useful to planners. In identifying connections that run between different types of information within an evidence base, the author suggests something much more expansive than the narrow definition of information identified by the positivist nexus in planning thought:

> The finding that responses from community consultation are sometimes referred to as 'evidence' deserves further comment. Material arising from community and stakeholder engagement is different from what is indicated in PPS12 [*Planning Policy Statement 12*] as 'evidence' … . Its use in developing and evaluating alternatives and as part of the justification of choices that are made is normal and appropriate however. The material that emerges from the engagement of stakeholders and the community can add real knowledge about the place and the community, because of the authoritative bodies involved and because of the familiarity with the area.
> … There is a reciprocal relationship between other types of evidence and community responses however. Information provided to those engaging in the process – through the issues and options consultation stage for instance – enables people to understand better what the local development framework is seeking to do or needs to do. This enables them to make informed representations that are likely to be more useful to the local planning authority, or more effective in influencing the emerging plan.

The underlying theme is a distinction between information derived from research of a positivist nature – housing and labour market studies, environmental impact assessment and habitats regulations – and that gathered through the participation of stakeholders and communities in consultation processes. On this account best practice for planners is constructed as gathering a wide range of information that can be attuned to local circumstances through community participation. To reinforce this point Nadin (2006: 21) concludes that:

> A wide and inclusive view needs to be taken of what constitutes evidence. Anything which assists in understanding a place and a community, and which is used in deciding what should be part of the plan should be seen as evidence.

But, of course, introducing more evidence does not remove the potential for those involved in the decision-making process to *use* that evidence to construct a selective reading of the 'facts' that supports a particular position they may have an interest in advancing. In short, broadening the evidence base does not overwrite the capacity of individuals and groups engaged in the planning process to act strategically. Under such circumstances – perhaps where one interpretation of the evidence might be inconsistent with another – how is the planner to evaluate what is the correct point of view (Pawson, 2002a, 2002b, 2006)? This echoes long-standing fears (see Schön, 1973, 1983) regarding the manner in which evidence may be misinterpreted, misrepresented and/or distorted in the practice of policy making that remain a concern for many, characterised by Parsons (2002: 43), paraphrasing Lindblom (1959), as 'from muddling through to muddling up' (see also S. Harris, 2002; Solesbury, 2001; Young *et al.*, 2002). Further general misgivings have been said to exist regarding the shelf life of evidence: the process by which evidence ages and potentially becomes 'out of date', descriptive of a past world and, therefore, no longer of practical use to policy makers. Such limitations resulting from a mismatch between cycles of evidence gathering and policy implementation may inhibit a truly evidence-driven approach (for example, Pawson, 2002a, 2002b; Sabatier, 1986). Regardless, in planning systems around the globe the impulse to collect as much data as possible – both quasi-scientific and qualitative – remains as strong as ever (Lord and Hincks, 2010). For example Faludi and Waterhout (2006a; see also van Gestel and Faludi, 2005) note the increasingly prominent role of evidence in the national planning systems of many states in continental Europe, including Germany, France and the Netherlands, as well as through the work of the European Spatial

Planning Observatory Network (ESPON) at the European Union scale itself. Similar observations have also been made in relation to the evolution of evidence-based planning in the United States of America (Hoernig and Seasons, 2004).

What does this mean for planning practice?

It is against this backdrop that, by the turn of the new millennium, planning systems across the globe have come to represent sophisticated arbiters of information. In most Western contexts this now means that planning decisions are predicated on a vast array of increasingly complex data, from the environmental science of sustainability appraisal and the geodemographics of neighbourhood change, to the no less urgent matters voiced in community centres and residents' committees. The result is a cacophony of voices representing a wealth of data to be sorted, understood and *used* to make policy. From this perspective, whilst evidence-based planning both as a concept and as a practice is not new, the dawn of the 'information age' means the context within which, and the purposes for which, information is being collected has changed remarkably.

In this respect, collating information and turning it into the knowledge that the expression 'evidence base' implies can be seen to be the crucial ingredient in the formulation of good planning: a way, perhaps now the *only* valid way, of explaining prevailing contextual circumstances and imagining possible future scenarios. Moreover, the demand embedded in many systems to include regular monitoring (Wong, Baker and Kidd, 2006) implies a way of linking actions with outcomes and the potential for an evaluation of 'what works' – and, crucially, what does not. The result is yet more data to be collected, interpreted and used to adjust the objectives and activities of planning practice.

This account of how urban and environmental management has evolved exposes the underlying theme of this chapter: what is the relationship between the information we collect and the knowledge we derive from it? At root this question speaks to an historical debate between an antiquated notion of the information used in planning practice as value-free and a more modern conception of how information, derived from broader sources, might be socially constructed into an evidence-base (Faludi and Waterhout, 2006a, 2006b; Nadin, 2006). This fundamental differentiation of a product, 'evidence', from its constituent, 'information', is significant as it forces us to confront the full catalogue of different types of information with which the planner might be confronted and ask how raw data is ultimately recast as evidence (Davoudi, 2006a, 2006b).

As an academic discipline and a professional practice it would be both intellectually immature and politically unrealistic to suggest that planning could or should draw back from this clamour to collect information and construct evidence. However, it might be argued that the acquisitive nature that has come to characterise planning's relationship to information has resulted in us losing sight of two things. First, how has the information we seek to gather found its way into the policy discourse in the first place? how are data-gathering priorities decided, what sources of information are available (and, equally importantly, unavailable), how is the pertinent separated from the superfluous and how is meaning constructed from data? Second, how is information, once collected, *used* to create or reinforce a normalised form of practice based on a set of options constrained to what the evidence suggests is feasible? The implication of such questions is that we must consider how information might be used strategically by individuals and groups to create an impression that one course of action is more viable or desirable than alternatives.

This acknowledgement that actors may use information tactically to manipulate the planning process forces us to confront some questions that, in the rationalist's interpretation of a clean world of data-led planning, simply do not arise: to what extent might the sources from which data is drawn have a vested interest in its interpretation?; how do we adjudge the veracity of the information with which we are presented?; does information come at a price, does it have different values to different interests and is it tradeable between interest groups in the planning process?

This volume outlines an approach to such questions premised upon a return to first principles regarding the epistemological basis for planning theory. As such, the arguments presented here are less concerned with historical debates about the genuine novelty of each identified 'new' incarnation of evidence-based planning in various contexts but rather the advocacy of a way of thinking about planning that seeks to redefine our superficial understanding of information as a discernible *thing* – either technical, positivist data or else normative statements of community consciousness – with an interpretation of information as constituted by and through its *use*. As Chapter 3 goes on to note, this represents an epistemological shift from the positivism of the rationalist position and the phenomenology of theory derived from post-positivist sociology to a position in keeping with analytic philosophy. Before we can begin to contemplate this fundamental transition in the theory of knowledge upon which our understanding of planning is premised, however, we must first investigate the existing treatment of how information is articulated in the forums through which planning practice is enacted, as provided by communicative planning theory.

2   Is there something wrong with planning theory?

The culmination of the previous chapter showed the positivist form of planning theory, dominant since the post-war period, to have reached an impasse perhaps best dated to the late 1980s/early 1990s, at which point it was said to be 'lost' (Poulton, 1991: 225). Whilst its technocratic basis has guaranteed it a continued relevance to some aspects of planning practice, its incapacity to adequately account for differences of opinion regarding the relevance of data renders it incomplete as a theory of planning, giving rise to the widely-held view that it has subsequently given way to a 'post-positivist' (Allmendinger, 2002a: 3) wave of planning theory. The result has been a flurry of activity over the last 30 years, much of which, in emphasising the desirability of citizen participation, has encouraged planning to engage with ever more normative data, therefore acting as a corrective to the previous rationalist paradigm. Such has been the intensity of activity in this more recent branch of thought that one of the most prominent writers in the field has remarked, 'planning theory has been in a hyperactive state since the 1980s' (Allmendinger, 2002b: 78).

Whilst this period of intense activity has also produced numerous hybrids of sociology, politics and philosophy to understand urban and environmental management – from philosophical neoliberalism (Pennington, 1996, 2002) and the public choice school (Ehrman, 1990; Evans, 1988, 1991; Lewis, 1992) to critical and Marxist analyses (Ambrose, 1994) – the most popular way of thinking about planning since the 1990s is that which has come to be known as the 'communicative turn'. Seminally stated by Forester (1980, 1989) and Healey (1991, 1997), the multifarious directions in which these ideas have been taken represent the bulk of the work in the post-positivist field, incorporating treatments broadly faithful to the original formulae (Sager, 1994); advances made by the school's pioneering theorists (Forester, 1993, 1999b; Healey, 1993, 2009; Innes, 1992; Innes and

Booher, 2010); adjustments to take into account philosophical prag-matism (Harper and Stein, 1995; Stein and Harper, 2003; Hoch, 1995, 1996, 1997; Healey, 2009); various strands of twentieth-century French post-modernism and post-structuralism (Beauregard, 1989; Fischler, 2000; Hillier, 1993; Gunder and Hillier, 2009; Sandercock, 1998); network governance (Hillier, 2000); and institutional analysis (Sager, 2006; Healey, 1991, 2007a). This restless landscape has been well described by Healey (1991: 12), writing during the height of the hyperactivity in the early 1990s, as resulting from a process whereby 'the post-war consensus on planning thought, as in many other fields, had blown apart into a diversity of positions'.

This apparent burgeoning of interest in planning theory can per-haps be best understood as coinciding with tandem demands made from within practice for theory/theories that could guide planning's practical development. This desire to make theory 'relevant' speaks to the tendency noted by Tewdwr-Jones and Allmendinger (2002: 213) as 'a longing for urban planning and urban planning theorists to provide an overarching theoretical understanding and prescription for planning – a desire that has been ridiculed for some time (Reade, 1987)'. For an academic discipline that hovers precariously between a heavily politi-cised and policy-centred real world of professional practice and an academic sphere of conceptual ideas and analytical frameworks, the internal tension in the planning academy to be at once practically relevant and theoretically robust is easily understood. Yet this well-noted 'theory–practice gap' (for example, Alexander, 1997) is made ever wider by those occasions where our academic theorising seem-ingly comes up short of the mark – prompting the revisions, adjust-ments and modifications that explain the multiplicity of nuanced accounts described as the 'explosion' (Allmendinger, 2002b: 82) in the planning theory literature noted above. Finding a bridge to make theory pertinent for practice is clearly no easy task, although an essential one.

Diagnosing the reasons for this apparent schism between theory and its practical utility is the principal objective of this chapter. By revisiting the epistemological basis of the two principal 'schools' of planning theory – the Comtian positivism of the rationalists outlined in Chapter 1 and, at more length, the phenomenology of the com-municative turn and its offshoots – grounds are found for reconsid-ering the relationship of planning theory to the types of information to which planning practice gives rise. As aspects of the critique of the rationalist paradigm have already been outlined, remarks in this chapter will be confined to philosophical arguments against positivism, its epistemological foundation, before the majority of this chapter turns to the development of the communicative turn including its articulations as 'collaborative' (Healey, 1997) and 'deliberative' (Forester, 1999a) planning theory. In so doing the great debt of placing the role of statements communicated by disparate groups in ordinary language at the core of these theories is acknowledged. However, their epistemological underpinnings are identified as inhibiting the communicative rationality's capacity to provide a strongly convincing account of how communicated information is translated first into knowledge and subsequently into policy and practice. In turn this creates a platform for a new approach to the conceptualisation of urban and environmental management based on a reconstruction of how we understand linguistic communication as set out in Chapter 3 and its application to outline a codified system of power relations in the second part of this volume.

What should planning theory seek to theorise?

For Taylor (1980) planning has two points of tangency with philosophy from which we derive the academic activity of planning theory. First there are epistemological questions that underpin the logic of the decisions we make in the name of urban and environmental management: what do we know about a state of affairs?; what do we *think* we know about a state of affairs?; how do we think we came to know it?; and so on. Second there are a series of ethical questions regarding how we might judge whether we have taken the right course of action: what grounds there are for believing that one planning decision is morally preferable to another; and what ethical assumptions are either explicit or implicit in the policies that emerge from this public activity of urban and environmental planning.

In relation to the first point Taylor, anticipating the post-positivist movement, goes on to successfully illustrate the limitations of what was, at the time, the prevailing rationalist response to epistemological questions at the core of planning theory. The Geddesian survey-analysis-plan approach, with which Faludi's (1973) 'rationalist' planning shared a positivist parentage, it was argued, falls foul of the same pitfalls as the philosophical school from which it is drawn – logical positivism (see Ayer, 1946; Carnap, 1959) – in that it rests on a very strict deductive method applied to an inevitably incomplete field of observation. To illustrate, when we say 'all forms of architectural style X are equated with crime and social distress', it takes just one witness of a counter-case to nullify the statement. As we can never

have a complete repository of all known examples, the circular verification principle of unfalsified empirical observation can never be
completed.

Even more tellingly, the 'verification principle' itself – that only
those statements that can be verified by empirical observation have
meaning – fails its own standard: as a statement it is a criterion of
significance that is not verifiable by recourse to any 'fact' in the
external world. The result is a philosophical position that allows only
analytic truths, the tautologies of mathematics and logic – true or false
by virtue of the definition of the signs employed in their statement
(such as the arithmetical operators: plus, minus, multiply, divide). The
extent of this reductionism resulted in a state of affairs where 'by the
late 1960s it was obvious that the movement had pretty much run its
course' (Fotion, 1995: 508).

Faced with such an unsustainable and degenerative philosophical
foundation a purely positivist approach to planning would not allow
us to even begin to analyse the wealth of statements made in the process by which some new buildings are brought into existence whilst
others are not; some old ones are demolished whilst others are set
aside for conservation; one set of environmental assets are protected
whilst others are surrendered to development. In a domain such as
planning, populated to a large extent by matters of opinion rather
than verifiable fact, it was perhaps most tellingly the incapacity of the
positivist paradigm to contend with any normative statement that
ultimately saw its theoretical wane. Seemingly, what would be needed
would be a theory that could speak to *both* an epistemology and an
ethics of planning.

It was against this backcloth that the approach to understanding
planning as a communicative activity emerged. Stated seminally by
Healey (1991, 1992b, 1993) and Forester (1989; 1993) this communicative turn sought to devise a far more expansive analytical framework: one that was embedded in the communicative processes that
typify the real life milieux of planning decisions. Drawing on an academic lineage that stretches back to the Enlightenment, the chief
architects of the school sought to root their thinking in the sociology
of discourse dynamics and, by marshalling concepts such as the 'best
argument' (Habermas, 1975), set out a theoretical standpoint that was
sufficiently wide to capture all those non-verifiable statements that had
slipped the positivist net. On such a reading it was argued that policy
making in the round, conducted openly through multi-stakeholder
engagement, would foster a situation that, even if it did not entail the
Habermasian paradigm of an 'ideal speech situation', would bring us

closer to a setting in which we could, first, understand the epistemo-logical grounding for planning decisions and, second, make ethical judgements about those decisions in light of the communicative pro-cesses by which they were brought about. The ethical quality of planning decisions could therefore be understood to be a function of the epistemological qualities of the communicative dynamics under which they were made: thus, Taylor's (1980) connection between the ethical and epistemological underpinning of how we understand planning could be forged.

Whilst this statement of the theory potentially obscures some differences between strands within the communicative turn – as Allmendinger and Tewdwr-Jones (2002: 6; see also N. Harris, 2002) note, the label is not necessarily indicative of one coherent position: 'what we today refer to as the communicative or collabora-tive turn in urban planning is in actuality a range of different theoretical pulses allied together by Habermasian and/or Giddensian thinking' – it does draw attention to something more important: their shared epistemological foundation.

To illustrate, we can take the work of the two thinkers principally associated with a theory of planning derived from communicative rationality: Forester and Healey. Certainly, for Healey, influenced perhaps as much by Giddens as Habermas, the emphasis on the rela-tionship between structure and agency in the decision-making process echoes Giddens's (1984) own contributions in the form of structura-tion theory. In the context of planning, Healey applies these ideas to develop an account, informed by institutional sociology and designed to better understand the interplay between micro-agency and meta-/meso-structural pressures through her identification of the role played by *style*, *representation* and *language* in the social construction of policy discourses. By focusing on these factors that condition the terms of engagement in the policy- and decision-making process Healey funda-mentally performs the service of placing the discursive arena within which the vast majority of planning decisions are made at the centre of planning theory.

Furthermore, by illustrating how the setting within which discus-sions take place might influence their outcome, Healey's contribution to planning theory has the added impact of suggesting policy applica-tions. If a *style* of engagement could be incorporated that ensured all participants had a voice; if a *representative* form could be adopted that diminished uneven power relations; and if a *language* could be encouraged that privileged perspicacity and veracity over obfuscation and dissimulation it follows that policy makers should have access to all the possible information that they might possibly need to arrive at a good decision.

Similarly the communicative turn's other principal theorist, Forester, allies his interest in Habermas with North American pragmatism (Forester, 1980, 1982), to outline a position similar to that of Healey, usually termed communicative and, subsequently, deliberative planning. The result is a difference of nuance which some have suggested is a function of the North American context within, and from, which Forester writes (Allmendinger, 2002b). Such contingent differences aside, Forester shares Healey's normative goals – 'let us stop rediscovering that power corrupts, and let's start figuring out what to do about the corruption' (Forester, 1999a: 9) – and seeks a similar response through the terms of a more integrative planning process: 'Reflecting alone, a practitioner learns; deliberating with others, practitioners learn together and craft strategies to act collaboratively' (Forester, 1999a: 4).

Seeing the conceptual promise of this Anglo-American theorisation of planning, a new generation of planning academics have set out to make their own theoretical modifications and put them to the empirical test, to the extent that, by the 1990s, the communicative turn was said to have become the dominant theoretical lens – in the West at least (Huxley and Yiftachel, 1998) – through which academics sought to understand urban and environmental management. Indeed, from the most significant statements of communicative planning theory (Forester, 1989; Healey, 1992b, 1993) until the high-water mark of its critique around a decade later (Allmendinger and Tewdwr-Jones, 2002), communicative planning theory had come, in the estimation of many, to occupy the position of a 'paradigm' (Alexander, 1998; Innes, 1995; Mandelbaum, 1996; Umenoto, 2001): although there has been much debate about what this label actually necessitates (Allmendinger, 1998; Allmendinger and Tewdwr-Jones, 2002; Huxley and Yiftachel, 1998). For policy makers, unconcerned by such academic hair splitting but instinctively persuaded by the theory, the search for the 'ideal speech situation' – a dialogue where undistorted communication can take place and in which the force of better reason expressed through persuasive argument can prevail – has been read into the reform of some of the world's best-known and well-studied planning systems such as those of the Netherlands (Voogd and Woltjer, 1999; Wolsink, 2003) and the UK (Kitchen and Whitney, 2004; see also Chapter 5 of this volume, Box 5.1). Consequently, devising forums and protocol that allow strategy to be developed in a setting characterised by the widest possible participation and in which the broadest range of voices could be heard and allowed to have an effect on the design of policy, which is at the heart of the communicative turn's transformative agenda, is now also at the heart of planning policy in some contexts.

However, for many commentators the promise of an epistemological-ethical marriage between Habermasian sociology and, variously, Giddensian structuration theory, North American pragmatism and, latterly, post-modern theory that underpins the most influential incarnations of communicative theory has left some important questions unanswered. As Taylor (1980: 159) presciently remarked, 'unfortunately, what is called planning theory still remains a vague mixture of philosophical judgement on the one hand and sociological theory on the other'. By the turn of the new century critique from many commentators writing from quite different traditions had exposed logical gaps in the edifice of communicative planning theory that seemed to weaken the case for its practical implementation. Some of these criticisms have been telling, although, as I hope to go on to show, not all. In response, there have been many attempts to make adjustments, sometimes subtle sometimes more radical, leading to the 'explosion' in planning theory identified at the beginning of this chapter. But how are we to understand the specifics of the critique that has led to this groundswell of activity in the defence and modification of communicative planning theory?

The communicative turn and its critics

Despite the undoubted influence of the communicative turn, and its merits in focussing the minds of theorists and practicing planners alike on the conduct of policy discourse, subsequent academic critique has posed a number of questions on which the theory is seemingly deficient. These may be broadly understood as falling into four categories, with references indicative of such critique in parentheses: that it does not mirror reality (Brand and Gaffikin, 2007; Tait and Campbell, 2000; Tewdwr-Jones and Thomas, 1998), that it is ill-equipped to explain the effects of transnational structuring forces, such as globalisation, on planning practice (Lauria and Whelan, 1995; Yiftachel and Huxley, 2000); that it focuses too much on process and insufficiently on outcomes (cf. Healey, 1990 and Innes and Booher, 1999 with Moote *et al.*, 1997); and that it undertheorises power relations (Flyvbjerg, 1996; Richardson, 1996). By far the most *theoretically* damaging of these is surely the gaps in the communicative turn's treatment of power relations (see also Flyvbjerg and Richardson,

2002; Mäntysalo, 2002). However, much of the oppositional literature has tended to conflate practical and theoretical weaknesses, using the empirical identification of some real world example said to be at odds with the predictions of the theory to illustrate its conceptual short-comings.

Rarely, if ever, has planning theory that draws upon communicative rationality been subjected to a systematic philosophical consideration of its epistemological basis – although this will be the objective of this and the following chapter of this volume. First, however, it is necessary to set out the principal objections directed at communicative theory by those dissatisfied with its seemingly limited explanatory value when applied to a real world context. To frame this discussion, we can employ two questions: first, what would it mean to realise communicative planning in practice? and, second, how would we know it if we did?

i. What would it mean to realise communicative planning practice?

What would communicative planning look like in practice? What steps should policy makers take to implement a genuinely communicative approach to planning? What forms of engagement, what structure of communication, would be required to encourage seldom-heard voices to be raised? For critics, on these vital questions communicative theorists have consistently offered insufficient advice.

Empirical attempts to sustain a connection between the theory and named examples from practice have usually focused on the specifics of a particular planning process emphasising the degree to which it/ they bear the communicative imprint (for example, Margerum, 2002). At their most forceful, these studies have purported to show that 'the technology is very well developed on how to create undistorted communication or ideal speech situations' (Innes, 2004: 11: see also Innes, 1992; Innes and Booher, 2000; Innes and Gruber, 2001; Innes *et al.*, 1994). Yet most research – even that emanating from within the communicative project itself – is less strident in proclaiming a formula for instituting mechanisms that will help achieve the Habermasian ideal of dominance by the best argument (Habermas, 1975). Rather, the majority of measured studies that seek to investigate the viability of implementing a communicative approach are generally much more tentative about the possibility of its realisation (see, for example, Hillier, 1998; Malbert, 1998; Woltjer, 2000; Van Driesche and Lane, 2002).

Much of the work in this vein has identified aspects of specific planning processes that appear to have fulfilled elements of what it might mean to conduct communicative planning, but researchers are often reluctant to specify how far down the road to an ideal speech situation we have been advanced by the institution of these protocols. Not that we would expect an example of an 'ideal' communicative encounter; but if such a thing is a theoretical possibility we should be able to establish whether the favoured methods – focus groups, community consultation exercises, residents' forums and knowledge-exchange workshops and similar – have brought us closer to a 'good' communicative setting and, therefore, correspondingly 'good' planning outcomes.

In response, sceptics have held communicative theory hostage to its seemingly grandiose aims and been scornful when it has, almost inevitably, fallen short of providing an example of unequivocally good, 'clean' communication that has led to Utopian ends. For this group the mismatch between 'collaborative planning in an un-collaborative world' (Brand and Gaffikin, 2007: 282; see also Neuman, 2000) is stark. This conception of a hostile and conflict-ridden real world of planning practice is said to be so at odds with the Habermasian goal of undistorted speech and the victory of reasoned argumentation that setting in train a process that could support better communication might, first, be impractical and, second, may not necessarily result in a more open form of planning practice at all (Allmendinger and Tewdwr-Jones, 1997; Moote *et al.*, 1997; Tewdwr-Jones and Allmendinger, 1998; Tewdwr-Jones and Thomas, 1998; Nienhuis *et al.*, 2011). In this respect Pennington's (2002: 194) critique is indicative of wider misgivings about the theory's realisation in practice:

> The communicative rationality approach appears to be suggesting that the epistemological problems of this sort could somehow be solved if only all the relevant stakeholders (in their multiple social and economic roles) could be gathered together in some sort of grand committee meeting to discuss the issues in hand (a logical impossibility in itself).

These impracticalities and their implications for the theory's empirical purchase have elsewhere been described by Flyvbjerg and Richardson (2002: 58): 'So Habermas neither provides an achievable model for planning, nor does he explain planning as it is actually done, to the exasperation of many practitioners. He therefore fails to provide guidance for those involved in bringing about change – he does not describe a world they inhabit'. Despite these shortcomings, in many contexts around the globe planners have been encouraged to 'strive to create deliberative contexts that, as far as possible, minimise inequalities of power and knowledge' (Huxley, 2000: 369). Yet why should we think that, even if we could realise it, this type of setting would entail more even power relations? In the original statement of Habermas's thought (1975, 1984) ideal speech situations rest on undistorted communication that might mean the emergence of more reasoned outcomes from more reasoned processes. But this emblem of clean communication clearly grates against what we have come to expect from the material world of politicised decisions and deal making.

Central in this is the 'planner' and the different type of conduct that this role might entail. As Huxley (2000: 376) points out, for communicative theorists, 'planners themselves are assumed to be people of goodwill who worry about ethics, inclusion and equality and are blessed with unusual reflexivity and insight into the constraints on their own and other people's understandings and actions'. For sceptics such as Allmendinger and Tewdwr-Jones (2002: 19–20; see also Tait and Campbell, 2000) such a view does not take sufficient account of the competing pressures to which planners might be subject and what effect their own normative biases might have on arriving at a planning decision. In stark contrast to the colourless, place-holding character at the centre of the planning process under the communicative school's conception, on this reading planners are said to have their own 'personal preferences' which may jar against the assumption of a benign, impartial official:

> To put it in the starkest terms, they reflect as autonomous individuals and learn how not to get caught out, either in adversarial settings, in politically charged debates, or at public meetings. Here under this scenario it is self-interest, career development and professional esteem that are the goals at the forefront of planners' minds, even if at times they are dressed up in the language of participation generation, fostering open and inclusive dialogues and mutual learnings.
>
> (Allmendinger and Tewdwr-Jones, 2002: 19–20)

Even Healey (2003: 109) notes that 'it is of course no surprise that many instances of practice are nowhere near the Habermasian criteria for an ideal speech situation'. In light of this admission it is surprising, but true, that 'the communicative planning literature often appears to suggest that planners can foster (relatively distortion-free) communication and that such communication can result in a consensus based on agreement to meaning and proposition with which no one disagrees' (Huxley, 2000: 374).

In light of these observations it is far from clear how the most frequently favoured methods of stakeholder engagement might result in the even-handed involvement of the full range of potential participants. This in turn has provided some with grounds to contend that other mechanisms might perform the task better. For Pennington (2002; see also Pennington, 1996, 2000; Lai, 2010), following Hayek, a marketised form of interaction allows for a more perspicuous engagement in which power relations are more clearly delineated and outcomes more easily analysed. However, it is unclear how the contractual form of planning advocated might begin to explain those numerous settings – development control decisions, appeals, the assignment of preservation orders – where existing practice is unequivocally communicative and probably could not be easily translated into a formal market.

By contrast, the systems of bargaining and voting highlighted by Allmendinger and Tewdwr-Jones (2002) as an alternative method of signalling preferences do align neatly with existing political and committee-based practice in many contexts. Moreover, with the case of voting, in having a clear principle by which preferences are signalled, such a method of engagement – usually one member, one vote – avoids some of the communicative turn's difficulties with power relations. Where it fails, however, is in understanding the multi-faceted nature of intention which is rarely captured by a stark, often binary, electoral choice: in all elections participants have the opportunity to vote *strategically*, the capacity for strategic behaviour being a point to which we will return repeatedly in this volume. In aligning choice with speech acts, communicative planning is a much stronger formulation than either of the alternatives outlined here as it envelops a much broader range of participants' positions and allows them each their own voice.

Nevertheless the problem remains: 'a more open approach will undoubtedly throw up a lot of information, opinions, facts, views, etc. which need to be organised somehow' (Allmendinger and Tewdwr-Jones, 2002: 10). How planners who seek to follow the prescriptions of the communicative turn might sort this information and make sense of it remains an open question: particularly when some have noted the tendency for data-gathering in planning practice to sometimes yield 'too much information' (Hanley, 2001; Karacapilidis et al., 1997). For some theorists the task of organising the form of

communicative engagement has been equated with weighting participants' roles and admitting, sometimes encouraging, the possibility of
distorted communication. For example, in an attempt to bolt on a
practical response to the potential for uneven power relations, Sager
(2006: 246), following Forester's (1993) critical pragmatism fine-tuning
of communicative theory, has suggested the invasive step of manipulating transaction costs – how readily a participant can enter and
influence the planning debate:

> Some stakeholders exploit their strong position in power relation
> to distort the communicative planning process and promote out-
> comes catering only to their own needs. If the planner can use her
> guidance of the planning process to realign their cost of acting in
> this manner, she might improve the capacity of other involved
> parties to implement a plan taking everybody's interest into
> account.

Others have argued that incentives should be offered to encourage,
and ultimately embed, a popular culture of civic participation in
planning (Olsson, 2009). Clearly such incentives might even further
skew the character and nature of participation, systematically creating
the conditions for bias to be introduced into the planning process.
Yet, for some this is entirely consistent with the communicative turn's
overriding normative goal to rebalance communicative power in
favour of voices from those discourse communities thought to be
inherently disadvantaged in the planning process (Connelly and
Richardson, 2004); however, there is rarely a strong justification for
why we might agree on this normative a priori assumption. More
significantly, few details are provided regarding how incentivised bias,
once introduced, might be controlled. What if the 'wrong' groups are
encouraged to be involved in planning decisions by pecuniary motivation?

In sum, the communicative turn lacks detail on critical issues
about, first, why it is logical to believe that the envisaged discourse
arena might privilege better decision making and, second, what to
do about the effects of contingent power relations. Using Taylor's
(1980) formulation of an ethics and epistemology of planning it might
be argued that the communicative turn's valiant attempt to devise a
socio-philosophical response to both satisfies neither. Certainly the
gaps in the conceptualisation of power relations and the unconvincing
and underspecified nature of the fixes suggested, using behaviour
manipulation by means of risk, rewards and pay-offs, represent an

excursion into a murky world with which the cynical economist is probably more familiar and better equipped to deal. Yet there have been few, and very limited, attempts made in the literature to use economics to rectify some of these issues – presumably as it is thought, erroneously, that this would entail the taint of positivism (see Chapter 5 of this volume). What remains is a rendering of the real world of planning practice which some have argued is almost naïve (Bengs, 2005). For example, if participation is engendered by appealing to the self-interest of participants, what reason is there for believing that this character trait will not be equally present in other aspects of their conduct during the exercise of their voice in the communicative planning arena? Might this ultimately have an impact on the decision-making process? Indeed, what guarantees are there that a communicative approach so orchestrated would result in the advancement of the 'best argument'? Moreover, how would we identify it even if it did?

ii. How could we recognise truly communicative planning: how should we come to know the 'best argument'?

Explaining the lack of prescription regarding what the 'nuts and bolts' of a genuinely communicative form of planning practice could comprise might be partly accomplished by reference to the fact that there are no clearly agreed-upon criteria amongst communicative theorists for tying outcomes to process, thus hampering any attempt at a meaningful evaluation of the degree to which 'good' process leads to 'good' outcomes (see Agger and Löfgren, 2008; Mandarano, 2008). The anxieties that prevent us from proclaiming one form of planning process to be closer to the Habermasian ideal than another are compounded by our uncertainty that 'better' speech acts lead to better outcomes. Fundamentally, the reason for this trepidation is epistemological and bound up with the communicative turn's roots in phenomenology. Furthermore, it is this basis that means that even if we were able to develop a truly communicative form of planning, by chance or design, we would have no mechanism for learning that we had done so.

Phenomenology forms the epistemological foundation for many of the forms of planning theory that might usefully be thought of as post-positivist. Indeed the thinker who has appealed most to planning theorists, Habermas, makes this connection explicit through the central role afforded in his work to the expression *Lebenswelt* or 'life-world', which was originally coined by the grandfather of phenomenology,

Husserl (Carr translation, 1970). Indeed this forms one of the most controversial aspects of Habermas's thought, particularly with respect to the route taken to connect the social interactions that he believes govern the parameters of meaning in the 'real' (objective, subjective and normative) worlds and this phenomenological 'life-world' that provides the structure and context within which these engagements take place (Outhwaite, 2009: 107). Finding a path from the 'linguistically constituted' (Habermas, 1984: 241) life-world to a separate reality of micro-agential communicative actions and back again poses a significant epistemological question to which many have found no satisfactory answer. In following this school of philosophic thought, planning theorists have adopted a stance to their subject that demands as intimate a connection as possible to the linguistic encounter – as this must be the site at which a connection to and from the life-world is made. The position, as it has come to inform the communicative turn, is best-expressed by Innes and Booher (2010: 21, italics added):

Phenomenology offers a more grounded form of knowledge, as well as one that can not only address the full complexity of a situation, but also explore it in a way that allows solutions to be tailor-made to unique circumstances. Phenomenologists argued … that knowledge is about phenomena as wholes, rather than divided into components, and the goal of knowing is understanding rather than explanation. The starting place for knowing is everyday life and the understandings of ordinary people, rather than abstractions like variables. Meaning is central, and intentions and beliefs are themselves constitutive of reality, rather than reality being out there to be discovered. Whereas positivist researchers would discount meaning as purely subjective, in the interpretive mode meaning and belief are basic data. From the phenomenologists' perspective, moreover, no one can be the neutral observer required by positivist thought. Instead the observer filters knowledge and therefore must be self-conscious about her own biases and how they may affect her perceptions. *The idea of intersubjectivity is central, as knowing depends on the ability to put oneself in the other's place.*

For Healey (2007b: 124), who also explicitly acknowledges the phenomenological origins of her work, this reorientation of investigators to their subject represents a core distinction between work in this post-positivist vein and the rationalists that came before: 'The planner, situated by the procedural rationalists as standing outside evolving realities, analysing and shaping them, was re-positioned as inside emerging realities, continually involved in the flow of practices, with complex dilemmas of understanding and of ethical conduct'. Whilst this might intuitively seem to be a practically/politically progressive step, it brings with it questions about how immersion in the setting of our subject allows us to have a better understanding of the features it might comprise. In short: how we can come to have knowledge of other minds?

Under the phenomenological outlook the importance of context and setting in situating meaning are central, as Taylor (1980: 169), pre-empting the germ of the communicative approach, points out:

> as far as planning is concerned, the adoption of such a phenomenological perspective suggests that planners should seek to identify much more closely with the subjective situation and perceptions of the communities for whom they are preparing plans, even to the extent of living amongst and being members of these communities themselves.

This phenomenological conception of the situated nature of meaning can be seen in some of the classic statements of communicative planning:

> Every field of endeavour has its history of ideas and practices and its traditions of debate. These act as a store of experience, of myths, metaphors and arguments, which those within the field can draw upon in developing their own contributions, either through what they do, or through reflecting on the field. This 'store' provides advice, proverbs, recipes and techniques for understanding and acting, and inspiration for ideas to play with and develop.
>
> (Healey, 1997: 7)

> Our challenge here is to learn through the friction of actual practice – to learn through the eyes and ears and hopes and dreads and difficulties and surprises of actual people, activists and ordinary – and often extraordinary – people who get up each morning and confront in messy detail the fears and distrust and scheming and self-interest and aggression of others that our abstractions otherwise so thinly render.
>
> (Forester, 2006: 574)

Stated alternatively, 'social actions are *meaningful* actions, that is ... they must be studied and explained in terms of their situations and their meanings to the actors themselves' (Douglas, 2010: 4, italics in original). The challenge is therefore clear: to learn meanings we must close down the gap between ourselves as researchers and the subject of our study – in our case, the communicative interactions that determine planning processes, decisions and their consequences. However, this brings with it its own epistemological demands. For the communicative turn these phenomenological origins mean that the capacity for each participant to articulate their own case on the basis of introspective reflection alone is taken to be guarantee of its perspicacity. We hope to truly learn their meaning by becoming as close to that testimony as possible. This may be intuitively appealing but if, as others have noted more widely of phenomenology (Dennett, 1987), we do not have an accompanying set of principles for how such context-specific meaning might be extracted and deciphered, we potentially run the risk of losing confidence in our capacity to develop a correct interpretation of speakers' meaning regardless of how proximate we are to their speech – the 'tentativeness' noted of empirical studies at the start of this, and the preceding, section. This tendency towards solipsism – the idea that the only mind of which we can be certain is our own – it has been argued, is epistemologically written into positions that rely on phenomenology for their theory of knowledge (Fodor, 1980).

For the communicative turn what is therefore needed is a rigorous account of how meaning, once uttered, is interpreted and, equally importantly, what steps might be taken to prevent misinterpretation. Instead, prescriptive examples of 'best practice', as opposed to a stronger philosophical defence, are proffered. Often this best practice is associated with paying careful attention to how dialogue is structured through manipulating the environment in which discourse takes place: for example Innes (2004: 12) argues that a cleaner form of communication, and therefore a more perspicuous understanding of meaning, can be encouraged by 'skilful management of dialogue, shared information and education of the stakeholders'. It may well be that such features encourage uninhibited dialogue from the speaker. They may even bring us closer to the Habermasian ideal of undistorted speech. Yet this is not a strong enough argument to prevent the slide into solipsism: even if it were possible to minimise error to allow for each speaker to be uncompromised in what they say, this does nothing to resituate our certainty that each listener hears the same thing and arrives at the same understanding, or that what is heard is what was *meant*. After all, we might be clumsy in how we articulate ourselves; we don't always say what we think we mean and our remarks might be misinterpreted, sometimes knowingly, sometimes unknowingly.

The implications for the communicative turn of this phenomenological epistemology are, as I hope to go on to show in Chapter 3, more significant than might be remedied by recourse to tinkering with the terms of the 'empty ceremony' (Wittgenstein, 1953: PI257) of manipulatively constructed communicative interactions. Instead we must confront the questions with which the communicative turn is epistemologically ill-equipped to deal: what if participants in the planning process are sometimes disingenuous?; what if the 'best argument' – as the decision-making planner understands it – is premised on misrepresentation or prevarication? Of course this might be deliberate: as we shall see in the second part of this volume human beings sometimes behave strategically. Crucially, however, this is not to say that we always show a tendency to behave strategically for selfish ends. In many instances strategic behaviour might be consistent with altruism. At other times it might be self-interested but of a qualitatively different nature, just as when we lie about our whereabouts when buying a gift for a loved one or to spare the feelings of a friend. Similarly it would not be too much to suppose that some portion of the discourse by which a planning policy or decision is made might be based on, at the very least, inconsistent, or more simply, inaccurate, information. Given what psychology, psychiatry and experimental economics (see, for example, Glimcher, 2004; Glimcher *et al.*, 2008) teach us about the complexities of individuals' behaviour when confronted by a dynamic decision-making process, it would seem, to again concur with Bengs (2005), naïve to premise our ideas about planning theory on the notion that, if we arrange our communicative protocols correctly, the truth will out, and we will be able to identify it as the truth, each time.

Later developments

Taken together these criticisms show the more significant limitations of communicative planning theory. As noted at the outset of this chapter, in response there have emerged many nuanced accounts that seek to make reparations to the theory by introducing fixes from, for example, post-modernism and pragmatism. Where these excursions have seemingly been most successful, thinkers have ultimately come to abandon core aspects of the communicative rationality and instead employ the work of Habermas's old philosophical opponent, Foucault (Flyvbjerg and Richardson, 2002; Huxley, 2000; Richardson, 1996; Stein and Harper, 2003). Such accounts of planning practice viewed through a Foucauldian prism make important contributions such as placing an emphasis on the often intransigent nature of power relations: the reality, and even desirability, of conflict and the materialisation of such features of planning practice through discourse. In prioritising a recognition of these features of realpolitik over a predefined theoretical-normative agenda regarding what the discursive practice of planning *should* entail, research in this vein emphasises a more open analysis of texts and discourse.

However, as Habermas (1987: 276) noted of Foucault, this lack of prescription might also be interpreted as a 'cryptonormative' stance in relation to the subjects under investigation that conceals the impulse driving our interest in them in the first place – our desire to effect social, environmental or political change. The result is a formula that potentially privileges description, or even redescription (Rorty, 1986), over genuine analysis. Extending this point, the preoccupation with textual and discourse analysis entailed by following Foucault, and other post-modernists, provides insights into, for example, the documentary reportage of how planning problems are (and have been) constructed, but it is unclear how a Foucauldian approach would circumvent the phenomenological problems associated with the Habermasian approach to interpreting speech acts. The crypticism of which Habermas accuses Foucault might make the phenomenological questions less conspicuous, but it does not hide the lack of prescription regarding a substantially altered methodological toolkit with which we might unpack the complex social interactions that comprise the lion's share of planning practice (for a discussion of the two thinkers, see Flyvbjerg, 1998a, 1998b, 2002).

Taking this challenge at face value others have sought to use complexity theory to understand urban and environmental planning. However the *mélange* of natural and social sciences – reminiscent of the systems and rationalist schools' preference for scientific metaphor (e.g. McLoughlin, 1969) – has often resulted in a theory that proceeds by analogy in which the social encounters of planning practice are said to mirror some, but rarely all, of the attributes that constitute the natural world and its relationship to scientific experiment – such as the capacity for replication, verification and falsification (for a review, see Chettiparamb, 2006; see also Byrne, 2003; Manson and O'Sullivan, 2006; de Roo and Silva, 2010). The result is a corpus that, depending on the epistemological predilections of the author, accommodates beneath the same banner both work that follows the positivist para-digm (Batty, 2007) and its polar opposite, an evolved form of com-municative rationality (see Innes and Booher, 2010). The epistemological cross-over can only ever result in a loose knot that barely ties the positivism of scientific method into the situated necessities of social enquiry (Horgan, 1995; Stewart, 2001).

In the final analysis accounting for the continued affection felt by many planning theorists for the communicative turn – indicated by the numerous attempts to rescue it by bolting on ever-more elaborate philosophical fixes – is accomplished by reference to its identification of linguistically grounded social encounters as the fundamental build-ing block of planning practice. Despite the myriad caveats and uncer-tainties outlined above, communicative theorists have performed the great service of focusing attention on this particular type of infor-mation that is central to the determination of decisions taken in planning practice – that resulting from the dialogue and actions that condition what we learn, and believe, about others involved in a planning encounter. Furthermore, its self-avowed normative desire, particularly strong in Forester (1989, 1999a), to rebalance power in favour of the systemically weak is a political objective shared by many working in both the planning academy and practice. If these are the debts owed to the communicative turn they might be repaid by repairing the epistemological problems that hamstring its practical application. For example when critics have challenged the theory to articulate how the practical components of power might be better theorised within the framework offered by a communicative ration-ality such requests have sometimes been waved away as the minutiae of the everyday:

> Collaborative planning is a plea for the importance of under-standing complexity and diversity in a way that does not collapse into atomistic analyses of specific episodes and individual achievements, or avoid recognising the way power consolidates into driving forces that shape situational specificities.
>
> (Healey, 2003: 117)

But, surely, for a theory to have explanatory value it should be able to provide us with an insight into the micro-rubric of its subject? The limitations of an ontology that requires for its fulfilment the aggrega-tion of a potentially limitless number of discrete, unique states of affairs, each entirely separate from the next and experienced differ-ently by every observer, was powerfully dismantled, through example, by Wittgenstein (1922) in the *Tractatus Logico-Philosophicus* (see also Russell, 1972). If what is required is a more systematic approach to understanding the logical formalisation of the speech acts that most agree form the basis of the commentary to our individual and collective socio-linguistic existence – in many respects the unstruck target of the communicative theorists' endeavours – we might be well advised to consider this form of ordinary language analysis pioneered by Wittgenstein (1953, 1958). In so doing we come to diagnose the epistemological limitations of previous attempts to 'theorise' planning as stemming from precisely this theoretical stance towards their subject. By reorientating ourselves from a theoretical to an analytically *investigative* position, it is argued, we might develop an alternative way of understanding the forces that shape urban and environmental management.

3 Is there an alternative way of understanding planning?

The fundamental objective of the theoretical perspectives enveloped by the communicative banner – to forge a progressive planning polity by rebalancing the communicative structure through which a significant proportion of planning decisions are made – is an admirable one. It is an objective, as Allmendinger and Tewdwr-Jones (2002: 7; see also Hooper, 1992) point out, that few would disavow: 'it is difficult to disagree with the sentiments expressed, but their meaning and implications remain obscure and contentious'.

As has been shown in the previous chapter, on a practical level it is precisely the 'obscure and contentious' nature of the prescriptions that communicative theorists have propounded that has led some to lose faith in using this brand of theory to either explain planning as it is, or to suggest alternative ways of managing urban and natural environments. Diagnosing the reason for this practice–theory gap led to the realisation that it was, at root, epistemological. The communicative turn's phenomenology, it was argued, undermined the capacity of researchers to make sense consistently of the testimonies they solicit.

To remedy this situation we need only take one step back. In agreeing with the post-positivists that communicative interaction is the correct site of investigation, we can retain an unerring focus on this setting but develop a non-phenomenological way of understanding it. Others have already alluded to how such an approach might proceed. For example, Flyvbjerg (1996: 391, emphasis added) states that the purpose of communicative planning 'is not to dissolve relations of power in a utopia of transparent communication but to *play games* with a minimum of domination'. Sager (2009: 7, emphasis added), in reflecting on the theoretical difficulties of adequately taking account of asymmetric power relations, uses a similar form of expression:

What if the planning theorist warns about the advantages that developers with access to money and expertise can have from dialogical, consensus-building processes instead of strict laws, rules and politically binding plans? What if the theorists try to devise ways for counteracting developer power in planning processes? Critics might say that this is all very well but it is not a solution to the problem. It does not change *the logic of the game* between developers, planners, politicians and local people.

When thought about in this manner, a much closer consideration of the 'logic of the game' (see also Wu, 1997) becomes the fundamental task that planning theory must confront. Moreover, such references to understanding communicative interactions as 'games' force a dialogue with analytic linguistic philosophy and specifically with the 'language games' upon which Wittgenstein's later philosophy was predicated. This chapter sets out to make explicit this connection between the analytic philosophy of Ludwig Wittgenstein and the types of question that we are preoccupied with in planning theory. In so doing, a platform is created for the development of a new way of thinking about planning: one that is directed to providing a full account of the interactions that give rise to the majority of the information that forms the currency of planning practice.

Planning and the philosophy of ordinary language

Wittgenstein is described variously as 'the leading analytical philosopher of the twentieth century' (Hacker, 1995a: 912) and 'iconic' (Stern, 2004: 1), and the works upon which his reputation has been founded, principally *Tractatus Logico-Philosophicus* (1922) and *Philosophical Investigations* (1953), represent two very different ways of approaching philosophy. Although both take the same form of presentation through a sequentially numbered series of remarks (here indicated by either TLP or PI, followed by the number of the remark to which reference is made), the *Tractatus's* articulation of logical atomism is understood as the 'early Wittgenstein' and the *Investigations'* critique of this earlier work is referred to as the 'later Wittgenstein' (Pitcher, 1968). In following this convention, what follows is a presentation of the later Wittgenstein's philosophy of language. In turn, the significance of this approach to understanding the source of linguistic meaning as residing in its use is shown to have potentially destructive consequences for the types of theory that rely on a phenomenological characterisation of meaning as introspectively defined.

The fundamental building block of the *Philosophical Investigations'* account of how terms come to signify meaning is the 'language game', used earlier in the papers that would become the *Brown book* (Wittgenstein, 1958) but given full expression in the *Investigations*. To introduce this concept Wittgenstein begins by positing the theory of linguistic meaning propounded by St. Augustine in the fourth century that retained much currency well into the twentieth century and had some similarity to his own thoughts as set out in the *Tractatus*:

> When they (my elders) named some object, and accordingly moved towards something, I saw this and I grasped what the thing was called by the sound they uttered when they meant to point it out. Their intention was shown by their bodily movements, as it were the natural language of all peoples: the expression of the face, the play of the eyes, the movement of other parts of the body, and the tone of voice that expresses our state of mind in seeking, having, rejecting or avoiding something. Thus as I heard words repeatedly used in their proper places in various sentences, I gradually learnt to understand what objects they signified, and after I had trained my mouth to form these signs, I used them to express my own desires.
>
> (St. Augustine, 1961)

This conception of how we understand the process by which language comes to be imbued with meaning Wittgenstein believed to be fundamentally mistaken for at least two reasons. First, as a representational theory of meaning – in which words picture a state of affairs that prevails in the material world – it does not account for all the other ways in which language might be used other than naming. Second, and more profoundly, the methodology employed in analysing language in this way has divorced it from the context in which it is used. It is this second point that is most significant for communicative planning theory as McGinn (1997: 70) demonstrates:

> It is not merely that Wittgenstein believes that the theories which Augustine presents are wrong in their details, but in the very first step of abstracting language from its application Augustine situates himself towards it in a way that makes it impossible for him to achieve the understating he seeks.

It is this separation of language from its context of use that Wittgenstein believes comprises Augustine's principal error, as it leads to a proto-phenomenological understanding of meaning – that the process by which we come to learn how to express ourselves in language is an internal one, something conducted in, and dependent upon, our own minds. The germ of Augustine's idea was given ultimate expression by the phenomenological movement's account of meaning (see Husserl, 1970; Merleau-Ponty, 1962) and, as was identified in the previous chapter, has been translated, in strains of varying strength, into the epistemological basis for many of the post-positivist theories of planning.

To persuade us that we should reconsider this notion Wittgenstein advances a series of propositions between PI243 and PI315 designed to illustrate the redundancy of thinking of language as a something that could function privately in this manner. This 'private language argument' is perhaps one of the most hotly debated parts of the *Investigations* with potentially devastating consequences for any episte-mology that shares Augustine's self-referential derivation of meaning. Chief amongst this group is phenomenology as Reeder (1979: 19) notes:

> Phenomenology often comes into criticism from linguistic analysts of the Wittgensteinian tradition who claim that the language used in phenomenological description must be an unac-ceptable form of language, due to the fact that the reflexive shift of the phenomenological reduction bars one from criteria of consistency of language.

That is, in showing that it is not an internal process in our own minds by which we come to learn meanings, Wittgenstein undermines the first premise in the theory of knowledge shared by Augustine and the phenomenologists. He points out that this would require us to determine meaning by creating our own definitions in isolation from the routine social applications that figure in daily life. Such a position is unsustainable as its status as a private language unknown to any other speaker entails that it would also be unknowable to the individual's own mind: as Hacker (1995b: 719) says:

> That the mutual intelligibility of a putative 'private' language is problematic is obvious. The originality of Wittgenstein's argu-ment is to show that it must be unintelligible to its speaker. For it presupposes the possibility of a private ostensive definition of a private mental sample functioning as a standard for the correct application of a word, and for a rule which cannot logically be

followed by another person, all of which are shown to be incoherent.

In relation to planning theory this is particularly significant for any position, such as the communicative turn, that rests on any form of philosophical phenomenology. If introspection can never lead to any form of communicable definition, it follows that communicative theorists, in seeking introspective testimony, elicit statements of indeterminate meaning: 'Introspection can never lead to a definition. It can only lead to a psychological statement about the introspector' (Wittgenstein, 1980: 212). Moreover, as McGinn (1997: 119; emphasis in original) notes:

> The thought that introspection is essential to our understanding of psychological concepts is a highly intuitive one. If the essence of psychological phenomena – what distinguishes them from physical phenomenon – lies in their possessing a *subjective* or *phenomenological* aspect, then it is surely by introspection alone that we discover the essence of this phenomena. To reject the idea that introspection is essential to a grasp of what, for example, a sensation is seems like a rejection of the distinctively subjective nature of sensations and a consequent blurring of the distinction between the psychological and the physical … . Yet he [Wittgenstein] also believes that our intuition here is a mistaken one; introspection, or looking inwards, does not prove a means by which we can grasp the nature of a given psychological state. Thus 'it shews a fundamental misunderstanding, if I am inclined to study the headache I have now in order to get clear about the philosophical problem of sensation' (1953: PI314). The act of turning my attention inwards to what is going on inside me, for example, when I feel pain or when I suddenly understand a word, does not tell me what a sensation is, or what understanding consists in. It is not that Wittgenstein wishes to deny that introspection is possible, or that its results may be of interest to us, but only to show that introspection is not a means by which we discover what sensations, thoughts, images and so on are; it is not a means to defining a psychological term.

So if a private language is impossible, how do we come to assign meaning to words? It is at this point that we might usefully introduce Wittgenstein's notion of a 'language game' – the situated process of practical linguistic application – as the antidote to the theoretical way that Augustine (as well as Russell, Frege and the earlier Wittgenstein) had sought to understand how language operates. This 'spatial and temporal phenomenon of language, not some non-temporal, non-spatial phantasm' (Wittgenstein, 1958: PI108) admits not just the representational forms of language that had preoccupied the mind of Augustine (again, as well as Russell, Frege and the earlier Wittgenstein) but also the multitude of other applications to which language is put in its everyday use, for example, 'giving orders, making reports, describing a scene, telling a story' (Wittgenstein, 1953: PI207).

This brief list is taken as indicative of the full, and infinite, range of propositions that might be concatenated from the terms employed in any language game. Taken cumulatively they represent the boundless limits of our language. The task for philosophy and philosophers as Wittgenstein now understands it is, when confronted with a problem, to uncover the grammar of the language games that the problem comprises. Thus, instead of the theoretical disposition towards language and meaning that we might suppose philosophy to require, he proposes something quite different – a therapeutic activity where the philosophical questions that we may have had can be dissolved, shown to have never really been questions at all, simply a misunderstanding of syntax resulting from a superficial engagement with the grammar of the problem we thought confronted us: 'philosophy simply puts everything before us, and neither explains nor deduces anything' (Wittgenstein, 1953: PI126). On such a reading the purpose of philosophical investigation is not theoretical explanation, much less prescription, but description. There are no ideals: each language game is simply what it is and the task of philosophy is to elucidate that game and the rules by which it is played, lay them bare and thereafter conclude the exercise complete.

Wittgenstein's implications for planning theory

Wittgenstein's work has had a profound impact on metaphysics, epistemology, the philosophy of mind and philosophical logic. It should be no surprise, therefore, that, in following Wittgenstein back to first principles in our investigative relationship to language, we also uncover issues that have a significant bearing on any attempt to devise a theory of environmental planning – particularly a communicative theory. Fundamentally there are three related areas in which the analytic philosophy outlined here shows the theories of planning that we have considered so far to be compromised.

The redundancy of theory

First, the ways of understanding planning discussed to this point all share a theoretical stance to the subject. In the case of the communicative turn this entails an overtly normative attitude to enquiry regarding what might and should be found. This feature is less conspicuous in other theories of planning, such as that of the rationalists or those following Foucault, but, as was noted at the end of Chapter 2, this may simply be that the communicative turn is more honest about the normative goals that its theoretical disposition entails and, therefore, the limited extent of information with which it is equipped to deal. Irrespective of whether planning is theorised by positivist, Foucauldian, pragmatist or communicative means, the desire to use theory of any sort in this way – to approach the subject with this theoretical posture – results in analyses imbued with the terms of that theory, whatever it might be.

By contrast, philosophy, as Wittgenstein construes it, is an activity entirely divorced from theory as well as its purpose, explanation. Rather, it is an 'investigation' based upon grammatical clarification. At its completion the result is the dissolution of the question that we thought confronted us, 'since everything lies open to view ... there is nothing to be explained' (Wittgenstein, 1953: PI126). This end-state of the philosophical method that Wittgenstein advances recasts philosophy from a 'bewitchment' (Wittgenstein, 1953: PI109) to a therapeutic activity. Significantly, as the goal is solely grammatical elucidation, we cannot have a positional attitude to the exercise; we are disinterested, although not uninterested, in the object of our investigations. Our task is simply to 'bring words back from their metaphysical to their everyday use' (Wittgenstein, 1953: PI116). As Hacker (1995a: 915) says:

> The task of philosophy is to clear away the conceptual confusions that stand in the way of accepting these rule-governed articulations in our language. There is no room for theories in philosophy, for in philosophy we are moving around within our own grammar, dissolving philosophical questions by examining the rules for the use of words with which we are familiar ... . Philosophical problems stem from entanglement in linguistic rules ... . The methods of philosophy are purely descriptive. The task of philosophy is conceptual clarification and the dissolution of philosophical problems. The goal of philosophy is not knowledge but understanding.

From this perspective the theoretical disposition that various schools of planning theory have adopted at the outset of their quest to make sense of planning practice effectively closes down their capacity to engage with the full range of information types to which their subject gives rise: the positivists are theoretically incapable of dealing with subjective data emerging from socio-linguistic engagement. Equally, the treatments of planning that use Habermasian sociology are theoretically antipathetic to an expert-technocratic construction of objective evidence from quantitative data. In both cases the fundamental problem is getting to grips with how information – whether it be of a positive or normative stripe – is used. For positivist accounts of planning this is a question that is not considered worthy of attention – just as all non-verifiable propositions were pejoratively dismissed as 'metaphysics' by the Vienna Circle (Carnap, 1959). By contrast, for the Habermasians and Foucauldians the question of how information is socially translated into opinion and 'facts' is a live one. However, the phenomenological origins of their approach to answering it are also fraught with epistemological problems.

The redundancy of phenomenology

The accounts that seek to rectify the positivist neglect of subjectivity by applying sociological theory attempt to do so by becoming as proximate as possible to their subject, acknowledging, even celebrating, that this runs the methodological risk of introducing normative bias. For example, in providing a communicative case study of environmental planning practice in Trondheim, Norway, Sager (2006: 238) states his own position clearly: 'the account which follows is openly non-neutral, siding with the planners to keep the recreational woodland as a public good. I am writing as an external observer'. Such an embedded attitude towards the case seems to directly contradict the assertion of observation from the outside. Nevertheless the impulse is clear and intuitively understandable: to really know a setting, surely the researcher must become as close as possible to the case?

For Wittgenstein this is an error arising from a desire to impose a brand of theory on the subject that searches for meaning through introspection rather than pursuing an investigation of meaning as socially determined by mutual use: 'To investigate the nature of a phenomenon is to *look closer*' (Geach, 1988: 3–5, italics in original). But, as identified above, we can never look closely enough to fulfil the demands of introspectively defined meaning; instead our quest for proximity only leads to us meddling in the language game that we seek to decipher: 'Philosophy may in no way interfere with the actual use of language; it can in the end only describe it. For it cannot give it any foundation either. It leaves everything as it is' (Wittgenstein, 1953: PI81).

The danger of losing distance between observer and observed is made especially perilous by the phenomenological origins of planning theory of this type. Regardless of whether we are a participant in, or detached from, the case that we seek to investigate, if we rely solely on introspection to define meaning, we admit the possibility of private definitions. The phenomenological origins of the communicative turn and the post-modern additions to it, place a strong emphasis on eliciting community opinion through precisely this introspective mechanism. It is then the seemingly embedded nature of this meaning that encourages the impulse to rush towards it and explains the erosion of distance between researcher and researched. But the phenomenological theory of knowledge snares this information in its situation: situated knowledge is knowable only to the situated. Applications of communicative theory – and other theories that rest on similar epistemological footings – thus seek in vain to overcome this difficulty, usually by engineering the environments in which speech acts take place in the hope that, if we can get the setting right, this might encourage us to really grasp speakers' meaning. But the phenomenological origins of this theorised stance towards the subject buries speakers' meaning in solipsism from where it cannot be excavated: 'The nature of the phenomena which constitute our world is not something that we discover by "digging" but is something that is revealed in "the kind of statement we make about phenomena"' (McGinn, 1997: 19).

Consequently the primacy that communicative rationality accords the speaker to frame their own unadulterated statements, without any corresponding treatment of how the hearer might understand them, degenerates into a set of circumstances where only the speaker can be sure of their capacity to speak their own mind: they can have no certainty that the hearer interprets the noises they make in the way they have intended. This results in the paradox whereby a theory of communicative interaction rests on a philosophical premise that will not allow for a mutual dialogue between two speakers/hearers, let alone a greater number. Wittgenstein (1953: PI38) illustrates how such a private language is impossible, as meaning is constituted through the mutual act of usage and not some 'remarkable act of mind'. This firmly eliminates the possibility of introspection as a mechanism of definition:

What the idea of a private language forces us to focus on, therefore, is the implication of the following two facts for our idea that we grasp what a sensation is on the basis of introspection. First the act of naming presupposes a grammar, or technique of employing a word within a language-game; and second, the mere act of looking inwards does not supply this grammar, or specify a technique of employment.

(McGinn, 1997: 128)

For the communicative turn it is the normative objective of empathy and strengthening the hand of the weak that demands opinion be solicited from every conceivable stakeholder by asking them to introspectively search for their own meaning and expel it in a communicative forum. Yet the barrier to collecting data from the widest possible set of sources is this very problem of introspectively defined meaning. No matter how hard the communicative planner wishes to learn about his/her subject and become their interlocutor, under a phenomenological epistemology the individual's understanding of their own preferences, pain, frustrations and joy is entirely that: their own. The uncertainty over each participant's capacity to understand the meaning of others makes each individual account literally meaningless; and, as each testimony is discarded, the terms of the language game close in until each speaker becomes mute, endowed only with their own private thoughts, incapable of meaningful articulation to another.

In light of these observations, replacing the phenomenological underpinnings of the communicative turn with Wittgenstein's detached understanding that it is in the act of employing language that it comes to have meaning might seem desirable. In planning theory an attempt to make a similar transition can be seen in the shift from communicative to 'deliberative' theory (Forester, 1999a) – although this 'fieldwork in a Habermasian way' (Forester, 2003: 46) still retains an inherent commitment to phenomenology and, therefore, the embedded nature of introspective meaning. Moreover, making a complete shift from the communicative rationality to an analytic understanding of how language is used in planning practice is inhibited as it would demand an additional modification that is further incompatible with the normative philosophical underpinnings of all variants of communicative/collaborative/deliberative planning theory. In addition to abandoning the impulse to theorise planning we would also need to reconsider the idea that some styles of planning practice are qualitatively better or worse than others – a central principle of the normative project to which this form of theorising gives rise.

The redundancy of the 'best' outcome

The normative idea of superiority evident in both the rationalist's conception of positivist data leading to evidence that could inform 'optimal' decision making and the communicative turn's quest for an 'ideal' speech situation and the 'best argument' contrasts markedly with Wittgenstein's eschewal of philosophy as an activity that should seek to adjudge relative epistemic values. This is of particularly acute significance for those theories of planning that purport to find a relationship between 'better' forms of communication and superior planning outcomes:

> There are *countless* kinds of sentence: countless different kinds of use of what we call 'symbols', 'words', 'sentences'. And this multiplicity is not something fixed given once and for all; but new types of language, new language-games, as we may say, come into existence, and others become obsolete and get forgotten.
>
> (Wittgenstein, 1953: PI23, emphasis in original)

So, if the set of language games is infinite, as this implies, the idea of 'best practice' or finding an 'ideal speech situation' becomes redundant: each language game is simply what it is, bounded in space and time, and the question of its epistemic value relative to another language game is not a meaningful question. In reflecting on the ostensibly simple language games that Wittgenstein introduces at the beginning of the *Investigations* to illustrate the idea, McGinn (1997: 50–51) narrates the point clearly:

> It makes no sense to speak of language as either complete or incomplete, for language represents a form of limit to those who speak it; it represents the point from which we judge. Our language is not superior to the language games Wittgenstein describes in the sense of being closer to some ideal or complete symbolism; it is simply richer and more complex. The concept of incompleteness, like the concept of completeness, belongs with the false idea of an absolutely correct or essential system of representation.

The quest for optimality, either in the ideal communicative situation or a data-based decision, is therefore a logical impossibility and a practical dead end.

The consequence of this position is perhaps the purest form of epistemic relativism (Boghossian, 2006; Rorty, 1979): the same form of relativism that has been identified in the work of other thinkers used by academics in trying to make sense of planning – for example Foucault and even Habermas (see Flyvbjerg, 1998b: 220). However, it would be a fundamental error to conflate this epistemic relativism with ethical relativism: 'Wittgenstein wasn't an ethical relativist' (Coliva, 2010: 1). On the contrary, ethical conundrums preoccupied much of Wittgenstein's personal thinking (Monk, 1991); but his philosophical method distinguished between understanding how we come to know the ontological character of a language game and matters of value that, for Wittgenstein, were the separate task of moral philosophy. What a language game is is determined by how situated participants use that language: whether, say, an accusation is better or worse than an apology remains situated in the language game but with their relative moral values a subsequent issue, separate from the first step of understanding the way in which they are used.

When we understand in this way, through grammatical investigation we have at our disposal the toolkit to confront any given language game and expose its syntactical form. This implies that the full and infinite number of potential language games are knowable without the requirement for the intimate resituation of the investigator within the language game itself. This is the polar opposite of the phenomenological dismissal of the potential for non-situated observers to understand a state of affairs that in turn afflicts positions derived from it with uncertainty about their capacity to always explain their subject: after all, how could we be certain that we could get close enough to speakers and that we might arrive at a correct interpretation of what they were saying? In the case of planning theory this reduces to the idea that there is no formula for developing the better processes from which better outcomes are said to stem; rather, each individual example of a planning game is a unique constituent of a wider catalogue: 'governance processes are not recipes. They are unique constructions in specific situations' (Healey, 2003: 110).

If we apply Wittgenstein's method to this apparent problem that an ethically prescriptive theory refuses to proffer practical steps to realise these ethical goals, we can see that this is precisely an example of the grammatical confusion in which, as Wittgenstein shows, all philosophical problems are constituted. Due to the epistemological constraints imposed by its theoretical disposition to its subject, the reason that planning theory that is derived from communicative rationality cannot set out what these ideal governance processes might be is not because they are not 'recipes' but rather because the theory turns them into 'secret recipes' known only to the situated and, as we cannot be sure of other minds, therefore, unknowable to anyone else. So, when the question arises, 'what might an ideal – or even a "good" – speech situation look like?', the communicative theorist must answer that it is beyond the reach of their theory to say: similar in grammar to 'it is a secret that cannot be told'. This plainly unsatisfactory conclusion leads us to unwind the argument back through the theory's uncertainty of other minds, into a private language and thereon to a form of solipsism.

If we can rebuild the world of language from this point by invoking Wittgenstein's public language, knowable to all through a dispassionate elucidation of the grammatical rules that form the basis for our language games, we have the means to provide a complete account of our linguistic encounters. Once we have regained our certainty in the possibility of intelligible communication, encompassing the full range of uses to which our language might be put:

> giving orders and obeying them, describing the appearance of an object, giving its measurements, drawing, reporting an event, speculating about an event, forming and testing a hypothesis, presenting the results of an experiment in tables and diagrams, making up a story and reading it, play-acting, singing catches, guessing riddles, making a joke, telling it, solving a problem in practical arithmetic, translating from one language into another, asking, thanking, cursing, greeting and praying ...
>
> (Wittgenstein, 1953: PI23)

we can show how these linguistic operators are understood within the context of the language games in which they are employed.

Where next?

The calming effect of Wittgenstein's *Philosophical Investigations* resides in its dissolution of questions. In setting out a philosophical activity of elucidation through grammatical investigation Wittgenstein shows us that epistemological questions are not questions at all when we understand the deep grammar of the language game from which they arise. The notion of 'theory' as the mechanism of explanation is replaced by one that shows how a thorough descriptive rendering removes the questions from view.

As has already been shown, the field of planning theory is replete with these types of question that are barely submerged in the surface grammar of the language games we play in planning: what should count as evidence in the decision-making process?; what circumstances would constitute an ideal speech situation?; how might we come to know the best argument? The kernel of these problems is the same: they seek an ethical answer to an epistemological question – 'The philosophical problem has the form: "I don't know my way about"' (Wittgenstein, 1953: PI123) – and this has given rise to the 'diverse and fragmented landscape' (Allmendinger, 2002a: 96) said to characterise planning theory at the turn of the twenty-first century.

If what is required in response is a way of understanding planning that takes a cue from Wittgenstein, it must be one that might allow us to uncover the deep grammar of the games we play in planning. But what would such a method comprise and how would it differ from previous approaches to understanding planning?

First, it would not be a theory of, in or about planning (Faludi, 1973) but, rather, in agreement with Flyvbjerg and Richardson (2002: 59), would be a planning 'analytic': a way of understanding the grammar of the language games we play in planning. Second, this non-theoretical stance to the subject would, therefore, also be non-normative: ethical judgements are sensible and desirable but they could only be well-informed once we have analytically dismantled the planning game itself. Third, the method would demand that we remove ourselves from the site of our confusion, from within the game itself: we don't need to collapse the distance between observer and observed because our understanding of meaning is one grounded in use, not introspective self-definition. Finally, it would be an analytical approach that had no preconceived preference for one methodological toolkit over another: if the subject of the language game is mathematics or physics, we must be able to understand it quantitatively; if it is about emotion, we must be able to understand it qualitatively. Often language games will have subjects where the two are mixed and may be co-constitutive; we must therefore have the capacity to unpack the planning game, whatever it might comprise. To meet these challenges, as the following chapters hope to show, we can look to an academic project that shares the same epistemological foundations as Wittgenstein's analytic philosophy: information economics.

4   The infusion of economics into planning thought

Wittgenstein's philosophy of language as articulated in *Philosophical Investigations* encourages us to pursue an understanding of semantics based upon syntax: by uncovering the grammar of how language is used we can determine meaning. When trying to understand a particular communicative interaction this forces us to reconsider our investigative relationship to the employment of language – Wittgenstein's language games, the speech situations of communicative theory – and present a dispassionate rendering of the ways in which language is used. In thinking about planning this would necessitate that we reorientate our focus from the theoretical stance that has been the dominant way for academics to approach their subject and instead pursue a value-free investigation of the grammar of planning process.

This intellectual project is problematised by the deep divisions between academic traditions that privilege one form of data over others (Russell, 1950). For example, in the natural sciences the objective of presenting analysis uncoloured by personal opinion is said to be the ultimate goal – despite acknowledgement from within that 'scientific findings do not fall on blank minds that get made up as a result. Science engages with busy minds that have strong views about how things are and ought to be' (Marmot, 2004: 906). By contrast, in large parts of the social sciences normatively imbued theory holds sway and has subjected 'devotees of positivism, objectivism, and foundationalism' to 'three decades of withering criticism by postmodernists, post-structuralists, postcolonialists, and all the rest' (Castree and MacMillan, 2004: 472). This raises two perennial questions: how might we become epistemologically neutral?; and, simultaneously, how do we devise an analytical framework that will admit statements and propositions that are both purportedly objective and value-laden? For environmental planning this is a particularly acute issue as the discipline finds itself at the confluence of multiple academic traditions that almost define this

state of epistemological and ontological loggerheads: finding a framework that could make sense of information relating to, for example,
environmental science-led conceptions of sustainability and the quality
of life in inner-city neighbourhoods is clearly no easy task.

Previous ways of thinking about planning have generally been well-
equipped to deal with one or other branch of information: the positivist
school spanning from Geddes (1905, 1915) to Faludi (1973) emphasises
the value of scientific method and so is perhaps naturally more aligned
with the types of information that might emerge from those quarters;
but it is particularly ill-equipped to contend with those sources that
produce normative data. By contrast, the communicative turn privileges this latter form of information but is sceptical of that which
purports to speak of objective truths.

To find a way of reconciling information of such different types and
to specify how, in doing so, we might live up to Wittgenstein's
demanding criteria of understanding through neutral investigation we
can turn to an academic discipline similarly conflicted by positive and
normative impulses: economics.

Planning and economics

The academic relationship between planning and economics has often
been fraught. As the currency of welfare economics has waned and
been superseded by the neoclassical paradigm, the historic justification
for planning – that our natural and urban environments represent a
collection of unique public goods that require careful management
through a system of statutory regulation – has been similarly diminished.
It is this regulatory nature of planning that has made it an emblem of
the types of state bureaucracy that neoclassical economics has been so
successful in criticising, particularly during the 1980s and 1990s.
Indeed, a small but vocal group of academics have directed their
attention to making the case specifically against environmental planning, identifying it with price distortions in land and property markets
in those contexts where the regulatory impact of planning is said to be
strongest. Examples include Pennington (1996, 2000, 2002) and Evans
(1988, 1991; see also Boyne, 1996), who draw upon the political science
counterpart to neoclassical economics – public choice theory (Niskanen,
1971) – in advocating a greater role for market logic to be introduced
into the act of urban and environmental management. This prescription
has found a waiting and willing audience in many policy circles
(Barker, 2003, 2004; DCLG, 2006; NHPAU, 2008) where the sustained
critique of writers such as Cheshire and Sheppard (2005: 660, 1989;

see also Bramley, 1999, 2007; Meen, 2005) has served to illustrate through the case study of the UK how an overbearing planning system might result in wildly divergent real estate prices:

> Over time, controlling land supply by fiat has generated price distortions on a par with those observed in Soviet-bloc countries during the 1970s and 1980s. There is a serious and growing problem of land supply in Britain – most obviously for residential development in regions of high demand. The constraints on land supply (more exactly, the supply of space for residential use) have over time fed through to an increasingly inelastic supply of housing. This chiefly arises from the combined effect of there being a highly income-elastic demand for housing and garden space (rather than for units of housing) together with a system of land use planning the major aim of which is to constrain space consumption irrespective of any price effects this may have. Not only has this caused the real price of housing and housing land to rise substantially over the past 50 years, but it has caused accelerating price volatility and very substantial price discontinuities for parcels of land that, while they are contiguous, are designated by the planning system for different uses.
>
> (Cheshire and Sheppard, 2005: 660)

The intellectual origins of work such as this in the neoclassical tradition provide its authors with the credibility of speaking to, and from, a position of entrenched orthodoxy. Their corresponding faith in the desirability of deregulation stems from a powerful analysis of the negative effects of planning on those assets for which prices can most easily be measured – most notably land and property. However, the theory's capacity to capture those aspects of planning practice that lie beyond a calculus of price and allocative efficiency, for example statements about the relative aesthetic value of a building or the public health implications of transport planning, is severely limited. Furthermore, whilst the econometric methods upon which such research is frequently premised chime with the positivist paradigm, many of the studies in this vein also carry with them a strongly normative neoliberal element, not noticeably less conspicuous than the similarly normative objectives – albeit of a diametrically opposed type – that can be identified in much of the literature within the communicative turn. The outcome is the strongly prescriptive position that declares the outcome resulting from a marketised form of planning practice to be the only legitimate or desirable outcome: the old TINA formulation – There Is

No Alternative. As we shall see later in this and subsequent chapters, there might very well be alternative choices that the neoclassicists ignore. Moreover if, following Wittgenstein, we seek a value-free way of describing the enactment of social, economic and political relations, such a strongly biased theoretical persuasion would not provide the appropriate framework.

Against this backdrop a subsequent wave of thinking from economics has come to infuse planning theory since the mid-1990s. In reflecting on, in her view, the principal shortcoming of her *Collaborative planning* published in 1997, Healey (2003: 115) dates this new dialogue between the two disciplines to around this time: 'I neglected attention to the contributions developing within the more mainstream branches of economics, particularly in rational public choice and transaction cost theory'. These areas of economics, in particular institutional, or 'transaction cost', economics, have subsequently gone on to provide some commentators with seemingly valuable insights into how planning is enacted and with what implications.

For planning academics the appeal of the framework offered by institutional economics over neoclassical interpretations resides in the fact that it carries with it far fewer normative commitments. In seeking to theorise the costs incurred as a result of making an exchange or entering into a contract for such an exchange, the institutional school follows Coase (1937; for example, Buitelaar, 2004; Alexander, 1992, 2001; Lai, 1994; Webster, 1998) in identifying how institutional arrangements structure the terms under which transactions take place. For planning theorists this prompts a fuller understanding of how the manipulation of such transaction costs might inhibit or stimulate different types of economic activity and so draws attention to their role in the development process. The resulting policy prescriptions take a conditional form: *if* the objective is to stimulate development and economic activity, usually in areas of social and economic deprivation, we might lessen the transaction costs imposed by a system of urban and environmental management in such areas; *if* we favour restricting growth, say on grounds of environmental protection, perhaps we should raise them.

However, as yet the development of this corpus into a full empirical account of case-based transaction cost determination remains largely unfulfilled. This is in part representative of the fact that the infusion of institutional economics into planning remains only partial due to the youth of the project. However, as has been noted in critiques of institutional theory (North, 2003, Yonay, 1998; see for a review, Holmwood, 2006), it may also reflect the incapacity of the toolkit at the disposal of theorists to go beyond the measurement of transaction costs and the role of formal institutions in setting them. Advancing the project will require a confrontation with its possible limitations when faced with the sub-institutional interactions that are uncosted, based on reciprocity, informal or even clandestine.

Viewed in this manner, the acknowledged antipathy (see Adams and Tiesdell, 2010 for an excellent review) between planning theorists and economics would seem to have some justification. The critique of planning offered by the neoclassical and related public choice literatures might carry the weight of positivist analysis but it also bears the excess baggage of a neoliberal normative agenda. Certainly planning has costs and creates price distortions but rarely, if ever, does this literature seek to balance such costs against any of the benefits that planning might entail – largely because the positive aspects of planning relate to unpriced public goods and are therefore not easily assimilated within the neoclassical view that a price exists for everything. Equally, the work in the field of institutional economics, whilst benefiting from a more distant attitude to its subject, therefore suffers from an incapacity to get sufficiently close to the informal, unofficial and unstructured components of planning practice – those aspects of practice that are human as opposed to institutional. If we are to realise a full account of how the micro-rubric of urban and environmental management is played out, equivalent in detail to the deep grammatical investigations of Wittgenstein's linguistic philosophy, we will need a toolkit that is both value-free and sufficiently precise to capture the multitude of games that individuals and groups use every day in the enactment of planning practice.

Information economics and planning theory

This volume argues that information economics, through its toolkit, game theory, provides just such an investigative method. As the most significant counterweight to the neoclassical paradigm in 'mainstream' economics, information economics has been defined as that branch of the discipline premised on a:

> recognition that information is imperfect, that obtaining information can be costly, that there are important asymmetries of information, and that the extent of information asymmetries is affected by actions of firms and individuals, has had profound implications for the wisdom inherited from the past, and has provided explanations

of economic and social phenomena that otherwise would be hard to understand.

(Stiglitz, 2000: 1441)

For information economists, how well-informed market participants are with respect to one another is a core issue. The relative symmetry (or asymmetry) of information held by counterparties is taken to be fundamental to determining the terms and conditions under which 'transactions' – widely construed to include social interactions of all types, not just market-based trade – take place. Information economists have been preoccupied with questions of how individuals and groups behave and what choices they make, subject to the fundamental constraint of differing endowments of information. In stark contrast to the neoclassical school, this has drawn those working in the field out of the typical areas in which economists work and into new territory, asking and answering questions about sociological conventions, markets for illicit commodities and contemporary geopolitical issues. Such 'rogue economists' (for a popular example, see Levitt and Dubner, 2007, 2010) have essentially popularised the burgeoning field of information economics by applying economic and econometric method to consider the choices we make, both individually and collectively, when confronted with differing types and degrees of information. In so doing they have pointed out the way in which information is used in our decision-making processes and what our actions reveal about the values and preferences we might have. Often such outcomes illustrate illogical and irrational behaviour that grates against a neoclassical interpretation of how *homo economicus* is supposed to behave.

With respect to urban and environmental management, the potential use of such methods to elucidate particular examples of planning practice are legion. To take one example to which we will return in Chapter 7, in considering previous research in the neoclassical tradition on the bargaining processes that underpin developer exactions policies ('impact fees' in the USA) Healey and Barrett (1990: 92) correctly argue that 'such models presume negotiation among agents as necessary but unproblematic in the processes of exchange, and assume certain structuring parameters, such as private property and a particular form of agent rationality. Thus, they do not explore negotiative processes empirically'. Accurate as this criticism is, unfortunately, as has been noted earlier in Chapter 2, the communicative turn does little to fill this gap of how power relations – in many instances strength and weakness being contrasting functions of being better or worse informed – influence the specifics of bargaining. By contrast, for information economists the area of interest is precisely the pattern of negotiation, analogous to uncovering the rule-governed grammar of a language game, as this *explains* the outcome of the interaction, just as the syntax of the language game explains meaning for Wittgenstein.

Building on the examples set out in Box 4.1, for information economics the most important questions in deciphering a theory of bargaining, such as that common to much of planning practice, are those that shed light on how counterparties seek to acquire, use and signal information: what is the information set and how is it distributed amongst counterparties? which agency 'moves' first and with what strategic intention? Applied to environmental planning, these questions entail an investigation of how participants in the planning process interact and with what strategic intention. In relation to the first question as to how agencies acquire information, this is an area of paramount concern for information economists and has been the subject of comprehensive theoretical conceptualisation. For instance, the seminal work of Spence (1973, 1974) on 'signalling' – the activity of conspicuously displaying information to resolve, or reinforce, an information asymmetry – and of Stiglitz (2000) on 'screening' are now well-established contributions for which each was awarded a Nobel Prize.

Box 4.1: Getting less than you bargained for: deficiencies in planning theory's account of 'deal making'

There is an urgent need for greater research on the specifics of bargaining in planning practice. The aggregate of knowledge in this area turns upon a recognition that there is an unspecified connection between 'the way social groups use their available power resources [and] their knowledge and capability to resolve their particular problems' (Brown and Rosendo, 2000: 212). Such observations have been supplemented by informal, long-hand accounts of the most basic features of bargaining in general that also characterise aspects of planning practice: 'for negotiations to be successful, all parties must desire to bargain. Some observers have referred to this as "ripeness" arguing that before effective negotiation is possible, the conflict must be one in which each party believes a bargained solution is the most cost effective way to end a dispute' (Burkardt et al., 1998: 877).

Aside from this intuitive understanding of what motivates bargaining in planning practice in the first place we apparently have a limited understanding of what the rest of the process might comprise. The specifics of how counterparts interact in the types of bargaining situation that characterise planning practice have not provoked significant interest amongst planning theorists. Perhaps this important gap in the research is redolent of the undertheorisation of power and conflict that has already been noted in Chapter 2 as having afflicted the empirical application of much of existing planning theory. For example, some have noted, but not elaborated upon, the centrality of power in understanding how planning encounters might work out:

> Conflict is part of the wider issue of power relationships and power has been defined as a form of social relationship whereby the behaviour of one group in society is dependent upon the behaviour of other groups. This wide-ranging and abstract definition can be delimited firstly by *describing power* in terms of magnitude (how much?), distribution (who controls?), scope (what is controlled?), domain (whom is controlled?) and secondly by *explaining power* by reference to the resources, skills, motivation and bargaining ability to establish relationships possessed by the groups concerned.
>
> (Ennis, 1997: 1947)

Helpful as these categories are, filling them with content is still some way off; maybe because we do not have a theory that can systematically explain the strategies that actors in planning practice might employ.

Such conjecture requires closer interrogation. What kinds of strategies and tactics characterise planning practice? Again, we only have broad-brush accounts to guide us. For example Brown and Rosendo's (2000) study of environmental depletion in Rondônia, Brazil found that interactions between the policy elite – NGOs, state actors – and local communities were characterised by 'strategic attempts to increase bargaining power by local actors that included the formation of alliances and the tactic of enrolling other stakeholders to their cause'. Instructive as this is, we still need a theory that could explain which alliances formed and why; why alternative alliances were not formed; to what extent existing arrangements were systemically durable; and what likelihood they had of securing their objectives. Similar questions remain despite studies such as Few's (2002: 31; see also Arce and Long, 1992) research on actor power in the enactment of planning arrangements that are designed to provide special protection for ecosystems of special significance: 'individuals and groups, including the marginalized, exercise power in negotiations between one another, making strategic trade-offs to give themselves room for manoeuvre and enrolling others to their cause'. Developing these valuable insights into a detailed understanding of how tactics and strategy are used, both by individuals and groups, will be the central business of Chapters 6, 7 and 8.

In many areas the application of information economics has yielded important insights into how any number of mechanisms – markets of various type, auctions, social interactions, discourse, political agreements, voting, negotiation, bargaining – work and, perhaps more importantly, why they sometimes do not work. Empirical applications have uncovered common forms of strategy such as 'information transmission' (Crawford and Sobel, 1982), 'competitive signalling' (Riley, 1975) and 'cheap talk' (Farrell and Rabin, 1996). Furthermore, the approach has been taken to set out specific empirical investigations of auctions (Laffont, 1997); markets for insurance (Rothschild and Stiglitz, 1976); credit (Bernanke and Gertler, 1995; Stiglitz, 1985); securities exchanges (Zingales, 1994); labour (Spence, 1974; Stiglitz, 1975; Weiss, 1995); and agriculture (Stiglitz, 1974; Shaban, 1987). If these areas are understood to fall within the compass of mainstream economics, the logic of information economics and its analytical toolkit, game theory, has also been used productively to analyse voting behaviour, bargaining and strategic interaction of different types in sociology (Petersen, 1994), political science (Brams, 1975; Ordeshook, 1986) and industrial negotiation (Bresnahan, 1989; Tirole, 1988).

When this replete corpus is allied to the numerous 'rogue' applications, it is perhaps surprising that the infusion of information economics into spatial planning has been far more recent and much more limited. Aside from a small number of early studies designed to incorporate game theory, the methodological toolkit of information economics, into conceptual work on land allocation (Batty, 1977; Berkman, 1965), there have been few significant subsequent attempts to use information economics as a lens through which to view the interaction of parties in the practice of urban and environmental planning. This is perhaps due to the fact that early attempts to use information economics and game theory to consider planning issues tended to focus on the theorisation of planning's effects on formal markets, most typically for land and property.

However, in light of the more recent confident application of information economics to areas traditionally outside the jurisdiction of economics, now might be a propitious moment to consider how information economics could be applied to specific, non-market-based examples of planning practice.

Game theory and planning

To explore the possibility of developing a dialogue between information economics and environmental planning first requires some preliminary engagement with its toolkit, game theory (for introductory texts, see: Bresnahan and Reiss, 1991; Dixit and Skeath, 2004; Fudenberg and Tirole, 1991; Maskin, 1999; Colman, 1995; Gintis, 2000; Snidal, 1985): an investigative approach to describing human interaction in any given setting. As Binmore (2007a: 1) describes it:

> Drivers manoeuvring in heavy traffic are playing a driving game. Bargain-hunters bidding on e-bay are playing an auctioning game. A firm and a union negotiating next year's wage are playing a bargaining game. When opposing candidates choose their platform in an election, they are playing a political game. The owner of a grocery store deciding today's price for corn flakes is playing an economic game. In brief, a game is being played whenever human beings interact.

In many respects the title game 'theory' is a misnomer as, far from being a theory in the sense of cognitive construction or a 'way of understanding' the external world, it is 'empirically empty' (Grüne-Yanoff and Schweinzer, 2008: 134). Instead, game theory is a methodological approach, or as it will be referred to here, a 'toolkit', that economists (and, increasingly, others) use to uncover the fine-grained details, often strategies, that define the myriad social settings implied by Binmore above. The consonance between this form of investigation and that advocated by Wittgenstein to unearth the deep grammar of our language games is well put by Bianchi and Moulin (1991: 187–88):

Game theory is not a theory which has as output a set of refutable statements, but merely a syntax articulating the vocabulary of interdependent rationality. Game 'theory' per se is no more empirically verifiable than an alleged translation from English into an unspoken language. Yet its application to specific economic political or social situations produces many testable statements.

Similar acknowledgements of the relationship between the analytic philosophy of Ludwig Wittgenstein and the method of game theory have been noted by prominent writers in the information economics tradition (Gintis, 2000; Hargreaves-Heap and Varoufakis, 1995). Taking this cue, many academics have gone on to apply game theory more and more widely to the long-run implications of the 'ordinary settings' implied by an analysis of ordinary language. Nowhere is this more apparent than in game theory's application to evolutionary biology (Weibull, 1997; see also Maynard-Smith, 1982). At its most ambitious, game theory has been used to synthesise a complete account of our social evolution, from a general account of the relationship between social behaviour and biological development (Gintis, 2009; Roughgarden, 2009), to the dismantlement and subsequent rebuilding of large parts of Western moral philosophy (Binmore, 2005). By comparison, the less ambitious task of using game theory to aid our understanding of urban and environmental management might seem a more manageable task.

This is not to understate the complexity attendant to the games we play in planning, but rather to emphasise the power of the toolkit that is available to decipher agents' (or, from now on, 'players') behaviour. Game theory allows us to reconfront the questions that have pre-occupied planning theorists in the past: do players of the planning game behave cooperatively or competitively?; what tactics do they use, and with what results? However, by using a game-theoretic framework we can provide a more systematic account of the way in which players play the planning game than might otherwise be possible using other theoretical approaches either borrowed from positivism, neoclassical economics or Habermasian sociology. To illustrate the value of approaching these types of question in this way we can use a famous game, first articulated in longhand by Jean-Jacques Rousseau (1755) and subsequently used by game theorists as a lens through which to consider a myriad of empirical issues, particularly international relations and diplomacy (for example, Stein, 1990): the Stag hunt.

In its original formulation, Rousseau used the analogy of a stag hunt to draw attention to the potential for social situations to

Player B

		Cooperate	Defect
	Cooperate	5, 5	0, 4
Player A	Defect	4, 0	2, 2

Figure 4.1 The Stag hunt game

incentivise cooperation or individualism (referred to here as 'defection'). The author conceives of primitive humans in a hunter-gatherer setting who are faced with a dilemma: they may either cooperate to catch a great prize, a stag, or behave individually (termed 'defect') to secure a 'lesser' hare for themselves alone. A game theory analysis of the problem begins from a recognition that each individual's best choice is dependent upon that of their counterparty. To illustrate, Figure 4.1 sets out a common game theory interpretation in which two players, A and B, play the Stag hunt game.

This practice of setting out the results, or *pay-offs*, of the game in tabular form is usually referred to as presenting the game in *strategic form*: the four pairs of integers reflect the outcomes to each player – with Player A's pay-off always written first – for any possible scenario that the game might take. It spells out a single interaction – or *one-shot game* – in which we might summarise what each player might do given the possible choices of the other. In this case, there are two potential 'best' responses summarised in the top left and bottom right corners of the matrix. If Player A chooses to defect, Player B is best served by making the same selection: the response secures a pay-off of 2 rather than 0. Equally, if Player A chooses to cooperate, Player B should follow suit again as that strategy results in a pay-off of 5 rather than 4. These 'best responses' are referred to as Nash equilibria after their discoverer, the game theory pioneer John Nash (1951).

For our purposes, with respect to urban and environmental planning and management, the Stag hunt game serves to demonstrate three vital lessons. First, the game does not have a single solution but rather a pair of best-response Nash equilibria: *cooperate, cooperate* and *defect, defect*. This means that there are two alternative 'states of the world' that can be understood to represent a 'best' outcome for both players: one is the unerringly non-cooperative solution that the neoclassical school has conditioned policy makers to think is representative of *all* optimisation questions, but the other is its polar opposite, an entirely cooperative arrangement. Explaining the perception that there is no alternative to the version of events that constructs individual competition as the hallmark of a well-functioning society is accomplished by pointing out that neoclassical economists have historically preoccupied themselves with abstract models that often have just one solution:

> I think that it is only because traditional neoclassical economics largely confined its attention to models with a unique equilibrium that it managed to get so far without paying any serious attention either to fairness norms or to all the many other institutions without which our society would fall apart.
>
> (Binmore, 2010: 245)

If the games we play in real life sometimes take a similar format to the Stag hunt, then we might do well to think of them as having more than one, possibly many, equilibrium solutions from which we select one. But which one should we pick? This question sets in stark relief the second lesson that we can learn from the Stag hunt game. The pay-off table shows that the cooperative solution yields the greatest return for all concerned (5, 5 versus the other Nash equilibrium of 2, 2 and the symmetrical non-equilibria of conflicting strategies 0, 4 and 4, 0). Yet, if players have chosen to settle on the less productive, non-cooperative equilibrium, *defect, defect*, making the transition to the more efficient *cooperate, cooperate* strategy is made more problematic by the fact that this will be incumbent upon each player being able to trust the other to accompany them in making a uniform transition from *defect, defect*, to *cooperate, cooperate*. To illustrate, should Player A seek to persuade Player B that this transition is desirable and that they (Player B) can rely on Player A to play *cooperate* next time, Player B's choice depends wholly on whether they believe Player A or not. In the event that Player A goes back on their word and continues to play defect, while Player B dutifully follows the terms of the agreement to change strategy, the outcome is summarised in the bottom left-hand corner of the grid: Player A becomes better off, with a pay-off of 4, whilst Player B's position worsens, with a pay-off of 0.

This raises the third and final lesson that we can draw from the Stag hunt game. For us to settle on the cooperative Nash equilibrium, the players must be able to trust that each other will stick to the selection that is mutually best for both. The strongest form of trust might be inculcated if the players have robust information that guarantees the cooperation of their counterparty; but our review of attempts to engineer cooperation in planning practice would suggest that, as simply encouraging cooperation is no easy task, *guaranteeing* it might be impossible. Perhaps only a well-codified, universally known and habitually obeyed set of rules would succeed in securing this outcome; but this is implausible. The closest approximation we have to such a state of affairs in planning practice is the rule book of planning law – the subject of the next chapter.

Establishing the rules of the game

Information economics offers the potential for a genuine marriage of planning and economics: its toolkit, game theory, allows us to conceptualise a degree of interdependent qualitative and quantitative complexity, present in even the most superficially simple interactions featuring just two actors. From this perspective, the fine-grained analysis that is the objective of game theory differentiates it from the use of institutional economics in planning theory in that it allows us to get beneath the formal institutional setting – important though this may be in setting the rules of how engagements are structured – and delve into the minutiae of strategy and tactics that exemplify all human interaction, as much in environmental planning as anywhere else. Furthermore, its consonance with analytical philosophy entails the eschewal of theory encumbered with normative baggage. This distinguishes it from neoclassical economics in its rejection of normative constructs such as 'economic man' and, significantly, through the acknowledgement of multiple Nash equilibria (even in simple two-player games), brings with it a recognition, shared with Wittgenstein, that many possible equilibrium 'states of affairs' exist: the task is to explain how the one that prevails has come to do so and with what effects.

Providing a game-theoretic interpretation of a social interaction, therefore, makes no claims for adjudging the desirability or otherwise of one equilibrium solution over others. By contrast, of course, this is precisely what policy makers might use game theory to do. If incentivising some uses of the urban and natural environments might be accomplished by instituting a rule book that encourages some types of planning game over others, the utility of a game-theoretic understanding of planning practice to policy makers is easy to see. Therefore, getting from one 'state of the world' to another will be a central preoccupation of this book. However, before we can arrive at an understanding of how transformation might be possible, we must first account for the state of the world that confronts us and consider how we make the rules for the planning game.

Part II

5 Introducing the planning game

Where do the rules that govern urban and environmental management come from? Stated alternatively, who sets them and why do they choose the rules they do? If we were to ask the same question of the language that we use in playing out this planning game, we could turn to Wittgenstein's philosophy of language, as discussed in the first part of this volume, which shows how individuals can be understood to frame their own rules and conventions about how terms are used and interpreted in the very act of using their language itself. Do the formal rules and informal conventions that condition the act of urban and environmental planning similarly emerge as a self-generated construction?

This question requires careful consideration and an extensive answer. Our superficial understanding of planning practice – just like our superficial understanding of language practices – is that it is inherently complex, contextually specific and the result of individual agents' choices and a macro-structure that sets parameters and standards by which norms are governed. A deeper reading inherited from Wittgenstein would emphasise the reflexive role that these individual actors play in establishing, and changing, the acceptance of what these norms should be.

In the following chapters the germ of this idea is cultivated to consider the various ways in which the actions of players in the planning game can be understood as conforming to this idea of response and adaptation to rules. This will encompass games of conflict (Chapter 6), games of dissimulation (Chapter 7), games of cooperation (Chapter 8) and games of direction (Chapter 9). However, before we can begin to dismantle and then rebuild the world of planning practice we must first set out the rule book of planning practice as it is.

Non-cooperative versus cooperative game theory: the 'classical planning game'

The last few pages of Chapter 4 set out the Stag hunt game. In its classic formulation the game illustrates how two entirely logical alternative states of the world might exist: the first, call it World I, where competitive individualism is the norm, and another, World II, where cooperation rules. We will return to this idea of alternative 'states of the world' in later chapters where it will be used to conceptualise how players come to refine their beliefs about the type of game they are playing – and, by extension, how they should play. For now it is sufficient to note that the entirely cooperative and wholly uncooperative alternatives revealed by the Stag hunt represent poles; in reality the games we play in planning are likely to be a blend of cooperative and non-cooperative behaviour.

This distinction speaks to a deeper conceptual schism between cooperative and non-cooperative game theory, the former being concerned with how, why and with what effect coalitions form, whilst the latter is preoccupied with the strategies and tactics that determine how a game might unfold in a competitive situation. As so many of the human interactions that game theorists have sought to investigate around the globe have turned out to run on competitive lines, non-cooperative game theory has come to hold sway as the dominant way for economists to think about and analyse everything from international relations and voting behaviour to terrorism and auctions. Similarly, in environmental planning many of the games we play seem to be characterised by some degree of conflict. Disputes over territory and the uses to which the natural and urban environments should be put represent the most enduring problem in planning.

This observation speaks most clearly to the legislative arrangements that must accompany a formal system of urban and environmental management. It is this legal framework and the recourse that it provides for a judicial third party to adjudicate in the event of dispute that leads Lai and Lorne (2006: 54) to conceive of an adversarial form of engagement as the hallmark of the 'classical planning game'. However, the impact of the formal structure provided by the law might be more far reaching than simply explaining courtroom encounters; it conditions the types of strategy that players of the 'classical' planning game might deploy long before informal conflict becomes a judicial matter. From this perspective the law itself and the institutions charged with upholding or dispensing justice provide not only the rule book for a 'one-shot' game in a courtroom but, rather, the wider context that governs how players who seek to play, or are forced into playing, games such as those that might arise in environmental planning behave towards one another. In short, 'institutions are the rules of the game' (North, 1990: 3). Planning provides an excellent example of how this rule-governed behaviour might be appropriately conceptualised using game theory. In thinking and writing on these issues many have used language that implies the consonance between the metaphor of a rule-governed 'game' and the types of engagement that might occur in planning practice. For example Jowell (1977: 65) has referred to a development plan as effectively 'a set of rules governing human conduct', a metaphor extended by Wu (1999: 1757) in his account of 'the "game" of landed-property production'. Indeed the chief architect of collaborative planning theory uses a similar vocabulary to describe the structuring influence of planning law:

> The *rules* of institutional organisation and political regulation govern the way material resources are used. Such rules may be formalized in law and administrative procedure, or exist as custom and practice. They express the specific form of the mode of regulation within which property development occurs as manifest in the way in which rules are used and adapted by agents; particularly significant are the rules governing the ownership and control of resources.
>
> (Healey, 1992c: 35, emphasis in original)

These intuitive ideas are supported by thinking from mainstream game theory. For example Cárdenas and Ostrom (2004: 310; see also Binmore, 2010; Ostrom, 1990, 1999, 2000) argue that:

> Studying the context of a game is crucial because institutions affect individuals' decisions to cooperate by performing at least three tasks. First institutions reinforce social norms that are consistent with the rules. Second they allow participants to gather more or less information about the behaviour of others. And third they entitle people to reward and punish certain behaviours with material and non-material incentives.

Naturally the type of planning game that arises as a result of the structuring influence of such rules differs from place to place and over time, giving rise to the strong tradition within the planning academy of comparative studies (Faludi and Hamnett, 1975). However, even where structural differences are greatest, for example between the federal USA and the unitary UK, some have identified a trend for the legislative-discursive aims, if not always the machinery of planning systems, to converge over the last quarter of the twentieth century (Elwood, 2004). This normalisation is explained, at least in part, as a response by national governments to an argument, popular in much of the social sciences, that the previously central role of the nation state – usually the principal author and enforcer of the planning rule book – has been eroded, largely as a result of globalisation. The complex, fragmented societies ushered in as a consequence of globalisation 'pulling up, pushing down, squeezing sideways' (Giddens, 1998a: 13), it was argued, have robbed the traditional locus of power, the national government, of its capacity for independent action. Such an explanation of the diminished capacity of nation states has been seen to fit neatly with collaborative planning's interpretation of an increasingly socially complex, urban world that would require new forms of state agency and an upsurge in participative democracy to design and deliver planning policy.

The resultant programmes of reform have often drawn explicitly on the work of authors such as Giddens (2002) and the planning theorists who have followed this lead, to justify the necessity for changing both the activities of planners and the scales at which planning operates. On the first of these two aspects of reform, in many contexts the day-to-day activities of the planner have been understood as having been 'deprofessionalised' (Tewdwr-Jones and Allmendinger, 1998), implying the diminution of a specific, multi-faceted, professional role to that of a coordinating activity, orchestrating the activities of others. The second component adds a further degree of complexity as the geographical resituation of planning has been incumbent upon whichever territorial scale has been in vogue in various contexts at various times (Deas and Ward, 1999, 2000). For example, in the UK repeated reterritorialisation of planning has seen the emergence, and subsequent discarding, of the 'new' localism (Imrie and Raco, 1999), the 'new' regionalism (HM Treasury, 2001), the 'new' city-regionalism (Urban Task Force, 2005; SURF, 2003) and even a second 'new' localism (DCLG, 2011).

This whirl of reform, both in the content of environmental planning and the scale at which it is delivered, has been the subject of a huge amount of research, giving rise to what are now well-rehearsed arguments – usually summarised by the dictum that the 1990s saw a transition from 'government to governance'. The attendant changes to planning of these reforms – often cloaked in the language of 'modernisation' (ODPM, 1998, 2005) – have been far reaching as governments have looked for solutions to developing planning systems 'fit for purpose' in the 'hollowed-out' (Rhodes, 1994) states of the twenty-first century. Often they have arrived at a remarkably similar prescription: a more open, 'stakeholder'-centred, potentially more permissive system.

Box 5.1: Making collaborative planning systems

The breadth of nation states in which planning reform has been instituted over the last quarter of the twentieth century is staggering. When collected together, the case-study research on the range of places effectively aligning their approaches to urban and environmental management covers much of the developed, and developing, world including: Albania (Nientied, 1998); Australia (McGuirk, 2005; McGuirk and Dowling, 2009; Searle and Cardew, 2000); Canada (Kipfer and Keil, 2002); the Czech Republic, Slovakia and Hungary (Nedović-Budić, 2001); Denmark (Majoor, 2008); Finland (Mäntysalo, 1999); Indonesia (Hudalah and Woltjer, 2007); Japan (Shibata, 2008); New Zealand (McDermott, 1998); Poland (Riley, 1997); Portugal (Breda-Vázquez and Oliveira, 2008); Russia (Shove and Anderson, 1997); the Netherlands (Nienhuis, *et al.*, 2011); the UK (Holgersen and Haarstad, 2009; Inch, 2009; Prior, 2005); and the USA (Elwood, 2002; 2004; McCann, 2001; Newman and Ashton, 2004).

In sum, these valuable studies leave the overwhelming impression that by the early years of the new century planning across much of the globe was a qualitatively different activity to what it had been 25, or fewer, years before. Furthermore, in virtually every case the rationale for change was that a more open system, in line with the prescriptions of the communicative school, was required to develop a planning system fit for the twenty-first century. Features common to all, in rhetoric at least, included the development of more public participation, partnership working amongst wide networks of 'stakeholders' and the redesignation of the planner from a specific, professional role to that of orchestrator, coordinating multiple stakeholders from, but most definitely not at, the centre of the process.

These aims, consonant with the prescriptions of the best advice of planning theorists at the time, have resulted in far more open planning systems across much of the globe. However,

the degree to which this opening up has had the effects that
theorists forecast is much less certain; as the rest of this chapter
goes on to show, some have contended that exactly the opposite
of a more progressive planning polity has emerged.

Spatial planning and the rise of neoliberalism

Rationalising the resulting states of affairs following the waves of
reform set out in Box 5.1 has often been officially accomplished by
reference to a purported transition from an adversarial style of land-use
planning, of which the 'classical planning game' is indicative, to a
system of 'spatial planning', in which all the stakeholders who might
conceivably have an interest in the development of a place are gathered
together and encouraged to arrive at locally-devised, consensual proposals. Yet, despite a host of attempts to define it, the term 'spatial
planning' has remained elusive. According to Faludi (2002: 4), the
Dutch/German origins of the term make the concept difficult for English
speakers to grasp and it does not resonate closely with nations that
have followed either a British approach to 'town and country' planning
or a US preference for zoning arrangements. Others (for example
Kunzmann, 2006: 43) emphasise the 'Euro-English' nature of the concept's
translation: a style of language that has become more and more
apparent as planning policy that has been formulated at the transnational
scale of the European Union has increased in significance for the
domestic planning polities of EU member states. As a result, significant statements of EU policy, such as the European Spatial
Development Perspective, have served to introduce such terms into
English usage and from there to the Anglophone world more widely.

The lasting impression is of an ill-defined expression used to
represent a variegated world of professional practice, perhaps best
summarised by Tewdwr-Jones (2004: 591) as 'an ongoing, enduring
process of managing change, by a range of actors, in the interests of
sustainable development'. Worthy as this sounds, in reality many have
identified the outcomes of the reforms outlined above as representing
something more sinister: part of a long-wave process of neoliberalisation
identified as having affected planning just as it had many other policy
spheres (Peck and Tickell, 2002). Perhaps the most significant outcome
of the neoliberalisation of planning is the emergence of concepts such as
state-led gentrification, revanchism and, where market conditions are less
propitious, the containment of social deprivation through, at best, ame-
liorative, at worst, vengeful neighbourhood-focused interventions

(Smith, 1996). When dismantled in empirical studies the hallmark of planning in this neoliberal period is the ubiquitous presence of conflict in the enactment of so many of the reformed systems that were designed to foster collaboration.

When collated, the lasting impression of work such as that outlined in Boxes 5.1 and 5.2 is of myriad planning systems across the globe being remade in the closing decades of the twentieth century around a neoliberal consensus regarding what the principal objectives of planning should be. Whilst the specific accommodations necessary to make such reforms 'work' *in situ* differ from one context to another, these contrasting features – the agents who may or may not be involved, the coalitions of interest that may or may not form, the strategies that actors may or may not employ – are said to be contingent. Continuity can be found in the all-pervading logic of neoliberalism. From this perspective the waves of reform can be seen as a recalibration of planning systems to facilitate rather than inhibit the territorialisation of economic growth whilst simultaneously containing and pacifying sites where the economic system has conspicuously unravelled. The result is a global trend for the subordination of planning's regulatory function to its capacity to grease the wheels of capitalist accumulation – through land assembly, encouraging deal making and generally providing an institutional framework for counterparts to bargain and negotiate. Whether communicative theory can be best understood as responding to, or driving, this programme of reform is an open question that others have already considered (cf. Bengs, 2005; Sager, 2005). In either case, by intent or otherwise, it is ironic that the political application of the communicative turn's ideas – borne of a desire to empower the systemically weak and amplify seldom heard voices – may have resulted in quite the opposite.

Box 5.2: Giving the game away? Spatial planning as a vessel for neoliberalism

When Manuel Castells asked in 1992, 'the world has changed: can planning change?' (Castells, 1992: 43), he posed a question that many academics working in the field had been contemplating repeatedly for many years. This perpetual self-examination is aptly put by Campbell (2003: 347): 'there has probably never been a time in history when somewhere a commentator was not penning the phrase, "planning is at the crossroads"'.

However, on this occasion, in the early 1990s, the question may have been particularly prescient as the date marks what in many countries was around 20 years' experience of a neoliberal period born in the late 1970s (Peck and Tickell, 2002; Harvey, 2005). The history and geography of neoliberalism now represent a replete corpus (see Brenner, 1999, 2004) but, for planning academics, Jonas and Bridge (2003) provide a great service in identifying a long-run understanding of urban and environmental management in much of the developed world that contrasts a post-war statist approach to the activity with one more closely aligned to market logic and neoliberal values that was in operation during the latter decades of the century – thus dating the 'crossroads' that many had been searching for to the late 1970s/ early 1980s. As Box 5.1 showed, the implications for urban and environmental planning of this 'roll-out' phase of neoliberalism have been geographically far reaching; however, it has also had a deep material impact on the content and character of planning practice across the globe.

Perhaps the most significant aspect of the reforms set in train in the neoliberal period is the seeming growth of conflict in planning practice. Whilst the adversarial nature of the 'classical planning game' serves to illustrate planning's 'intrinsically conflict-ridden position within the state' (Inch, 2009) some commentators have drawn attention to the irony that, in implementing a programme of reform at least superficially designed to enhance collaboration – often explicitly supported by the communicative school's prediction that a more open system would create space for wider participation – the opposite has actually occurred: domination by the most powerful interest groups.

Evidence of newly instituted forms of collaborative planning resulting in more overtly conflicted relationships that degenerate into neoliberal settlements is widespread. A good example of a typical tale can be found in Kipfer and Keil's (2002) account of the decades-long struggle between two groups in Toronto's city politics: a left-leaning group of advocates for social justice and the commercial interests of the business community. The latter's enhanced capacity to engage with a formal system remodelled along communicative lines, the authors argue, presented them with a significant advantage in representing their case as the only viable option and the one that should be implemented urgently if the city were to be prevented from losing out to international competitors. The currency of the argument resulted in the conversion of once-dispassionate professionals responsible for checking and balancing these two competing groups since the

1960s (see Filion, 1999) to the new orthodoxy: 'Many planners, consultants, and developers with reform roots have become exponents of neoliberal entrepreneurialism, even as they continue to promote the "emotional values" associated with sophisticated downtown urbanism'.

Research from other settings – good examples include London (Holgersen and Haarstad, 2009); Frankfurt-am-Main (Keil and Ronneberger, 2000); and Newark, New Jersey (Newman and Ashton, 2004) – corroborates the above account and lends credence to the view that the reformed systems of planning are now, in many contexts, explicitly part of the neoliberal project. By extension, planners' active role in animating these systems has seen them understood by some researchers as complicit in the aggressive gentrification of some urban spaces and in the erosion of the natural environment. These material implications resulting from attempts to enact communicative planning have led some to acknowledge that 'communicative and collaborative planning ... provide an extremely attractive way for neoliberals to maintain hegemony while ensuring political stability' (Purcell, 2009: 140).

For others, the transition to 'spatial planning' systems that in actuality crudely ape some, but far from all, of the visions of the communicative theorists is best understood as revealing the true degree of conflict that previous, post-war accommodative systems masked. This point is well made by Aylett (2010: 479), who argues, in a case study of urban and environmental management in Durban, South Africa, that 'conflict is not only unavoidable, but also a legitimate and potentially beneficial form of participation'. Pre-empting a question to which this volume will return, the same author (Aylett, 2010: 492) persuasively argues that, 'far from being in opposition, conflict and collaboration constitute mutually re-enforcing elements of an ongoing political process'.

The consequences, a widely-experienced landscape of domination by the powerful and increased frustration amongst those traditionally peripheral to the decision-making process, leading to more hostile forms of engagement, suggest that the crossroads at which planning once again finds itself represents the dilemma of how to reconcile conflict in the neoliberal age. This task is problematised by the fact that our experience is not of a uniform transition to increased conflict and competition but, rather, as Aylett (2010) correctly points out at the end of Box 5.2, a situation where cooperation and conflict are inextricably linked through the *strategies* employed by players of the planning game: for example where threats of conflict are used to subdue dissent. This throws into sharp relief the way in which superficial accounts of practice and process in environmental planning reveal how little we *really* know: when we observe conflict, are we witnessing an episode essential to encourage ongoing collaboration or an expression of genuine systemic differences between competing parties? A useful way of thinking about the researchers' position to questions such as this might be found through analogy. In this respect Healey's (1997: 275) 'black box' – used to critique the rationalist conception of planning as a vessel to be filled with data – becomes a particularly rich metaphor for the task that now confronts planning theory itself. However, rather than the 'impenetrable black box of "taken-for-granted" knowledge', it rather becomes a vessel for the myriad of competing agential strategies that might be deployed by the various actors, and coalitions of actors, involved in the planning game.

Lifting the lid on the 'black box' of planning practice

As Boxes 5.1 and 5.2 have illustrated, the subtle contextual differences that comparative studies teach us, serve to differentiate one planning system from another, can, from a different perspective, alternatively be understood as contingent aspects of a wider international trend for planning to be remodelled along neoliberal lines. These differences in the 'nuts and bolts' of what each black box of planning practice might contain represent a specific challenge to empirical researchers: how to make sense of the strategies and tactics that players of the planning game might employ. What are the 'moving parts' in the machinery of spatial planning?; what should we expect the black box to hold and how should we unpack it?

Previous chapters have shown that the rationalists' dream of finding an empty black box and filling it with pure, objective facts was, as the collaborative school quite correctly pointed out, a fantasy. However, the collaborative turn's hopes that the box might contain an ideal speech situation, mutual collaboration and the possibility of a politically progressive settlement were also often frustrated because they 'ignore the permanence of conflict, inequality and domination' (Bickerstaff and Walker, 2005: 2139) that, in the neoliberal age, frequently lies within. In response, more recently some writers have turned to complexity theory in recognition that, often, the contents of the black box are

tangled and not easily understood. This has resulted in mixed interpretations of what will be required of the academic project that begins
from an acknowledgement of this complexity. For example some
understand it to demand the production of computer-simulated visuali-
sations, 3-D mapping and ever more elaborate geographically weighted
regressions (for example, Batty, 2007; see also Batty and Longley, 1987;
Batty and Xie, 1999). Others respond to the challenge by developing
the work of the communicative turn to conceptualise increasingly
complex urban societies (for example, Byrne, 2003). It remains to be
seen if this project can be made into a coherent whole that is capable
of delivering a consistent theory of urban and environmental planning
or whether the disciplinary divisions that seemingly remain intact
beneath the common label will undermine its integrity.

By contrast, this volume argues that a theory that can adequately
conceptualise the planning game must have recourse to a suite of
methods that will allow the black box to be systematically unpacked,
whatever it might contain. Ironically the analytical framework
suggested to meet this challenge, game theory, uses the same metaphor
of a black box to conceptualise the questions to which it is
applied. For example Binmore (2007a: 141), pre-empting many of the
themes that this volume will seek to explore in relation to urban and
environmental planning, conceives of:

> an unmodelled black box whose contents somehow resolve all the
> problems of commitment and trust … . In economic applications,
> one can sometimes argue that the black box contains all the
> apparatus of the legal system … . In social applications, the black
> box may contain the reasons why the players care about the effect that
> behaving dishonestly may have on their reputation for trustworthy
> behaviour in the future.

This illustrates game theory's versatility. Through the lenses of
cooperative and non-cooperative method, in which qualitative answers
are often provided to quantitative questions, game theory allows us to
tackle the full range of social interactions: those governed by a formal
rule book, such as that provided by planning law, and informal
encounters where the terms of engagement are self-determined. As a
result, unlike other theorisations of planning, game theory is prepared
for the black box to hold any contents. For example, to address the criticism outlined above – that planning theory has historically not dealt
sufficiently with 'conflict, inequality and domination' – what if we
think of the black box as containing all the ingredients for outright,

undiluted conflict? In such an event we would be confronted with a situation well-represented by the class of games of which the Prisoners' dilemma is the most famous example.

The Prisoners' dilemma

In its classic articulation the Prisoners' dilemma presents a game where two suspects are being held separately on suspicion of committing a crime. Each is being questioned individually and has the binary choice of confessing to the crime, and thus implicating the other captive, or denying any involvement. The consequences of the available choices to each prisoner are described as: if one prisoner were to confess and the other deny, the confessor would be freed, whilst the denier would be incarcerated for six months; if both were to deny involvement, a technicality would be used to award each a one-month sentence; if both were to confess, each would be held for three months. Presented in its strategic form in Figure 5.1, the game has pay-offs.

Player B

		Confess	Deny
Player A	Confess	−3, −3	0, −6
	Deny	−6, 0	−1, −1

Figure 5.1 The classic Prisoners' dilemma

If we consider the game from the perspective of Player A, whatever Player B does, the optimal strategy seems to be to confess: if Player B decides to deny, Player A is set free by choosing to confess; equally, a confession on the part of Player B is best matched by a confession on the part of Player A as this results in a three-month, rather than six-month, custodial sentence. As the game is symmetrical, the same conditions apply for Player B: their optimal choice is also to always choose 'confess'. The conclusion is that the game strongly incentivises individualism – choosing confess is the only Nash equilibrium in the game, but it represents a betrayal of the other prisoner.

However, here we are assuming two things: first, that both prisoners are interested in securing the best individual outcome for themselves and, second, that they do not have any information about what the other will do. If we relax these assumptions, we can see that there is an alternative conception of optimality. Thinking collectively, the best solution is for each to deny involvement as this results in both prisoners receiving a sentence of one month. As this is the best collective outcome we can say, in the language of economics, that it is Pareto efficient: it is the optimal solution where no player can be made better off under a different scenario without simultaneously making another player worse off. But now imagine that one of the prisoners is extremely confident – or better, knew – that their accomplice would obey this cooperative arrangement of denying any involvement. With this knowledge, the best individual choice is now even more decidedly to choose *confess*, and so double-cross the other prisoner, as the pairing *confess, deny* (and *deny, confess*, as the game is symmetrical) results in the confessor being set free whilst the denier serves the full six-month sentence. The conclusion is that it can never be individually rational to choose the cooperative *deny, deny* in a one-round iteration of the Prisoners' dilemma.

The Prisoners' dilemma is a simple game that illustrates a number of core concepts. First, it provides us with two separate notions of optimality, depending on whether we are thinking individually or collectively, and shows that the two might lead to completely different outcomes. Second, it illustrates the critical value of information. If one player is better informed than the other, it throws into sharp relief the moral hazard of whether we behave collectively or individually, honestly or duplicitously, when we know more than our counterparty. For environmental planning, this lesson is important as it illustrates how acquiring information about the structure of the planning game might yield important insights into how conflict is likely to materialise.

Even though it is an extreme example, it is not inconceivable, as the following chapter (see particularly Box 6.1) goes on to show that the black box of planning practice might contain games close to the type of strongly incentivised individualism that is well described by the Prisoners' dilemma. Under such circumstances the framework offered by non-cooperative game theory allows us a very powerful way of thinking about conflict, as Chapters 6 and 7 illustrate. However, it would be odd if all the games played in planning practice took this form: at other times and in different places some form of cooperation might emerge relatively intact from the black box. Where this is the case, as Chapters 8 and 9 investigate, we can ask why the particular form of collaboration that prevails does so and with what effect, using the language of cooperative game theory. It is this versatility of game theory to capture conflict and cooperation – particularly where they co-exist – that it is argued here makes the theory so applicable to the tangled contents of the black box of urban and environmental planning. Readying oneself for the possibility that the black box of planning practice might contain degrees of conflict and cooperation is made easier by a confidence that game theory offers us both cooperative and non-cooperative paradigms with which to greet its contents – providing we don't make the error of having preconceived ideas about what the black box *should* contain:

> the big mistake is … seeking to furnish the black box of cooperative game theory with nothing more than the fond hope that conflict would disappear if only people would behave rationally. Much conflict in real life is admittedly stupid but we won't make people less stupid by teaching them that their hearts are more rational than their heads.
>
> (Binmore, 2007a: 461)

This conclusion forces us to confront the fact that often the black box of planning practice contains the conditions for some degree of conflict and competition to co-exist with collaboration and cooperation. In seeking to understand the entirety of the planning game – not just the 'classical' courtroom encounter – we therefore have to expect that its players will act 'strategically' in the course of their interactions. As the rest of the volume goes on to consider, this might mean that players compete (Chapter 6), signal information about themselves (Chapter 7), or partner with others (Chapter 8). The value of knowing the structure of the planning game is clear: if we understand the origins of competition and conflict, and we can agree that in a particular planning game they are in some sense deleterious, we can intervene to correct or rebalance power relations and perhaps even encourage cooperation, should we think it a worthwhile objective (Chapters 8 and 9).

Unpacking the 'black box'

Getting to grips with the contents of the 'black box' is equivalent to the unravelling of one of Wittgenstein's language games: the black box represents a prevailing state of affairs for which the attendant intellectual project is to dismantle the contents and lay them bare.

Specific to planning practice this will mean carefully setting out how actors' behaviour is explained as a function of various forms of 'information': that codified in the rule book of planning law; the informal norms of engagement explained by what is customary; and, perhaps most importantly, behaviour *in response to, or anticipation of, what we know about the actions of others*. Because we cannot know what the black box might contain, we have to be prepared for any eventuality. As it is entirely possible that the box might contain degrees of either conflict or cooperation, perhaps even mutually coexistent conflict and cooperation – such as where threats of punishment are used to engineer compliant collaboration – theory needs to be able to explain every such possibility. Game theory provides just such a framework because: 'game theory is actually about both conflict and cooperation, because realistic games usually contain the potential for both' (Binmore, 2004: 6).

In the course of the following chapters it will be argued that game theory allows us a way of unpacking the black box of planning practice whatever its contents might be. In circumstances where we have a well-codified set of rules – such as those given by planning law – it allows us to consider how agents interact and with what effect. Where no such rule book exists, we can consider self-determined solutions: for example, the emergence of self-assembled coalitions. It even allows us to develop a reflexive understanding of how rules emerge out of chaos and who the author of the rule book is likely to be. However, before we can get to this point we must first ask how the games that are apparently not well covered by existing theory – games characterised by degrees of competition and conflict – might be better conceptualised.

6   Conflict, power and risk

The opening moves in the case for thinking of planning as a 'game' made in the last chapter really introduce a planning game of two parts: first, the strictly rule-governed 'classical planning game' of the courtroom and, second, the wide range of informal interactions that, whilst they might be conditioned by the rule book of planning law, are actually a material representation of strategies enacted either by individuals or groups. The implied complexity of the games that we play in planning – and the attendant issue of whether they are best dealt with by cooperative or non-cooperative game theory – prompted the introduction of the 'black box' as a metaphor to describe those parts of planning practice that are in some senses hidden, beyond the reach of existing theory.

Conceived in this manner, the black box contains both the 'local' legal framework through which urban and environmental management takes place, as well as the equally 'local' cultural conventions and customary practices by which players respond to these rules. As noted in Chapter 5, despite a widely experienced transition to neoliberal forms of urban and environmental management across the globe, developing an understanding of the specifics of how these individual planning games work out will be incumbent upon contingent aspects of location, for example: ecology and ecosystems; the heritage value of historic architecture; geodemographic change; and political regime.

To capture this variation, which is implicit in so much of the popular work in the comparative planning tradition, we can turn to the concept of a 'state of the world' (Rasmusen, 2007: 54) at the core of game theory. The circumstances that define a particular state of the world – spanning variations in the pay-off/outcome structure that might prevail in different settings, how players' subjective beliefs are formed and their respective endowments of power – are fundamental to understanding the terms of engagement and, by extension, how a game might work out. Using this idea to advance the project of developing a way of thinking about planning that is born from information economics is accomplished by acknowledging that context is a fundamentally significant structuring variable, the role of which can be elucidated through the toolkit of game theory.

Ultimately this chapter seeks to investigate this issue of how the structure of an encounter – the 'state of the world' that prevails – is of primary importance in understanding systemic aspects of power. In so doing it paves the way for an account of how agency might respond to the structure of the game – the power relations established at, or prior to, the outset of a game. In time – in Chapters 8 and 9 – this will be developed into a wider game-theoretic understanding of how players might have an ongoing role in shaping and reshaping the structure of the games they play through the degree to which we make our own rules. To get to this point, however, we must first address a suite of preliminary questions: to what extent is the strength or weakness of the position of a player in the planning game a function of the rules of the game itself?; does having the right to make a 'first move' carry an advantage or does it reveal something about a player that might be used to the advantage of an opponent? In short, before we can make ethical judgements about the patterns of engagement to which the rule book gives rise, we must first be able to say something about the power that individual players might have and the extent to which those power relations are actually inherited from the rules of the game.

Ubiquitous and enduring conflict

The struggle for control of space and the assets situated within it has always been the most fundamental issue in planning, to the extent that, for Hamelink (2008: 291), the binding theme in a 6,000-year urban history of the globe is competition for space: 'as long as there have been cities, there has been urban conflict'. Yet, despite it being a defining characteristic of city life and resource exploitation from time immemorial, we do not have a fine-grained conceptual understanding of the anatomy of conflict as it might play out in urban and environmental planning.

This is not to say that planning academics have not been fascinated by conflict – they have – but rather that the focus has primarily been on conflict as a given feature of planning practice, something to be diminished or 'managed'. This has resulted in a large body of inductive research, conducted over a prolonged period, that provides insights into contingent aspects of conflict in particular settings (for example,

Hoch and Cibulskis, 1987; Murtagh, 1998; Peltonen and Sairinen, 2010). By contrast, the corresponding contribution of theorists on the subject has been less voluminous and has often begun from the same proposition as empirical work – that conflict is inherently undesirable. Indeed, in an era in which the communicative school has gained the ascendency as the dominant theoretical lens through which to regard planning practice, the primary task of analysing the existence of conflict and competition for resources has been overwritten with a quasi-normative reification of collaborative working practices. In turn, the empirical research that has followed has focused on the subjectively predefined 'good' aspects of practice – categories such as collaboration and consensus building – to the detriment of that which they are designed to overcome – conflict and competition. The result is that there are extremely few studies that show in a conceptual sense how conflict, as the common characteristic of the games we play in planning, might be more systematically understood. As Chapter 5 has illustrated, where theory has led, practice has followed, to the degree that, in many contexts around the globe, attempts to engineer collaboration without first having a full understanding of the conflict that it was supposed to replace have given way to cooperation and accommodation with the neoliberal consensus.

Dissent from, principally, those following Foucault (see also Pløger, 2004) has resituated questions of conflict as central to understanding planning processes and has somewhat diminished the urge amongst theorists to encourage practitioners to suppress or subdue conflict as a matter of course. Nevertheless, many still hold to the process goal that engineering more widespread cooperation in planning is itself a desirable outcome. But is collaboration always a worthwhile objective? Whilst it might be intuitively appealing to think that collaboration is inherently preferable to competition, is this really the case? Are there circumstances where a totally open attitude on the part of the planning profession potentially means discarding an information advantage that might be used in some way for the public interest or to secure a sustainable future for the environmental assets that our planning systems are designed to protect? Moreover, at what point does collaboration dissolve into a relationship of unhealthy or even improper proximity? The identification of a '"bribery-blackmail" continuum' (Ennis, 1996: 146) and 'abuse by collusion' (Saxer, 2000: 265) on the part of local planning authorities, particularly in dealings with the property development industry, has been the subject of illuminating descriptive research. But, without a supporting theoretical framework within which to make sense of those occasions where overenthusiastic cooperation has occurred, the identification of its potential preconditions – either structural or agential – is inhibited. We must, therefore, ask what causes conflict; can we understand specific instances of conflict over the resources that planning seeks to steward as a function of the systemic advantage or disadvantage handed down by the prevailing rule book of planning law? In summary, how can we develop a fine-grained account of conflict related to agential power relations given some wider structuring set of rules?

These questions demand not only an account of conflict but also of the power relations that determine its outcome: again, a commonly identified deficiency with the communicative turn's understanding of planning. Having discussed this critique at length in Chapter 2 it must, however, also be noted that alternative approaches have not resulted in a notably more elaborate approach to how power relations might be conceptually understood. As Few (2002: 29) notes in his study of power differentials in planning processes, 'relatively few in number are those studies that explicitly aim to unravel the mechanisms involved in the exercise of power by human actors'.

In what follows it is contended that game theory offers a potential corrective to some of these identified gaps in how we think about conflict in planning. A series of games are marshalled to illustrate how the concept might be unpacked before the chapter culminates in a discussion of how game theory uses risk to unlock an explanation of power that in turn can be deployed to account for the conditions under which conflict might arise – and, therefore, should we deem it desirable, how it might be resolved.

Planning and non-cooperative game theory

If conflict is the defining characteristic of the games we play in urban and environmental management, this suggests a point of tangency with the branch of game theory that takes this very subject as its principal focus: non-cooperative game theory. Indeed, as conflict is endemic to so many walks of life, not just environmental planning, work in the non-cooperative field has grown massively over the second half of the twentieth century and now endows us with a huge corpus of conceptual work that can be usefully applied to aid an understanding of the types of conflict that characterise struggles over the natural and urban environments.

At its most extreme, implacable, systemic conflict can be represented by a set of circumstances that pit two opposing parties in such a way that the outcome of each interaction results in the gains of the winner being identically equivalent to the losses of their opponent. The structure of such a game in its most basic form would be the same as many parlour pastimes, such as the common childhood game of 'matching pennies', where two players simultaneously reveal a coin to each other, their choice being heads or tails: if the choices match, Player A takes both; if the choices conflict, Player B takes both. Each round of the game is described in the matrix set out in Figure 6.1:

Player B

Player A		Heads	Tails
	Heads	1, −1	−1, 1
	Tails	−1, 1	1, −1

Figure 6.1 Matching pennies

As ever, the first digit in each cell of the matrix is the pay-off to Player A, the second being that to Player B. The outcome of each one-shot game results in a certain outcome of one player losing a coin and the other gaining a coin. This is sometimes called a zero-sum game as, in a game of pure conflict, the pay-offs to both participants set out in each cell of the table sum to zero. All games of pure conflict are zero-sum games. However, the term is routinely misused in the literature on dispute resolution in planning to describe an encounter where pay-offs are simply uneven across a set of players. Very few, if any, of the games we play in planning are likely to have a structure similar to that of a zero-sum game; most are characterised by pay-offs that are skewed, incentivising *degrees* of conflict or cooperation (see Box 6.1).

To illustrate this we can return to the core building block of so much of elementary game theory, the Prisoners' dilemma. This game, introduced at the end of Chapter 5, demonstrates how the choice to either act cooperatively or independently can become a conundrum in those situations where the rational choice (given the pay-off structure of the game) is a form of moderated individualism that results in a less desirable outcome for both players than if cooperation could be engineered and guaranteed. In the example from Chapter 5 this moderated individualism was manifested by the choice 'confess' emerging as the logical selection for both players, given their uncertainty as to the choice their accomplice might make – hence 'moderated' individualism.

To use the idiom of information economics, this 'toy' version of the game shows how each player, given the relevant pay-offs, would logically choose to confess rather than deny the crime. Stated alternatively in the language of game theory, under two-sided ignorance, 'confess' is the optimal strategy for each captive, regardless of what the other chooses to do, as it is the strategy that results in the Nash equilibrium (in the example from Chapter 5, each player being sentenced to a term of three months' imprisonment). Under any game that follows this pattern, we can see that ensuring individual outcomes is incentivised over cooperation – providing that one or more players do not have an information advantage, or even a strong belief about how other players will behave. If this condition of two-sided ignorance is not satisfied, cooperation may be possible, providing that the prisoners are sufficiently empathetic to privilege the common interest.

If each player could count on the other to cooperate, a better solution for both could be achieved with a mutual response of *deny*; but this in turn would leave the door open for a stronger, unmoderated form of individualism in the guise of a double-cross by one or other player, as the pair of strategies, *deny, confess* and *confess, deny*, result in the best individual outcomes for Player A and Player B respectively. Therefore, thinking individually, it is never logical to choose *deny* in a one-shot Prisoners' dilemma.

This illuminates a crucial point for environmental planning. If, instead of months of incarceration, we think of the pay-offs as revenue from the extraction of some natural resource or reductions in greenhouse gas emissions, we could imagine games where the structure of engagement between two counterparties incentivises various degrees of cooperation and non-cooperation in real life situations where the outcome would have significant implications for the encouragement of sustainable development. To illustrate, if, following game theory convention, we retain the same pay-off matrix as at the end of Chapter 5, but change the labels from 'confess' and 'deny' to 'defect' and 'cooperate', we can see that the same logic applies: both players choose to act as competitive individuals, or 'defect', resulting in the pay-off pairings in the upper left corner of the strategic-form game matrix. Moreover as Ward (1996) points out, to retain the grammatical integrity of the game, we merely need to illustrate that (ignoring signs), if for Player A $s > p > q > r$ and for Player B $s' > p' > q' > r'$, the Prisoners' dilemma, with the same corresponding non-cooperative Nash equilibrium, could be notated as shown in Figure 6.2.

Player B

		Defect	Cooperate
	Defect	p, p$'$	r, s$'$
Player A	Cooperate	s, r$'$	q, q$'$

Figure 6.2 The Prisoners' dilemma (formal)

For our application to environmental planning, the implications of the game format are hugely significant, as Carraro *et al.* (2005: 1) note:

> in many issues related to natural resource management the characteristics of a Prisoners' Dilemma game are present: the dominant strategy for players is not cooperative and the resulting equilibrium is not Pareto efficient – the pay-off for at least one individual could be improved, without some other individual being made worse off.

The veracity of this statement can be confirmed by re-examining either the formal iteration of the Prisoners' dilemma above or that of Figure 5.1. Both Player A and Player B could be made better off by the Pareto-efficient, cooperative strategy of *deny, deny* (labelled 'cooperate, cooperate' in Figure 6.2) – but the structure of the game does not incentivise this choice.

Applied to the real world of environmental planning, the issues thrown up by the Prisoners' dilemma illustrate a micro-encapsulation of the collective action problem identified by Hardin (1968: 1243) in his famous 'The tragedy of the commons'. Indeed, Hardin used the metaphor of a game of tic-tac-toe to illustrate the central problem of those circumstances where a common resource is overused because private profits and collective costs are skewed in favour of the former: using the language of the Prisoners' dilemma, the scenario is one where a cooperative strategy is individually sub-optimal. Under the terms of 'The tragedy of the commons', as envisaged by Hardin, the overuse of a natural resource by agents acting to maximise their individual pay-off from the resource results in a negative externality of reduced productivity borne by all other users of the resource and ultimately by the selfish users themselves. Game theory provides us with a useful way of thinking about such conflicts over the exploitation of environmental assets (see Box 6.1).

Box 6.1: Game theory, cooperation and sustainable development in the USA and Mexico

Whilst game theory has been applied to an eclectic range of disciplines and questions, perhaps the most logical starting point for an application of the theory to environmental planning is with respect to how natural resources are used and managed. One such resource that has been the subject of extensive game-theoretic consideration is water, with 'tragedy of the commons'-like dilemmas found in the work of, for example, Dixon (1999; see also Clarke *et al.*, 1996), where the competitive extraction of groundwater leads to overexploitation and an unsustainable use of the resource.

As water is subject to demand from both increasingly resource-hungry urban centres and agricultural uses, frequently in contiguous, and often conflicted, space, it is clearly a resource issue at the centre of what it means to be engaged in urban and environmental management. Logically, therefore, large population centres in arid settings represent an excellent test case for the utility of game theory as applied to the sustainable management of hydrological resources. In this respect, game theory has been used to model complex water resource-sharing problems such as that between the states of Colorado, Nebraska and Wyoming (Supalla *et al.*, 2002) and in Guanajuato, Mexico (Raquel *et al.*, 2007) – with the potential for overexploitation, degradation and permanent loss noted in each.

Some of the most illuminating work in this area, however, has allied a theoretical advance with empirical application. For example Loáiciga (2004: 23) sets out to 'develop a game-theoretic approach to calculate sustainable ground water extraction rates': specifically, a level of exploitation that would not entail 'overdraft', a situation where groundwater extraction rates exceed aquifer replenishment. From this starting point the author seeks to establish what would constitute sustainable levels of extraction with a view to considering whether users could be encouraged to cooperate at that level and with what implications for their profitability.

Using environmental characteristics of an aquifer facility in Santa Barbara, California (see also Loáiciga and Leipnik, 2000), the author finds that game theory offers a solution for how users could be coordinated in such a way that not only engineered a sustainable rate of extraction but also greater revenue for users; in short, 'sustainable aquifer mining pays better' Loáiciga (2004: 32). However, for this rate of extraction to be accomplished across the aggregate of users would require each to behave cooperatively in their use of the facility. As noted by the author – and explored further both formally and empirically later in this chapter – encouraging such cooperative behaviour to ensure long-term sustainability is sometimes inhibited if actors are faced with an opportunity to 'defect' in the interest of short-term profits: 'Non-enforceable cooperative equilibrium strategies in free markets tend to be unstable, as has been demonstrated by Nash (1951), and amply confirmed empirically (Samuelson and Nordhaus, 1995)' (Loáiciga, 2004: 25).

The author's conclusion was: 'for cooperation to yield its benefits, enforcement must be effective' (Loáiciga 2004: 32). Perhaps environmental, and in other contexts, urban, planning offers just such a form of enforcement.

Games in extensive form

As it has been analysed so far, the Prisoners' dilemma has been treated as a one-shot game of two-sided ignorance. Of course this need not be so. Later in the chapter we will relax the second assumption to investigate how information, coupled with a player's attitude to risk, provides for a game-theoretic understanding of power relations. Prior to this, however, we can remove the first assumption: games are rarely one-shot affairs: they are often played over a series of consecutive rounds. We therefore have to allow for an extended version of the Prisoners' dilemma in which our participants play the game repeatedly. If they know they will have to play a subsequent round of the game, and so face the same opponent again, will this have any bearing on how players conduct themselves from the very first round?

The results of experimental economics and empirical application suggest so. The critical importance of time in modelling games in extended form is that it effectively mirrors the reality that, in many circumstances, choices are not a one-shot, cast-in stone decision but are rather the cumulative function of additive actions. As a result, many experiments (see for a review, Cárdenas and Ostrum, 2004) illustrate that players will choose the Pareto-efficient strategy 'cooperate', thus signalling their willingness to 'play fair', despite, as has been shown, a non-cooperative move of 'defect' being individually optimal. Fundamentally this allows us to open game theory up to take account of normative factors in determining the manner in which players conduct themselves in a game. Sometimes the strategies illustrate the worst, as well as the best, in human nature.

For example, the most punitive approach to the extended Prisoners' dilemma is the 'grim trigger' strategy, whereby, having started the game by playing 'co-operate' on each round, a player who is then double-crossed by an opponent acting selfishly in one round by a move of 'defect' retaliates by playing 'defect' in every subsequent round until the end of the game. Over a sufficiently long sequence of rounds grim trigger has frequently been shown to be dominated by other, more nuanced, strategies. Indeed, the strategy reputed to be the most successful in experimental trials has been 'tit for tat', where a break by one player from the conciliatory choice of 'cooperate' is punished by their opponent with a retaliatory move of 'defect' for one round only, the next. On the victory of the largely, but not wholly, cooperative 'tit for tat' at the game theory 'Olympiad' in the early 1980s, the competition's convener, Axelrod (quoted in Binmore, 2007a: 80), remarked:

> What accounts for tit-for-tat's robust success is its combination of being nice, retaliatory, forgiving and clear. Its niceness prevents it from getting into unnecessary trouble. Its retaliation discourages the other side from persisting whenever defection is tried. Its forgiveness helps restore mutual cooperation. And its clarity makes it intelligible to the other player, thereby eliciting long-term cooperation.

In the years after the Olympiad, debate has raged amongst game theorists about whether experiments in which individuals play the Prisoners' dilemma cooperatively are best explained by reference to an allegedly intrinsic human preference, born either of culture or biology, to act cooperatively or as a result of an initial miscalculation of what is the optimal strategy to play, which changes as individuals become more experienced players. A school of behavioural game theorists has been instrumental in arguing the former case (see essays in Gintis *et al.*, 2006), whilst others such as Binmore (2006) argue the reverse, to paraphrase Axelrod (1984), and that it is actually conflict rather than cooperation that emerges as, the more experienced a player becomes, the more likely they are to behave as a competitive individual. In reality both positions are behavioural and raise an important question for the empirical application of game theory: how can we know what an individual *means* by their actions?

There is no short answer to this question. Instead the longitudinal nature of games in extended form explains in part how we can begin to devise a qualitative understanding of strategy: just as, when a speaker uses a word for the first time in a language game they specify its meaning by *how* it is used, a meaning that is then clarified by its repeated use over time and its incorporation into the vocabularies of other speakers, so, too, the nuances of strategy and tactics might be understood by observing *how* they are used. For example, the strategy tit for tat is *defined* by its particular format of being responsive to the strategy played by an opponent, thus providing Axelrod with the opportunity to *define* it in qualitative terms, as one might define a word, as being 'nice, retaliatory, forgiving and clear'. Understanding what a strategy might mean provides a necessary first step in applying game theory to the real world, such as the encounters that characterise urban and environmental management.

Box 6.2: Tit for tat in Taipei

Perhaps the clearest example of an application of the extended Prisoners' dilemma to the games we play in planning practice can be found in Chiu and Lai's (2009) study of locally unpopular land uses or, as the authors term them, NIMBY (Not In My Back Yard) developments.

The facility that the research took as its subject was a proposed landfill site in the Neihu district of Taipei. In modelling the costs and benefits to the two parties involved in the negotiation over whether the development should take place or not – government (in this case Taipei City Council) and the local community – the authors noted that the negotiation could be analysed by the format offered by the Prisoners' dilemma. Both parties had well-defined payoffs that mirrored the logical symmetry of a classic Prisoners' dilemma in relation to the financial implications of the facility being approved and both had a choice to either acquiesce to or contest the development (labelled 'cooperate' or 'defect' in keeping with tradition).

To investigate how the negotiations might work out the authors (Chiu and Lai, 2009: 960) ran an experiment in which 20 rounds of the Prisoners' dilemma were played between eight parties, four representing government planners and four the local community. Each of the subsets of four groups played one of a series of strategies in the negotiations: tit for tat, where the player only deviates from cooperation in the event that their opponent defects, whereupon they respond with one round of defection prior to reverting to their preferred default of cooperate; 'grim trigger' (termed 'trigger punishment' by the authors), in which a default position of cooperate is broken by an opponent's defection, and thereafter the player defects in each subsequent round until the end of the game; a 'faithful' strategy in which a player always chooses to cooperate regardless of the choice of their opponent; and a random strategy in which the choice to either cooperate or defect is made in an entirely random pattern.

To determine which was the most successful strategy for each to employ, the researchers ran the Prisoners' dilemma experiment over a limited number of rounds between the actual participants before the results were extrapolated over an unlimited number of rounds to consider whether conditions changed over time.

Qualitatively, the results are illuminating. The authors (Chiu and Lai, 2009: 963) found that 'in the case of a limited number of iterations just 25% (five subjects) of the residents wished to cooperate initially with the government ... the residents were reluctant to cooperate with the government right from the start'. However, this reluctance to cooperate diminished as more rounds of the game were played: 'as the game proceeded there was an apparent increase up to 45% (nine subjects) of residents who chose to cooperate. This finding corresponds with the notion that cooperation emerges'.

Quantitatively, the research confirms the general theoretical proposition that tit for tat dominates other strategies in a Prisoners' dilemma of this form. Indeed, this was true of both the run of the game limited to 20 rounds and that over an unlimited number.

The conclusion of the research is that 'the tit-for-tat strategy proves to be more beneficial than other strategies, not only to the local government, but also to the society as a whole', meaning that Axelrod was again vindicated in his assertion that even in urban and environmental planning tit for tat is the most successful strategy – not because it is uniformly cooperative but rather because it combines traits of being 'nice, retaliatory, forgiving and clear' (Chiu and Lai, 2009: 966).

Making your best move: information, belief and knowledge

Box 6.2 reports empirical evidence of various approaches to playing the Prisoners' dilemma over multiple sequential rounds. This conception of a game in extensive form can be represented by a tree diagram in which each 'node' represents an action point for a specified player, each 'branch' represents a possible choice of strategy and each 'leaf' specifies the outcome of that choice. For any complete strategy the pay-offs to Player A are located in the bottom left hand corner of the leaf, with the corresponding pay-off to Player B in the top right. To illustrate, we can consider an adaptation of Rasmusen's (2007: 50) game, Follow the leader, in which Player A and Player B are neighbouring planning authorities trying to decide whether they should have a permissive or restrictive attitude to development.

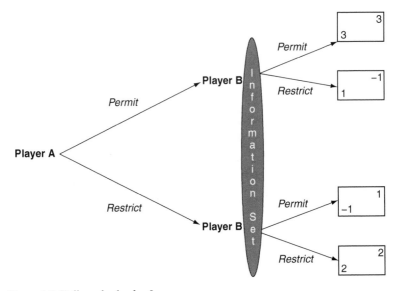

Figure 6.3 Follow the leader I

Close inspection of the game tree in Figure 6.3 illustrates the central proposition at the core of game theory: that information is intrinsically valuable. The diagram describes alternative conceptions of what would constitute a best response for Player B dependent upon the choice that Player A makes first. If Player B knew that Player A had chosen to permit development, she would surely choose to do the same, as the pay-off (3, 3) is superior to the alternative, of being restrictive (1, −1). Equally, if Player A chooses to restrict development, Player B would make the same choice (hence 'Follow the leader'), guided by the superior pay-off (2, 2 versus −1, 1). In sum, the array of pay-offs describes a world where the proceeds and externalities of development are unevenly distributed across a territory when contiguous planning authorities have policies that conflict. Conceptually, game theorists account for the centrality of information to the outcome of a game such as this by speaking of *information sets*; the aggregate of what is known to a player at the points in the game that constitute their 'turn' is here denoted for Player B by the shaded area around the nodes at which they must make a choice.

What is known to a player at their information set is critical in understanding and accounting for the strategy they adopt. It is at that juncture that the epistemological parentage of game theory is most explicit as, to complete a game-theoretic analysis – any game-theoretic analysis – we need to be clear about what is known to participants when they make their move. This forces us to take into account all conceptions of knowledge – what a player knows about the rules of the game they are playing, what they have learnt from their counterparty's move (should they already have made one, or more) and what the relationship is between their beliefs and knowledge about the world they inhabit.

Overlooking these features of game theory's epistemological basis has led critics at various times in history to argue that the discipline is rigidly preoccupied with rules and logic – features that, some have argued, bar it from practical application. For sceptics (for example, Hechter, 1992; Tullock, 1992) all that is contingent – the 'unforeseen circumstances' and 'acts of God' that characterise the realpolitik of the material world – appears to prevent the theory from meaningful empirical fulfilment where rules are often disobeyed, actors sometimes behave irrationally and pay-offs are uncertain.

Game theory has proven remarkably resilient to such critique. Whilst the rules of a game may be contested and/or participants may act differently from how neoclassical economic theory might suggest they would, explaining why, often by reference to qualitative variables and participant psychology, is a central aim of game theory; this is largely by virtue of its epistemological foundations, inherited from the analytic philosophy of which Wittgenstein is so emblematic. These shared epistemological objectives – to uncover the 'state of the world' that prevails and give it perspicuous articulation – necessarily situate information and the contextually embedded beliefs that players might have at the forefront of an understanding of the limits of what is possible within their world. As a result, game theorists have provided an account of those features of real life that might otherwise seem superficially random – the very 'acts of God' and 'unforeseen circumstances' that are taken to be contextually specific by other theoretical perspectives and explained away as contingent. More specifically, by interpreting the acquisition and modification of players' subjective beliefs as a shifting array of probability distributions about the type of world in which the game is being played out, game theorists accurately render structure and agency as two mutually reflective, inextricably linked components of a game.

Follow the leader provides us with an excellent opportunity to consider some of these issues. The structure of the game is indicative of the type of relationship that might prevail should two neighbouring local planning authorities acquiesce with the terms of some meta-scale planning system designed to cover a national or sub-national territory – for example a municipality/local authority area, a regional state space such as a German *Land*, a federal state of the USA or even a national state space such as in the UK's unitary system of government. However, we know from numerous inductive case studies that local planning agents frequently respond differently to the terms of the system imposed from above – they don't always 'follow the leader'. This may be because, as Ennis (1997: 1947) has noted:

> all planning systems have a statutory basis and policy guidance which provide a set of objective standards against which assessments can be made. The problem here is that often policy guidance can be ambiguous and open to a number of interpretations.

So how might game theory capture such differences of local agency in examples where the rules are unclear, open to interpretation or perhaps just not 'common knowledge'?

The way in which game theorists have come to think about this relationship between what a player knows about the game in which they are engaged and what their competitors know is called the 'Harsanyi transformation' after Karl Harsanyi (1967, 1968a, 1968b). Harsanyi identified that games of incomplete information could be characterised by an infinite regression to mutual ignorance of the form: Player A does not know Player B's position in the game; Player B does not know what Player A believes to be Player B's position; Player A does not know what Player B believes about what Player A believes Player B's position to be in the game, et cetera ad infinitum. To circumvent this infinite regression Harsanyi conceived of a structuring agency, called 'Nature', that moves independently of the players, often, although not necessarily, first to determine the rules of how the encounter will be played out. It is this initial move by Nature that sets the 'state of the world'.

Making your mind up: Bayesian updating and the discourse universe

Precisely what is meant by 'Nature' here requires elaboration. Far from being a mystical first mover, Nature is really just a reflection of the beliefs that each of the players have about one another: the sum of the players' beliefs defines the state of their world. Again, to draw a connection between information economics, game theory and associated academic traditions, the features of a game are self-explained without any reference needed to a hidden hand – as with Darwinian evolution or one of Wittgenstein's language games.

This means that, in analysing an encounter, the rules of the game are themselves a function of what the players interpret them to be and how they respond to them; structure depends upon agency and vice versa. The expression, a 'state of the world' (Rasmusen, 2007: 54) reflects this: the decisions that players make and the strategies they employ are understood to reflect their judgements about which state of the world prevails. For any possible scenario, the full range of possible formats that the game might potentially take – the complete set of possible states of the world that could prevail – is referred to as the 'universe of discourse' (often denoted by the Greek letter, Ω; see Binmore, 1992). This again demonstrates information economics' intellectual lineage: analytic philosophy's understanding that the limits of language in some sense coincide with the limits of the knowable world is closely analogous to the idea that a 'universe of discourse' delimits the epistemic possibilities of any given game: '*The limits of my language* mean the limits of my world' (Wittgenstein, 1922: 5.6, italics in original). To illustrate, we can consider alternative ways in which the game, Follow the leader, could have been played had it had a different structure, alternative pay-offs and, therefore, different best responses. The possible states that 'Nature' could have created may have represented a totally different world to that of Follow the leader I, for example that of Follow the leader II (Figure 6.4) or Follow the leader III (Figure 6.5).

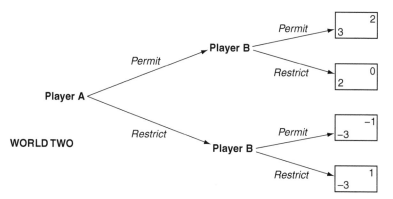

Figure 6.4 Follow the leader II

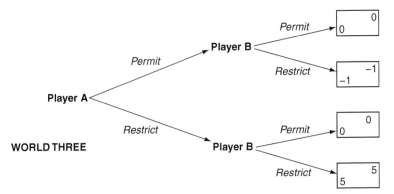

Figure 6.5 Follow the leader III

Indeed a continuum of possible alternative worlds might be imagined. But how should our players judge which one prevails?

Although we might produce the same analysis for many others, for simplicity's sake let us assume that these three worlds comprise the full set of alternatives. Now, suppose that Player B attaches a 60% probability to the world in which they live being that depicted in Follow the leader I, a 20% probability to it being that of Follow the leader II and a 20% probability to the world in which they live being Follow the leader III. If Player A plays *permit*, should Player B change their beliefs about the world in which they live; should they 'update' what they believe?

The process by which beliefs are modified is known in game theory as Bayesian updating, as the method of calculation is analogous to Bayes's Rule (for a formal derivation see Rasmusen, 2007: 55–56). Ultimately our objective is to establish the likelihood that our prior beliefs about the world are correct, given that we now have a little more information: an observation of an opponent's move. Therefore, to arrive at our 'posterior' (our updated belief about the world in which our game is played), we must measure the ratio of two probabilities: that the move we have witnessed is consistent with our prior belief, against the probability that the observed move is consistent with rational play in an alternative state of affairs. So, for Player B to arrive at an updated belief about the likelihood that they inhabit the world they thought they did, we should measure the extent to which a move of *permit* by Player A is more or less likely in Follow the leader I than it would be in Follow the leader II or III.

Given that we have established that Player B begins from the prior belief that they inhabit World I (that of Follow the leader I) with a 60% probability, World II with a 20% probability and World III with a 20% probability, we can begin to think about whether these beliefs should be modified after an initial move of *permit* on the part of Player A by proposing an equilibrium. Consideration of the game trees set out above would suggest that, given a move of *permit* on the part of Player A, Player B might discount the possibility of the world being that of Follow the leader III, as such a move would be inconsistent with a rational choice on the part of Player A: either subsequent response available to Player B would result in a return to Player A of 0 or −1, whereas the alternative fork in the game tree, a move of *restrict* by Player A, opens up the possibility of a return of 5 should Player B 'follow the leader' and respond with *restrict*. As a result, we could represent Player B's updated posterior belief that they are playing Follow the leader I by using Bayes's Rule: Player B's prior belief about the world being that of Follow the leader I as a ratio of their beliefs about it being some other conceivable world (in our example, Follow the leader II of World II):

$$\text{Probability World I}|permit = \frac{(1)(0.6)}{(1)(0.6) + (1)(0.2) + (0)(0.2)} = 0.75$$

The arithmetic above (to be read, 'probability that this is World I, given Player A's move, *permit*') shows us that, once they have seen Player A make a move of *permit*, Player B updates their belief that they are playing either Follow the leader I or II. Moreover, their initial best guess, summarised by the prior probability of 60% that they attached to it being Follow the leader I, is now a stronger belief: having seen A play *permit*, B now believes it 75% likely that the world is World I and will therefore respond with *permit* in the belief that, on 75/100 occasions upon which the game would be played, a pay-off of 3, 3 would result.

Changing the rules

Of course in any game of sequential rounds, circumstances – the rules, the pay-offs – may change. For example, most formal systems of environmental planning, understood now to be the rule book of the planning game, have been reformed and moderated from time to time. Again, this might be thought of as a move by Nature to which players would respond by updating their beliefs about the characteristics of the game they were now playing.

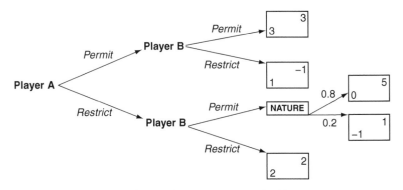

Figure 6.6 Follow the leader I with an intervention by Nature

To illustrate how this might work, we can introduce an additional node in the Follow the leader I game tree (see Figure 6.6). Here we can see that a new actor, Nature, intercedes in the game that was previously restricted to Players A and B – perhaps the terms of the planning system to which the two parties respond has been the subject of reform – with the result that the sequential choices *restrict, permit* carry revised pay-offs to both players governed by two probabilities – effectively the beliefs that the two players have about the implications that set of choices might have. In this example, the players' beliefs are understood to be 80% probability that the choice for A to be restrictive whilst B is permissive (0, 5) will result in development migrating to B's territory and a 20% chance that the combination of choices will see no change to the *ex ante* state of affairs (−1, 1). The structure of the game becomes a reflection of the players' expectations: in this case, a set of circumstances that might predispose the two neighbouring planning authorities to compete for development, something that our empirical understanding of the world bears out (see Box 6.3).

Box 6.3: Who competes in environmental planning? Local authority competition in the USA and Britain

Chiu and Lai's (2009: 966) analysis of the disputed NIMBY development using the framework offered by the Prisoners' dilemma in Box 6.2 concludes that further game-theoretic work could be useful:

> in similar real planning situations that are reminiscent of prisoners' dilemmas including a local government as

regulator versus a private land user as developer; a private land user versus another private land user, both as developers; a private land user as developer versus a community group as landowners; and a local government versus a higher tier or neighbouring local government, both as regulators.

Taking this cue, one area where nascent work has begun to address this research agenda is competition between local planning authorities for development to occur within their, rather than a neighbour's, jurisdiction. Whilst more research is needed in this area there are a number of studies that have begun to use the language and logic of game theory to conceptualise precisely these forms of competition. For example in Saxer's (2000) study, 'Planning gain, exactions and impact fees: a comparative study of planning law in England, Wales and the United States', the author begins by contemplating two hypothetical neighbouring local planning authorities – City 1 and City 2 – and how they relate to one another in the competition to host development:

> For example a new superstore may generate additional traffic in the general vicinity, but City 1 may receive all the benefits from the developer in exchange for planning permission, while nearby City 2 receives only the burdens caused by additional traffic. The unequal distribution of benefits and burdens creates intergovernmental conflict and competitions between local communities, but neither England and Wales nor most jurisdictions in the United States have successfully addressed this problem.
>
> (Saxer, 2000: 32)

This inter-governmental conflict describes the trade-off between the benefits of development and the externalities that, sometimes literally, spill over into a neighbouring jurisdiction that have been found to be a common feature of urban and environmental planning the world over. Nevertheless, the results of the research show that the games we play in planning might be structurally quite different on either side of the Atlantic. In contrast to warring local planning authorities in the USA, competition in the UK was said to be largely confined to the private sector:

In contrast to the competition that occurs in England and Wales, market competition for land development in the United States is more likely to occur among municipalities than private developers. In the United States municipalities compete for tax revenue and attempt to avoid the externalities by shifting them to a nearby municipality or forcing the developer to internalise any infrastructure burdens.

(Saxer, 2000: 24; see also Saxer, 1997)

So, competition occurs to varying degrees, dependent upon context, amongst the private development industry and between local planning authorities for the attentions of those developers. But how does this competition become manifest and with what effects? In short, how do we explain the outcome of these competitive urges that are apparently so common amongst all players of the planning game?

Is knowledge power?

When combined, the concepts behind a game like Follow the leader and the realities implied by empirical work such as that reported in Box 6.3 reveal an intuitive truth: we learn which game it is that we are playing by the act of playing itself. Just as Player B learnt something about the state of the world that prevailed from observing Player A's move, so too in many other situations revealing information to a counterparty might endow them with an advantage in, for example negotiating over the terms of a planning decision – the subject of Chapter 7. Moreover, unwinding Follow the leader takes us right back to the confluence of game theory and epistemology and, specifically, the limits of what might be known to our players (cf. Wittgenstein's philosophy of knowledge in Chapter 3). How did our players arrive at their initial beliefs about the state of the world that Nature had bestowed in which their game was played out? The answer for game theorists is that the set of possible 'states of the world' that players must decide between comprises the 'universe of discourse' that corresponds to the Wittgensteinian idea that there is a continuum of possible 'states of affairs', with the task of philosophical investigation being to decipher which of those possibilities prevails. Game theory uses the same underlying principles to unpack the specifics of an engagement and gradually deduce how players have conducted themselves and based upon what information.

The logical conclusion is that the games we play in real life might be characterised by players deploying strategies to elicit information. As Chapter 7 will go on to show, once obtained, this information may in turn inform a more refined approach to strategy with respect to how players seek to represent their character – or, in the language of game theory, their 'type'. Knowing your standing in a game informs how you choose to play and often knowing more than an opponent may be a significant advantage. However, the trite dictum, 'knowledge is power' neglects to take into account the capacity of its holder to *use* that knowledge. In the final analysis of Follow the leader, the first move by Player A revealed a valuable piece of information to Player B that allowed them to update their belief about the nature of the game in which they were a competitor. How well placed Player B was to use this information to their advantage in securing what they might perceive to be a desirable outcome, however, would depend greatly on the extent to which they occupied a position of strength or weakness.

To illustrate this fundamental concept we can use the Ultimatum game, where an anonymous benefactor makes an award, usually set at $100, to be split between two players. To decide on how the fund should be apportioned, one player, the first mover, has the right to make an offer to the other. If the offer is accepted, the money is divided according to the terms of the accepted offer; if the offer is rejected, the award is withheld and both players receive nothing.

Whilst it may sound like a television game show, Ultimatum illustrates several important characteristics that carry over into other more complicated games that have considerable value in explaining the choices that policy makers might make. In many games in the real world, as in Ultimatum, the first mover – the one making the offer in this toy game – is at a considerable advantage. But how much of an advantage? The supposedly rational choice – the prediction of how the game might play out that some neoclassical economists might make – is frequently at odds with how players conduct themselves in practice. In Ultimatum, the strength of the first mover's advantage is such that we might expect them to offer their counterpart just $1. If they refuse, they receive nothing and, as we assume $1 is preferable to $0, they would be foolish to decline the offer. However, in numerous experiments the offer made is much closer to a 50:50 split: players frequently cede the advantage that their status as first mover affords them and make a conciliatory offer (for a review, see Güth and Tietz, 1990; Kirchsteiger, 1994). Moreover, even where an offer is made that 'prices in' the first-mover advantage to a quite modest degree, it is often refused. In many experiments, offers of a 70:30 ratio in favour of the first mover are routinely declined: it would seem that some players would rather punish a quite reasonable offer that they perceive to be a slight, rather than accept that the first mover's advantage should bring with it a larger share of the endowment.

Bargaining for power

Games such as Ultimatum have conflict written into them. What we may think is a reasonable offer might be refused by a player who feels scorned. This illustrates the qualitative power of game theory as, to explain the outcome of the game, we marshal concepts such as pique, vindictiveness or 'envy' (Kirchsteiger, 1994) to account for outcomes that deviate from what neoclassical scholars tell us *homo economicus* would or should do.

The qualitative aspect of explanatory game theory is particularly relevant in those cases where counterparties bargain. In Ultimatum, as the name implies, there is no opportunity to dispute what would be a reasonable, just or mutually acceptable settlement; it is just a one-shot game in which a brief encounter results in a binary choice between an offer either being accepted or rejected. In the real world, though, how 'fair shares' are decided is likely to be a more complicated business: negotiations might be a sequential game of offer and counter-offer in which players choose to represent themselves as having some quality that gives them a competitive advantage – perhaps they may wish to appear to be a 'tough' negotiator, for example. In other circumstances, as has been demonstrated, it might be more advantageous to move second if the choice of the first mover reveals some information about their position. Engagements may be time-limited, meaning that the capacity to use 'delaying tactics' could be a powerful advantage. If there are many players, they may choose to arrange themselves into subsidiary coalitions. Whichever combination of such contingent factors prevails – themselves respectively the subjects of Chapters 7, 8 and 9 – power relations will almost invariably be uneven.

Before we can begin to consider the complexities of games characterised by these various forms of tactical behaviour in the next chapter and coalition formation in Chapter 8 we must first address the primary issue of power. As has been illustrated in Part I, the undertheorisation of power is perhaps the most damaging criticism of the account of planning process offered by the school of planning theory that follows Habermas. It therefore follows that, if information economics is to make a contribution to how we understand urban and environmental management, it must be able to fill the gaps in our qualitative understanding of the role played by uneven power relations in planning practice.

To do this we can look to the work that game theorists have done in conceptualising the circumstantial advantage or disadvantage of players in a game relative to one another. The resultant analysis provides the basis for a thorough account of the factors that together comprise advantage or disadvantage in a game: players' attitudes to risk, their character 'type' and subjective beliefs combine to provide a nuanced account of the various factors that together constitute the bundle of attributes typically passed over in many of the existing treatments of planning practice as underspecified 'power relations'. The first step towards constructing this game-theoretic understanding of power and tactics is to consider the degree to which players' attitudes to risk place them at a systemic advantage or disadvantage.

Risk: explaining the conditions for conflict and cooperation

To say that an individual is risk averse, risk neutral or a risk seeker is to say something specific and quantifiable about the character of their tastes (for a very clear articulation, see Varian, 1996: chs 3 and 4). Consequently, the determination of attitude to risk is a fundamental component of the toolkit of positive microeconomics. Using the concept of utility, economists have set out an analytical framework that describes individuals' preferences as an expected utility function, sometimes referred to as a Von Neumann-Morgenstern utility function, after the authors of the first codified account of game theory (Von Neumann and Morgenstern, 1944). Essentially, the expected utility function sets out a measure of an individual's taste for risk by obtaining a rank of whether that individual prefers a current endowment of some asset (typically money) or an investment proposition with well-defined return probabilities. Any individual who chooses the risk-free current endowment up to or beyond a point at which the average return from the investment is equal to or greater than the endowment is said to be risk averse. Equally, any individual who chooses the investment over the current endowment when the average return specified by the probabilities attached to it are less than that guaranteed by the current endowment is behaving as a risk seeker. Indifference between the two alternatives, resulting in an affine relationship, implies a neutral attitude to risk. This relationship is specified by the slope of the expected utility function (Figure 6.7). As Varian (1996: 221) notes:

> Thus the curvature of the utility function measures the consumer's attitude towards risk. In general the more concave the utility function the more risk averse the consumer will be and the more convex the utility function the more risk loving the consumer will be.

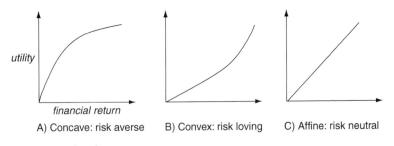

A) Concave: risk averse   B) Convex: risk loving   C) Affine: risk neutral

Figure 6.7 Utility functions

The value of these observations resides first and foremost in describing how the outcome of a game can be thought of as attributable to the type of conduct that, all other things being equal, would be consistent with a player's attitude to risk.

For example, if we imagine two counterparties, A and B, bargaining for some asset or endowment, we could present the set of possible splits of that asset as a bounded frontier, X, in the two-dimensional space between the axes along which we measure the possible outcomes that might result following the two counterparties' bargaining. If A and B fail to come to an agreement, then we can conceive of some default allocation within the set of possible divisions that prevails, or remains the case; we can call this the 'conflict point' because it represents a status quo allocation that both parties find undesirable/unacceptable and would wish to contest. The bargaining situation is represented graphically in Figure 6.8.

Under such circumstances, what would be the predicted outcome of the bargaining game? The game theory pioneer John Nash (1951) set

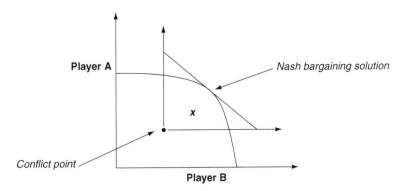

Figure 6.8 Nash bargaining programme

out a solution (known as the Nash Bargaining Programme) in which the utility scales of A and B are recalibrated to the conflict point and a tangent is drawn to the boundary of the set. Nash reasoned that the two counterparties would logically choose a point on the edge of the set, as any split further within X would be sub-optimal: both players would be better satisfied by an alternative agreement on the edge of the set. The optimal solution is indicated by the point of tangency between the 45° tangent and the bargaining set, as this marks the furthest point on the extremity of the set from the conflict point and therefore the best outcome for both counterparties.

The issue of fundamental importance here is that there are two key determinants of how the endowment, resource, good or asset under consideration is divided: the position of the conflict point and the shape of the bounded area that represents the set of possible allocations. Moreover, both tell us something about the circumstantial position of the two parties. First, the location of the conflict point indicates the position of what would be an unsatisfactory allocation of the asset under consideration for both counterparties: however, the level of endowment that triggers conflict or, equally, that each finds just satisfactory, might be lower or higher for one player relative to the other. Second, the shape of the bounded set describes the players' attitude to risk: a concave set, as is depicted in Figure 6.8 above, would indicate risk aversion, but the specifics of its shape would, in the event of a difference in attitude to risk between players, specify precisely what the character of that difference was. It is really this fundamental underlying concept that determines the result of the Nash bargaining game. Where we have two players who are equally risk averse, the outcome will be an even division, or 50:50 split. However, it is far more realistic to acknowledge that counterparties will usually have different attitudes to risk which in turn will have attendant implications for how well they do out of the game; as Binmore (2007a: 150) states, 'the more risk averse you are, the less you get'.

It is these features of the Nash Bargaining solution that has led many to question its moral attributes (see Sen, 1970; Hausman and McPherson, 1996). In the course of applying bargaining solutions to conflict resolution with respect to ecosystem management Shields *et al.* (1999: 81) spell out such concerns more fully:

> The problem here is that a Nash solution disadvantages the poor because their conflict point is low. And ... risk averse players are at a disadvantage because their utilities increase more slowly as a function of their pay-offs than is the case for less risk averse, risk

neutral or risk seeking players. Hence their utility gains in the solution will be less than those of other players.

So systemically weak players are, by virtue of their risk aversion, almost preprogrammed to settle for an outcome that they find less satisfactory than stronger, less risk averse, players. Or, perhaps they are weak *because* they are risk averse? But what makes a player risk averse and what can be done to overcome the uneven power relations that these varying attitudes to risk explain? These questions regarding the subtleties of bargaining and negotiation will be the subject of Chapter 7.

7 Bargaining, negotiation and tactics

The utility functions set out in the final section of the last chapter describe the preferences that an individual might have. They specify a profile of a player's attitude to risk that provides a vital starting point in explaining the prevailing power relations in a game. When supplemented with an account of how players might form and revise their beliefs, game theory can incorporate qualitative variables, which are essential to a complete rendering of how a game might work out. Ultimately this allows us to use game theory to investigate fully those situations where reality deviates from the predictions of what would constitute rational play and so set out in qualitative terms how players might exercise their agency. For example, the Ultimatum game illustrated an example where the character of the players – namely their capacity to act vindictively, given a perceived slight – played a central role in explaining how empirical experiments based on the game worked out. The purpose of this chapter is to extend this analysis of character and beliefs by considering how a player's 'type' and tactical skill come even further to the fore in the analysis of bargaining and negotiation.

The requirement for conceptual work in this area is bound up with some given features of environmental planning in all situations where it takes place. First, much of planning practice, almost regardless of context, has negotiation and bargaining at its core (Claydon, 1996; Claydon and Smith, 1997; Goodchild et al., 1996); second, the outcome of such encounters is shaped by the relative strength of counterparties (Callies and Grant, 1991; Tiesdell and Oc, 1991). As game theory takes the explanation of such processes of bargaining and negotiation to be a central theoretical objective, it follows that it may offer substantial insights into the specifics of this core element of planning practice.

Negotiation in planning: gaps in the theory

Academic interest in negotiation in urban and environmental planning is a relatively recent phenomenon despite recognition that it is a long-standing feature of planning practice in many national contexts (Claydon, 1996; Claydon and Smith, 1997). In the UK, where curiosity seems to have predated most other contexts, many of the most significant contributions in the area date from the 1980s and early 1990s; for example, the work of Claydon (1985); Heap and Ward (1980), Healey *et al.* (1982, 1993), Bruton and Nicholson, (1987) and Elson (1986) stand out as examples of work that has discovered and sought to explain specific examples of negotiation in planning practice. These studies have subsequently been complemented by others relating to different planning systems, where negotiation and bargaining, albeit of a systemically different type, are also prevalent in the day-to-day work of planners, such as those of France (de Carlo, 2002, 2006) and the USA (Shmueli *et al.*, 2008).

In seeking to understand the encounters it uncovers, research of this type has typically sought to marshal a brand of negotiation theory quite separate from the treatment offered by information economics. This negotiation theory is principally summarised by the work of Fisher *et al.* (1991; see also Bacow and Wheeler, 1984, Kriesberg and Thorson, 1991) and, specifically in relation to environmental questions, by the work of Susskind and collaborators (Susskind and Ozawa 1984; Susskind and Cruikshank, 1987; Susskind and Field 1996). Taken in aggregate, this material seeks to distinguish between two different styles of negotiation, principled and positional, with the aim of showing the former to be the more desirable approach for negotiators to take.

To elaborate, principled negotiation is understood to be driven by three core objectives. First, it should produce a 'wise' agreement; second, it should be efficient, in the sense that no better outcome could be envisaged; and third, it should be amicable and not provoke a deterioration in relations between the negotiating parties. Where it might have been successfully implemented, principled negotiation is said to have resulted in agreements being made that not only meet the individual aspirations of each of the counterparties but also result in mutual conciliation. Such a 'wise' decision is one that 'meets the legitimate interests of each side to the [best] extent possible, resolves conflicting interests fairly, is durable, and takes community interests into account' (Fisher *et al.*, 1991: 4).

This contrasts with positional bargaining in which, according to Fischer *et al.* (1991: 7) 'each side takes a position, argues for it, and makes concessions to reach a compromise'. Whilst advocacy of this competitive style of bargaining can be found in some of the mainstream literature on business administration and management (for example, and most influentially, Kennedy, 1982, 1988, 1992; see also Kennedy *et al.*, 1980), in planning it has been explicitly disavowed by most theorists. For example, in commenting upon this corpus in a paper on the development of negotiating skills within the French planning profession Bobot (2008: 185) remarks that:

> my view is that whilst the advice may be helpful in purchasing second-hand cars or haggling in a market, it has the fundamental disadvantage that gains to one party are losses to the other; in other words, a zero-sum game.

Recalling from Chapter 6 that a zero-sum game is one of pure conflict, it is unlikely that the result of many negotiations in planning could be usefully thought of in this way; as Binmore (2007b: 10) points out, 'the games we play in real life are seldom games of pure conflict'. This aside, the same author is surely much more accurate in summarising the sentiment shared by others regarding the desirability of a principled over a positional negotiation: 'standard strategies for negotiations often leave people dissatisfied, worn out or alienated – or frequently all three' (Bobot, 2008: 185; see also Fisher and Shapiro, 2005).

Given its contention that reasoned argument is, or should be, the essential ingredient in engineering consensus, it is perhaps unsurprising that communicative planning theorists have strongly favoured the idea of principled over positional negotiation; after all, the notion of 'planning through debate' (Healey, 1992b) or 'deliberative planning' (Forester, 1999a) is strongly consonant with the objectives of principled negotiation. Indeed, many of the school's principal theorists have explicitly incorporated it into their work (for example, Innes, 1998, 2004).

Emphasising this conceptual connection between communicative planning and principled negotiation also serves to highlight the fact that the most significant questions posed of communicative theory in Chapter 2 might also be sensibly asked of principled negotiation theory: how should we adjudge what constitutes a wise decision?; how could we come to learn a counterparty's BATNA (Best Alternative to a Negotiated Agreement, broadly analogous to Nash's conflict point set out in Chapter 6)?; how do we know that all players are behaving in a principled fashion? – how is it possible for an observer to differentiate between a principled and a positional strategy? Ultimately, why should we believe that a principled approach would lead to a better outcome than a positional one? In fact, the reverse may be true. For any player who knows that others are playing in an open, honest and principled fashion, the attendant information advantages of principled players laying their cards on the table may provide an incentive to play strategically, as the principled players are often 'too quick to equate satisfying interpersonal relationships with overall success' (Leach and Sabatier, 2005: 255).

These questions aside, the most curious aspect of the marriage between communicative planning theory and principled negotiation is that the epistemological cornerstone of the latter is objective fact – precisely the type of information that the communicative turn was born to contest as part of a progressive planning polity. However, on this matter the chief architects of principled negotiation theory are clear: to realise a situation where personalities and problems are separated and in which innovative solutions to conflict can be designed, both parties must first be willing to submit to the primacy of objective criteria, 'independent of each side's will' (Fisher *et al.*, 1991: 45). More fully, this world view – consistent with a systems or rational-positivist account of planning theory – argues that negotiators should ensure that 'some fair standard such as market value, expert opinion, custom, or law determine the outcome. By discussing such criteria rather than what the parties are willing or unwilling to do, neither party need give in to the other; both can defer to a fair solution ... . *Insist on using objective criteria*' (Fisher *et al.*, 1991: 42, italics in original).

The inconsistency of this position's marriage to mainstream communicative planning theory is quite straightforward, although it is instructive to illustrate it by running the argument through: negotiation is a contingent aspect of virtually all planning systems; negotiation is a communicative activity and, therefore, one would imagine, a core area of interest for communicative planning theory. Communicative theorists reject the positivism of systems and rational planning theory and instead argue for empathetic debate over adversarial competition; by extension, communicative planning therefore advocates principled over positional bargaining. Yet principled bargaining requires positivist information and objective facts to set standards around which consensus might be engineered. The unwind is clear to see; if post-positivist theorists are to provide an account of negotiation, either they have to admit the centrality of positivist facts to conflict resolution, thus abandoning their epistemological parentage, or they must concede that they are theoretically ill-equipped to offer an account of positional bargaining, one of the central activities of planning practice. Neither position is tenable.

By contrast, information economics, and by extension its investigative method, game theory, has no predisposed normative commitment to one style of negotiation or bargaining over another. Instead, given that bargaining is a long-term feature of many planning systems, it would seem likely that in some instances in environmental planning a positional style has been adopted; indeed, the practice of positional bargaining might be the norm, as Baccaro (2006: 186) notes: 'real actors rarely deliberate; they bargain'. Consequently, whilst it might be desirable that everyone behaves in a principled fashion, where the games we play in planning are characterised by positional bargaining – regardless of our personal feelings about this style of engagement – if we are to explain them, we will need a framework that can capture their characteristics.

These features of everyday practice might be out of kilter with the naive's view of pure planning in an impure world – 'bargaining over positions creates an incentive to negotiate from an extreme position, making small concessions and deceiving the other side about views on the issue' (Ennis, 1997: 1946) – but the alternative is the wholly unsatisfactory state of affairs where theory can only describe a form of practice of which it approves: a form of practice that, if it has been truly realised at all, represents a marginal addition to the mainstream and, therefore, small comfort for practising planners who are told that, more often than not, they 'must expect practice to diverge from theory' (Shmueli *et al.*, 2008: 362).

Negotiating or bargaining?

In the literature surveyed above the expressions, bargaining and negotiation, are often used interchangeably. Whilst this is understandable on stylistic grounds, the two concepts do have subtle but important differences. The *Oxford English Dictionary* states that to bargain means to 'discuss the terms of a transaction', whilst negotiation is 'to confer with others in order to reach a compromise or an agreement'. Semantically this would imply that negotiation is a more wide-ranging activity that does not necessarily preclude discussions that do not result in a settlement. This contrasts with bargaining, which implicitly includes the idea that an agreement will be reached but with specific terms to be determined. This small difference may seem pedantic but, particularly in environmental planning, it is an important distinction, as the nature of the discussions that might characterise planning practices are likely to differ depending upon the stage at which they take place; pre-application *negotiation* has been shown to give way to a qualitatively different form of post-application *bargaining*:

> Much in the debate about negotiation depends on how the planning process is measured and how much importance is attached to the supposed benefits of discussion. Negotiations can occur at three stages in the development control process: before an application is formally submitted (pre-application negotiations); while an application is being processed; and after a decision has been taken ... . We may even argue that those negotiations that occur after an application is lodged are more significant in their impact than the more open-ended discussions that take place before an application is made.
>
> (Glasson and Booth, 1992: 67–68)

The core reason explaining why the character of discussions differs dependent upon the stage in the planning process at which they take place is the changing temporal dynamic of power relations between counterparties. As the planning process becomes more advanced, the local planning authority's strength grows as it gains more information about the specifics of a given proposal and can control a hugely significant bargaining advantage: the potential for delay. This use of positional strategies like 'holding out' or 'delaying tactics' is well noted in practice with examples from contexts such as the UK (Sheldon and Claydon, 1991) and the USA (Forester, 1987: 304; see also Box 7.1) and is conceptually well described by a subset of non-cooperative game theory that explicitly considers timing. At their most effective, such games illustrate those circumstances where a façade of nonchalance masks a competitive urge in which the primary choice of the player is as to at what stage they allow their real intentions to be made apparent. Examples include *War of Attrition*, which is designed to model those circumstances where, under longitudinal conflict, rewards are allocated to the player with the greatest endurance – the player who 'holds out' longest. Other examples include various forms of Duel, where the model of confrontation between two players takes the form of a pistol duel, with the business of locating an equilibrium typically being the determination of the distance from their opponent at which it is optimal for a player to initiate their action (in the toy example, to 'open fire'). Finally, this class of games also includes the pre-emptive group such as Grab the dollar, where two competing individuals playing a time-limited game have to decide how long they should hold out before trying to seize the prize for which they compete (for an introduction to each, see Dixit and Skeath, 2004; Fudenberg and Tirole, 1991; Rasmusen, 2007).

Player B

		Continue	Swerve
Player A	Continue	−3, −3	2, 0
	Swerve	0, 2	1, 1

Figure 7.1 Chicken in strategic form

A simple game that can be used to illustrate some timing aspects of relevance to planning practice is Chicken. This symmetric game essentially models commitment to a course of action and what the result of such commitment might be. It takes its name from a scene in the film *Rebel without a Cause*, in which competition between James Dean's character, Jim Stark, and Buzz Gunderson (played by Corey Allen) is given figurative expression by a race towards a cliff edge; the last man to swerve receives the kudos but, if that choice is made too late, he pays the ultimate penalty of plunging over the cliff to an almost certain death. In strategic form the game can be represented as shown in Figure 7.1.

To give the game narrative explanation: if both players choose *continue*, the worst possible result ensues and both meet their end, summarised here by the pay-off in the top left-hand corner of the matrix. Should one player choose *swerve*, whilst the other plays *continue*, the result is a pay-off of 0 to the one who swerves and 2 to their opponent, representing the enhanced standing that motivated their participation in the foolish game in the first place; this is captured by the upper right and bottom left corners of the strategic form table. Finally, should both players 'chicken out', resulting in the bottom right-hand corner of the matrix, their shame is nullified and each receives a positive pay-off for having participated but not met an untimely end.

Essentially, the game gives fuller expression to a tendency already noted in environmental planning for disputes to be highly influenced by time and, particularly, the potential for players of planning games to manipulate commitment, subject to time-related qualitative variables such as desperation and the 'escalation of commitment' (Shubik, 1971). Whilst this might be positional bargaining at its most stark, the alternative, principled approach allegedly encourages rapid decision making and potentially surrenders the advantages that being able to play a 'waiting game' accord. In advocating principled negotiation Fisher *et al.* (1991: 8) contrast tardy positional approaches with the implied efficiency and swiftness of principled negotiation:

> Bargaining over positions creates incentives that stall settlement. In positional bargaining you try to improve the chance that any settlement reached is favorable to you by starting with an extreme position, by stubbornly holding to it, by deceiving the other party as to your true views, and by making small concessions only as necessary to keep the negotiation going. The same is true for the other side. Each of those factors tends to interfere with reaching a settlement promptly.

Whilst principled negotiation may well lead to more rapid decision making, we must not lose sight of the fact that, particularly in environmental planning, a rapid decision may sometimes be better thought of as a hasty and irreversible one. Having the opportunity to manipulate players by using delaying tactics is potentially the greatest advantage that professional planners have, something conceptually well described by Chicken. However, the game does a great deal more in that it represents a simple example of a class of games known as signalling games, where the pay-off structure incentivises players to signal something of their type to their opponent: in Chicken this may be that they are single-minded in their commitment to a chosen course, in the hope that this will encourage their opponent to 'blink first'. So, do planners play Chicken? (see Box 7.1).

Box 7.1: Playing a waiting game: do planners use delaying tactics?

Planning can be a slow business. In most countries the principal reason for delay in the process by which planning decisions are made is attributed to the existence of pre-application negotiations and post-application bargaining. But how do we explain 'delay'? Is it simply a necessary aspect of planning practice resulting from the complexity of the discussions that might take place or do planners knowingly use delaying tactics to gain a competitive advantage in these discussions?

A good deal of empirical research would suggest the latter. For example, in the English system – which admittedly relies heavily on negotiation (Goodchild *et al.*, 1996: 166) – it has been argued that 'planning authorities hold a very valuable negotiating position, the ability to delay, and it is this trump card which has secured bargains, even blackmail settlements, for the issue of valuable planning consents' (Osborn, 1989: 30). Similar conclusions were found in Bunnell's (1995: 93) study of the English system of negotiated settlements:

> When interviewed in connection with this research, planners working for Boroughs in Greater London expressed the view that delay in processing planning applications was a powerful tool which could force developers to agree to terms sought by the local authority.

Interview testimony from Ennis' (1996: 155) research perhaps puts the case most starkly '"Delay", one developer commented, "is the local authority weapon"'. But does this mean that developers are powerless? Almost certainly not. Once the game has started the planning agency may have time on their side, but the developer has the first-mover benefit of choosing when to initiate negotiation. As Glasson and Booth (1992: 76) note, 'The other point that has to be made about delay is to note how much of the period from inception to the first return on investment is in fact under the control of the developer and not the local planning authority. The decision on how and when and with whom to conduct negotiations and when to lodge an application rests entirely with the developer.'

This takes us straight back to game theory and the question of who has the greater advantage the first mover or the player of a waiting game?

Time on your side: are planners good at bargaining and negotiating?

The discussion of delaying tactics in Box 7.1 demonstrates two things. First, it illustrates that planners are quite astute in recognising that their primary advantage in the planning game is their capacity to delay development. Moreover, it would seem from the empirical evidence that they have historically been adept in using this advantage, despite a well-recognised deficit in the provision of negotiation training in university planning education (Bobot, 2008) and a popular image of planners as somehow by professional nature ill-equipped to bargain or negotiate effectively:

> While all of the actors require negotiating skills, the significance for the planner is that the need for such skills marks a difference from the perceived role of her/him as understood in the traditional planning model. While the planner may retain some of the kudos of the 'expert' ... he/she needs to be a skilled negotiator. This provides a sharp contrast with the understanding of planning as a rational scientific, technical exercise which identified the planner's role as one of implementer, utilising a known means to a certain end. What become of significance are the dynamics of the negotiating process.
>
> (Ennis, 1997: 1944)

Second, it shows that, in many, perhaps even most, examples of negotiation and bargaining in planning, the activity is of a positional nature. But these positions may mask underlying interests. To continue the Chicken analogy, planning authorities and developers might each know that they will choose *swerve* and will in all probability know at which stage in the process they will make that selection. However, it would be extremely unwise to make this known to their counterparty and so they may choose to project a position that is at odds with their real intentions. As Shmueli *et al.* (2008: 360; see also Fisher *et al.*, 1991; Lax and Sebenius, 1986) intuitively point out:

> Positions are the demands that parties make, or their preferred action to address a particular problem. Interests are the concerns that motivate proponents to advocate specific solutions, the 'why' behind positions. These positions represent solutions that satisfy proponents' underlying interests. Typically, parties hold firmly to their positions, which they present as the only acceptable solution ... positions often mask underlying concerns.

So, there is evidence that planners accept that positional bargaining is an essential aspect of their professional life. But what makes a good bargainer?

To answer this question we need to unpack in far greater detail the individual attributes that together comprise effective bargaining practice; for example, to what extent would a good bargainer be able to infer a counterparty's *real* position from what they choose to reveal in a game? Questions such as this are perennial in game theory and have given rise to a large subset of the discipline – signalling games – of which Chicken can be used as an example. For example, how should we interpret players' approaches to playing a game like Chicken when the pay-off structure is not well known either to one or both players – termed one- and two-sided ignorance? Introducing the wholly realistic notion that information might be incomplete illustrates that, to get to the bottom of the game, we have to consider a player's 'type' and how this affects their decision-making process when they weigh up the possible pay-offs they might receive from the various 'moves' open to them: perhaps some players are more concerned than others about the increased social standing that might result from appearing to be a daredevil in front of their peers. By extension, we also have to consider what an opponent believes a player's likely type might be in determining what is the best course of action for them: perhaps a genuine daredevil will be more committed to the folly of racing towards a cliff edge if they perceive their opponent to be lukewarm about the idea. Clearly, therefore, it may be tactically advantageous for a player to signal to their opponent something of their type, or alternatively to try to dupe them into a false belief. To summarise this in relation to Chicken, Binmore (2007a: 98) succinctly notes of his version of Players A and B, Alice and Bob, that 'when people play chicken in real life they look for clues that may signal the type of their opponent. Is Alice driving a dented old pick-up truck? Is Bob wearing a dog collar?'

Imperfect information, types and signals

Considering the concept of a player's 'type' forces us to contemplate how the structure of a game is determined prior to its commencement. For an 'encounter' to be deciphered using non-cooperative game theory it must have a structure given by a set of rules that govern how it is to be conducted. As we saw in the various examples of Follow the leader in the previous chapter, there may be many possibilities for what this structure is and how the rules are determined. Moreover, it is not necessarily the case that each player has complete knowledge of the rules, much less complete knowledge of what each of their counterparties knows about the game, its structure and rule book. In thinking about this relationship between what a player knows about the game in which they are engaged and what their competitors know we invoked the Harsanyi transformation (1967, 1968a, 1968b) in the last chapter to introduce 'Nature' as the first mover in setting the structure of the game and the types of each of the players. These two aspects of the particular format of the game and the beliefs of its players are intimately related. Again, as noted in Chapter 6, Nature's role in selecting a state of the world is really just a reflection of the beliefs and expectations each of the players has about the game that they are playing and the character types of their opponents. Whilst each player learns their own type through introspection, their opponent(s) has (have) to learn that type by assigning probabilities to the range of types that the player(s) *might* be before amending their judgement as their type is revealed by their conduct throughout the game. Therefore to complete an account of any game of imperfect information we need to say something about a player's type.

To illustrate the importance of type, belief and the role of Nature we can run a famous game that speaks to many of the types of interaction that empirical studies of positional bargaining in planning practice suggest might prevail: Cho and Kreps' (1987) Quiche-beer game, here referred to as Quiche. In what follows I have used an adaptation based on Binmore (1992: ch. 10) and Govindon and Wilson's (2008) account of the original game.

Imagine a negotiation scenario in which two types of Player A vie for some asset that is within the gift of a gatekeeper, Player B: such as a scenario where two competing developers seek planning consent, for example. Player B would prefer to award the asset to the player who is the toughest negotiator as they do not want to antagonise a hard bargainer. To differentiate a hard from a weak bargainer, Player B considers their dietary preferences with a choice of quiche, understood to be synonymous with a weak bargainer, and beer, as the mark of one who drives a hard bargain. We assume that Player B is correct in their understanding of the relationship between dietary preferences and player type: tough bargainers prefer beer and weak types prefer quiche. Therefore, both types of Player A will take two things into consideration when making a choice about what they consume: their tastes (in this case dietary preferences), known only to themselves, and their desire to persuade Player B that they are worthy of the prize.

So, for example, if Player A were a tough bargainer, they might be confronted with the game tree shown in Figure 7.2.

Player A's pay-off (the bottom left corner of each 'leaf') shows that drinking beer results in Player B correctly inferring that they are a tough bargainer and awarding the prize to Player A. Note that the award of the prize to Player A in the event that they have eaten quiche is less rewarding as the player has consumed something they find unpalatable. Finally, as Player B's preferences are always to award the prize to a tough bargainer, second-guessing the truth of the signal, beer, and thus denying the prize to Player A when they are a tough bargainer (as in the game tree in Figure 7.2) results in a pay-off of 0 to

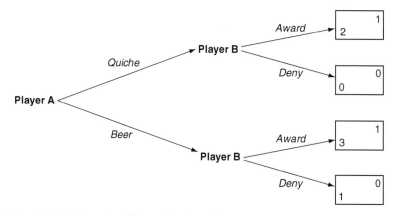

Figure 7.2 Quiche when Player A is 'tough'

Player B (as would the other option, to play *deny* when a signal of quiche is uncritically read by Player B to imply that Player A is weak). Similar logic can be applied to the game tree that might confront Player B if they were faced with a weak variant of Player A (see Figure 7.3).

A player's preference or, perhaps more accurately 'taste', for quiche or beer is known to them alone (and correspondingly whether they are strong or weak). As neither Player A nor B knows the other's type, simply drinking beer, for example, may be a signalling ploy by a weak bargainer to encourage Player B to believe that they are really of the tough variety and award the prize to them as *beer, award* (2, 0) is a superior outcome for a weak Player A to obeying their preference for quiche and having Player B correctly interpret this with a

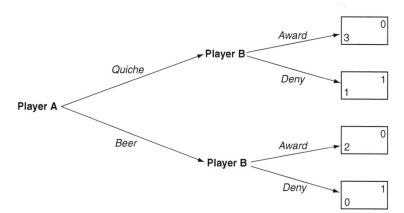

Figure 7.3 Quiche when Player A is 'weak'

corresponding move of *deny* (1, 1). The only logic that Player B is able to apply to the problem of to whom the prize should be given is to make a judgement about the type of world in which they live and weigh the probability that the signals with which they are presented are true or false indications of each players' type.

To model this we can introduce a first move by Nature in which players' types (tough, weak) are assigned at the outset of the game. As illustrated previously in Chapter 6's run of Follow the leader, this move will be a reflection of Player B's beliefs about the limits of their world: the set of possible player typologies within the universe of discourse. So, for example, if Player B believes that Nature endows her world with three weak bargainers (denoted *r* in the tree in Figure 7.4)

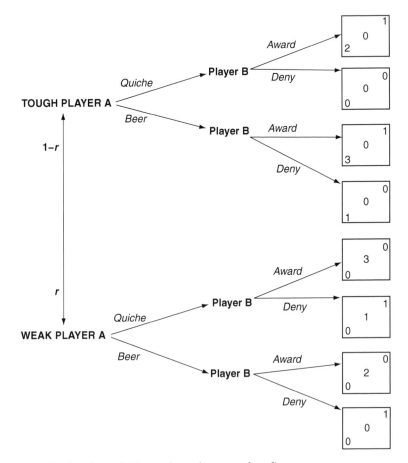

Figure 7.4 Quiche with Nature (complete, unreduced)

for every two toughs, her beliefs can be summarised prior to any signalling that each player has a 0.6 probability of being weak and a 0.4 chance that they are tough. Working through the example in stages we can construct the complete set of outcomes as in Figure 7.4. Here, the pay-offs at the completion of each possible scenario that the game could take under these terms have three entries, one for a tough bargainer in the southwest corner of the leaf, one for a weak bargainer in the centre and one for the gatekeeper, Player B, in the northeast. After a choice has been made by Nature, the non-participation of the unselected character type is reflected by an entry of zero: so, for example, in the bottom half of the figure in which Nature has chosen a weak type to make a play for the prize, each entry in the southwest corner of the grid is completed by an entry of 0 to denote that Nature's choice means a tough bargainer has not been selected to play. The same logic in reverse can be applied to the top half of the diagram: each middle entry in the leaves in that half of the draw contains a zero, as a tough bargainer and not a weak one has been chosen by Nature to play the game. For neatness, the non-choice of players can be cancelled out to give the reduced form presented in Figure 7.5.

So what should our players do? Should a weak type drink beer to project the image of a tough bargainer in the hope that the act of dissimulation will fool Player B into awarding them the prize? If both types of Player A make the same dietary choice, how will Player B be able to differentiate between them? Is there a Nash equilibrium for the game?

If we search for a Nash solution we can look in turn at each of the four strategies available to each player with subscripts t and w denoting tough and weak and q and b denoting quiche and beer. As described in Figure 7.6 these would be for Player B on the column labels: *refuse a signal of quiche, refuse a signal of beer; refuse a signal of quiche, give to a signal of beer; give to a signal of quiche, refuse a signal of beer; give to a signal of quiche, give to a signal of beer.* Similarly, the strategic choices available to the variations of type that might exist for Player A represented by the rows are explained by: *A chooses quiche when tough, A chooses quiche when weak; A chooses quiche when tough, A chooses beer when weak; A chooses beer when tough, A chooses quiche when weak; A chooses beer when tough, A chooses beer when weak.* When the incidence of weak to tough bargainers is 3:2 (that is 60% probability 'weak'; 40% probability 'tough') the game tree of Figure 7.5 can be set out in strategic form as in Figure 7.6.

The table summarises the average expected pay-offs to all players across all possible strategies. So, for example, to take the first pair of

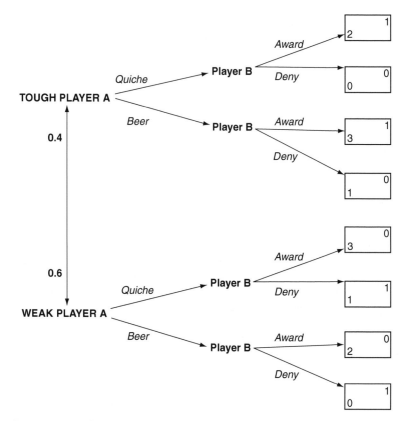

Figure 7.5 Quiche in reduced form where Nature chooses types

	R_q, R_b	R_q, G_b	G_q, R_b	G_q, G_b
q_t, q_w	3/5 3/5	3/5 3/5	2/5 2 3/5	2/5 2 3/5
q_t, b_w	3/5 0	0 1 1/5	1 4/5	2/5 2
b_t, q_w	3/5 1	1 1 4/5	0 2 1/5	2/5 3
b_t, b_w	3/5 2/5	2/5 2 2/5	3/5 2/5	2/5 2 2/5

Figure 7.6 Quiche of figure 7.5 in strategic form

pay-offs in the strategy space, Rq, Rb; qt, qw, the southwest corner of the pair represents the expected pay-off to Player A from their choice of eating quiche when they are either tough or weak, which is met by a uniform strategy of refusal by Player B. Reading off from the game tree of Figure 7.5 for the 40% of occasions upon which Player A is tough, that player type's least preferred outcome, a choice of *quiche*, coupled with a response from Player B of *refuse*, results in a pay-off of $(0.4) (0) = 0$. This is then added to the pay-off that results from a choice of *quiche* when weak being similarly met with refusal on the part of Player B of $(0.6) (1) = 0.6$. The same logic is applied to the corresponding outcomes for Player B to arrive at their pay-offs, here summarised in the northeast corner of each cell of the table.

The purpose of the table is to inform our analysis of the game by providing an alternative visual representation of the game from which we can search for a 'solution' to the game: or, more correctly, a Bayesian-Nash equilibrium as we are effectively looking for best responses – hence Nash – that turn on a player updating their beliefs given an opening move by 'Nature' – therefore Bayesian. In the language of game theory the universe of discourse only contains four possible potential states of the world: where both potential types of Player A make the same selection (qt, qw and bt, bw), we are searching for a 'pooling' equilibrium; where both potential types of Player A make a different selection (qt, bw and bt, qw), we are searching for a 'separating' equilibrium. As there are only four possible strategies for Player A, two pooling and two separating, each can be investigated in turn.

Providing that they know that a separating strategy has been used across the two possible types of Player A, the specific strategy, *beer if tough, quiche if weak* (bt, qw), results in Player B updating their beliefs. To demonstrate this, Bayes's rule can be invoked to measure Player B's updated belief that Player A is of the tough variety, given a signal of 'beer' – noted 'Probability Tough|Beer' (to be read 'probability that Player A is a tough bargainer, given a signal of "beer"'). Using the same method as for Follow the leader in Chapter 6:

$$\text{Probability Tough|Beer} \quad \frac{(1)(0.4)}{(1)(0.4) + (0)(0.6)} = 1$$

The above equation simply summarises that, in this particular separating scenario, Player B uncritically interprets the signal of 'beer' to always indicate a tough bargainer: that is, when Player B knows the type of separating strategy deployed, they will strengthen their prior beliefs to the degree that a signal of 'beer' will make them certain that they face a tough bargainer. Using the same logic, under the same separating strategy, a signal of 'quiche' ensures that Player B updates to a position of certainty that they face a weak bargainer. Again, using Bayes's rule:

$$\text{Probability Weak}|\text{Quiche} \; \frac{(1)(0.6)}{(0)(0.4) + (1)(0.6)} = 1$$

To check this, we can read off from the strategic form of the game in Figure 7.6. Here we can see that Player B, faced with the strategy bt, qw will respond with Rq, Gb (refuse quiche, give to beer) as, with their beliefs strengthened that the signal they receive is a genuine indicator of player type in this separating scenario, Rq, Gb is the only logical strategy as it gives a pay-off of 1 (north east corner of cell at coordinate bt, qw; Rq, Gb) as opposed to $\frac{3}{5}$, 0, or $\frac{2}{5}$ for any of the three alternatives. However, is it recommendable for Player A to simply obey their tastes; is bt, qw an equilibrium?

Given that we know that Player B will choose the response Rq, Gb in this separating scenario we can work backwards to see if bt, qw is optimal for either potential incarnation of Player A. For the tough variety of Player A, *beer* is definitely an optimal choice, given Player B's choice of Rq, Gb, as it means that they both win the prize and consume something they like resulting in their maximum possible pay-off (3). For the weak variety of Player A, however, whilst they consume their preferred snack, that choice precludes them from ever winning the prize under this separating scenario with the corresponding pay-off of 1. In fact the weak variety of Player A would be better advised to choose 'beer', as that would result in Player B awarding them the prize and the corresponding pay-off of 2. In short, the strategy bt, qw cannot be a Nash equilibrium.

The alternative separating strategy would be quiche if tough, beer if weak, qt, bw, but this makes no sense: if Player B knows the game being played is bt, qw, they are now certain about their ability to decipher each type of Player A – their beliefs have hardened to certainties, for the reasons stated above, yet under this separating scenario both players now consume something they find unpalatable. Clearly this cannot be an equilibrium either.

All that remains are the two pooling choices of beer when tough, beer when weak (bt, bw) and quiche when tough, quiche when weak (qt, qw). Using Bayes's rule, again we can investigate what the choice witnessed by Player B leads them to decide about the veracity of their prior beliefs. If we start with beer when tough, beer when weak (bt, bw) Bayes's rule enables us to work out what Player B believes about Player A once they have seen them drink beer by measuring the ratio of what they have seen against the potential likelihood that they are facing a Player A of either type:

$$\text{Probability Tough}|\text{Beer} \ \frac{(1)(0.4)}{(1)(0.4) + (1)(0.6)} = 0.4$$

Updating shows us that the pooled set, bt, bw, is understood by Player B as meaning that they face a tough bargainer on 40% of the occasions upon which a uniform choice of 'beer' is observed and a weak one the remaining 60% of the time. In short, this pooling strategy reveals nothing to Player B: they begin with the prior belief that Nature has created a world with two tough bargainers for every three of the weak disposition, so, even when Player B knows that the game being played is bt, bw, their best guess is still that viewed through the filter of their prior beliefs. So what should Player B do? what is their best response to bt, bw?

Looking at the strategic form of the game set out in Figure 7.6 helps us here. When the game being played is bt, bw, the pay-offs to Player B mean that they have no best response: they are indifferent between two strategies Rq, Rb and Gq, Rb. That is, as Player B always prefers to give the gift to a tough bargainer, and with their prior belief intact that weak bargainers outnumber tough bargainers 3:2, they will choose to refuse any signal of beer. However, the parity between Rq, Rb and Gq, Rb effectively means that a choice of quiche is indeterminate; Player B does not know what to make of the signal.

Getting to the bottom of the game

To find our way out of this puzzle we can consider the thought processes that Player B might bring to bear to work out how they should respond to a uniform signal (either all quiche, or all beer). We can begin by considering Player B's preferences. We know that they prefer to give to the tough type and refuse the weak type of Player A. So, Player B's pay-offs describe a temperament that wishes to make an award for any state of affairs where they believe that the probability of their counterpart being a tough Player A, call it x, is greater than the probability that they are weak, call it $1 - x$. Stated alternatively, whenever confronted with either possible uniform choice of qt, qw or bt, bw, Player B will choose 'award' whenever $x > \frac{1}{2}$ and 'refuse' whenever $1 - x < \frac{1}{2}$.

As we know from the discussion above that a uniform signal of quiche is indeterminate for Player B – when faced with this dietary choice there is no pure strategic response – it must therefore be the case that, in equilibrium, Player A is pursuing a mixed strategy, deviating from a consistent selection of quiche or beer. To explore why this is the case it must be that Player B has arrived at the conclusion that, when confronted with a particular choice set, of which we know *quiche* must be an element, they are unable to distinguish the likelihood of them being either 'tough' or 'weak'. Player B must believe that the two probabilities are equal; $x = \frac{1}{2} = 1 - x$. Somewhere in the game Player B's prior knowledge has been updated to the degree that they are unable to judge whether it is more or less likely that they are facing a tough or weak bargainer. For this to be the case it must also follow that Player A of either incarnation is randomising their dietary choices. Furthermore, in response, Player B must also be randomising in equilibrium between their two options of 'award' and 'deny' when confronted with this particular choice set: but at what point in the game is this happening?

To answer this question we can follow the analysis of Binmore (1992: ch. 10). If we put ourselves in the position of Player A we can ask, what is the probability that they should drink beer or eat quiche in either of the pooled strategies, bt, bw or qt, qw? The probability that a tough variant of Player A should drink beer in the game bt, bw could be referred to as B and the corresponding probability that they should eat quiche in the game qt, qw could be called Q. The two must sum to 1, as each player always seeks to use their dietary choice to transmit a signal: they always consume *something*. Equally, for Player A of the weak variety we can ask what is the probability that they should drink beer or eat quiche in either of the pooled strategies, bt, bw or qt, qw? The probability that a weak variant of Player A should drink beer in the game bt, bw could be referred to as b and the corresponding probability that they should eat quiche in the game qt, qw could be called q.

As we know that Player B is adopting a randomised strategy somewhere in the game, either under qt, qw or bt, bw, we know that they must be indifferent between their two options: a player would only randomise in a situation where they are indifferent between their two choices. Therefore, as Player B always prefers to reward a tough bargainer and refuse a weak one, their reading of at least one of the pooled scenarios must be that $Q = 2q$ or $B = 2b$: either that the probability that Player A eats quiche when tough is equal to the probability that Player A eats quiche when weak; or that the probability that Player A drinks beer when tough is equal to the probability that Player A drinks beer when weak.

If we start with the hypothesis that $Q = 2q$ we can see both algebraically[1] and intuitively that the implication this has for the alternative information set (*beer*) means that there cannot be a mixed strategy deployed by Player B when confronted with a uniform signal of 'beer'. From the discussion above we know that Player B will meet a pooled selection of bt, bw with a response of 'refuse'. In the case of the tough type of Player A the choice is clear, selecting 'beer' accords with their preferred tastes and results in them being awarded the prize. For the weak variety of Player A the answer is quite different; if they know they will be refused anyway there is no incentive to drink beer – they may as well follow their dietary preferences and eat quiche. If it is therefore certain that a weak A would eat quiche and a strong A would drink beer, such a straightforward separating strategy would not require Player B to mix their response; quite the reverse, they would be certain of their capacity to 'read' their opponent and we would no longer be playing a pooling game.

To investigate what happens to Player A of the weak variety, we can look at the other hypothesis, the only remaining possibility for a mixed strategy for Player B, $B = 2b$, by again looking at what this would imply happens at the other information set (*quiche*). If $B = 2b$ then we can substitute these terms for their inverse expressions $(1 - Q) = 2(1 - q)$. This in turn can be re-expressed as $2q = 1 + Q$ which, as therefore $2q > Q$, simply states that the probability that Player A eats quiche when weak is greater than the probability that Player A eats quiche when tough. Consequently, Player B must refuse a uniform signal of quiche as they believe it more likely that they are facing a weak than a tough bargainer in accord with their prior belief that there are three weak bargainers for every two toughs. However, a tough Player A gains nothing by eating quiche if they know they will be refused anyway, so they will certainly drink beer. This gives us our first two certain results: it is always an equilibrium strategy for a tough Player A to drink beer; it is always an equilibrium strategy for Player B to refuse a signal of quiche.

Given that we now have some certain pieces in our puzzle, one of which relates to the equilibrium strategy for Player A – that a tough Player A will always choose to drink beer – we can represent this as $B = 1$ in the statement of potential areas in the game where a mixed strategy might be deployed and thus unlock the rest of the game. If a tough bargainer always drinks beer, $B = 1$, then re-presenting our initial hypothesis shows that where $B = 2b$ then $1 = 2b$ and so $b = 0.5$. That is, our weak version of Player A is consuming beer with probability 0.5 at the information set, *beer*. Correspondingly, if $b = 0.5$ then it must also be the case that $q = 0.5$ (as the two probabilities must sum to 1; each player always consumes something): in equilibrium, weak versions of Player A are randomising between choosing quiche and beer on a 50:50 basis.

So weak Player A is indifferent between quiche and beer: they play them equally frequently. As we know that Player B always refuses a signal of quiche, Player A of the weak variety must be indifferent between the pay-off of 1 that they get from that outcome (qw, Rq) and a pay-off of 1 whenever they play beer. As the best pay-off that a weak Player A can hope to get by playing beer is 2 (when Player B is fooled by the signal and awards them the prize), it must be the case that Player B is also randomising to the same 50:50 degree when confronted by a uniform signal of beer.

The conclusion is that the equilibrium state for the game is for a tough Player A to always select beer and for Player B to always refuse a signal of quiche. Player A of the weak temperament should adopt a mixed strategy choosing quiche and beer equally frequently to either fulfil their taste preferences or to dupe Player B that they are a tough bargainer and worthy of the prize. In response to this mixed strategy on the part of weak Player A, Player B must also randomise in equilibrium when confronted with a choice of bt, bw. Just like the action of weak Player A that prompts the mixed strategy on the part of Player B, Player B oscillates between refusing and giving to a probability of 0.5 when confronted with a uniform signal of *beer*.

Understanding signalling

Quiche is an example of a signalling game – where participants can choose to take costly decisions to signal something about themselves that may or may not be an accurate indication of the truth (Spence, 1974). In this example the cost incurred is that to, say, the weak bargainer of consuming something that they find distasteful to signal something, in this example false, about their character. Within this class of signalling games Quiche is a relatively straight-forward example. Of course, just as with any game, the structure of the chosen illustrative form might have been different – for example we might have run the game for a world where Player B believed there were four weak bargainers for every one tough, or where Player B preferred to make an award on the grounds of need and favoured weak over tough bargainers (for different articulations of the game, cf. Rasmusen, 2007: 174; Binmore, 1992: chapter 10; Govindon and Wilson, 2008). The specifics of the example are almost irrelevant; the method of deciphering its outcome is the important element of the analysis.

The power of this method resides in its capacity to reveal the intricacies of positional bargaining, specifically the manner in which players of a bargaining game might seek to mask their real intentions through dissimulation. Of course this does not have to be through behaviour-based signals. As Farrell and Rabin (1996: 104) note 'we suspect most information sharing is not done through Spence-style signalling ... it is done through ordinary, informal talk'. Some of this information sharing through conversation may be equally disingenuous, as in the case of the weak bargainer who chooses to drink beer; but where it is costless (i.e. where it does not inconvenience the player in the way that consuming something they might find unpalatable would), game theorists have termed this form of information sharing, 'cheap talk'.

This recognition that signals are often (usually) expressed in ordinary language takes us back to Wittgenstein's language games. Moreover, the introduction of 'cheap talk' highlights the fact that, where communication is costless, the language game may be characterised by many signals and counter-signals of indeterminate meaning: hollow threats, empty promises. It is precisely this form of bargaining that characterises planning practice, although the specifics of each encounter will be conditioned by the terms of whatever planning law prevails in a jurisdiction, meaning that bargaining may be qualitatively different from place to place. However, as we have already seen, for example in Box 7.1, the rule book of planning law in myriad jurisdictions effectively provides systemic advantages and disadvantages to players of planning games that make positional bargaining accompanied by signalling – some of which may be true, some of which is likely to be false – almost inevitable. It is this feature of urban and environmental planning policy – where protagonists' behaviour is marked by tactical duplicity – that makes game theory potentially so illuminating in the investigation of the situations and circumstances that arise as a result. So, by now we know that some planners play a form of Chicken. Do they also play a form of Quiche?

Box 7.2: Quiche and the planning gain game

The propensity for players of the planning game to behave duplicitously is well noted. Often this may be due to the uneven distribution of information between the public and private sectors, as Rydin and Pennington (2000: 159) note: 'Rent-seekers are typically better informed about the issues which directly affect them and may fill the information vacuum created by rational ignorance, disseminating selective or distorted data to other participants'.

One area of planning practice where this dissemination of misinformation might be particularly common is in the determination of developer exactions: financial contributions made by a developer to a local planning authority to offset the impact of development. Known variously as 'planning gain' in Britain and 'impact fees' in the USA, but practiced throughout the majority of nation states that have a formal system of urban and environmental management, whilst the specifics of each system vary, the process by which a contribution is agreed almost inevitably requires some form of bargaining between planning authority and developer.

To take an example, in England, although the formal legislation that sets out how developer contributions might be agreed has changed on several occasions even in the recent past, Loughlin's (1981: 89) observations remain an accurate portrayal of the system's enactment: 'The process is discretionary, with few formal controls imposed on the use of powers to negotiate gains'. The result is a set of circumstances that provide an opportunity for tactical bargaining.

But do players of the planning gain game respond by behaving strategically in the way that games such as Quiche would suggest they might?

For evidence we can turn to the most complete empirical study in this vein: Bunnell's (1995) account of developer contributions in Cambridgeshire in the east of England. First, the author considers the relationship between the political stripe of the local authority and the types of bargaining tactic that this might imply. In so doing the author dispels the myth that the politics of developer contributions conform to an ideological distinction between Labour-controlled authorities, assumed to be in favour of maximising community benefits from development, and Conservative-run councils' presumed preference not to interfere with the free market:

> It has often been assumed that Labour authorities have been more inclined to try to force developers into making excessive contributions than Conservative local authorities. However, evidence that political affiliation has affected willingness to negotiate contributions is largely anecdotal and

inconclusive ... . According to Marsh (1990, interview), Conservative local authorities in outlying areas have often been particularly aggressive in negotiating planning gain. 'These are areas where stockbrokers live and these financial people participate in local government and understand deal-making. They favour policies of tight constraint and at the same time drive a hard bargain'.

(Bunnell, 1995: 14; see also Barlow and Chambers, 1992)

Second, on the other side of the transaction – with planners as 'Player B' – the research found that planners' gate-keeping position accorded a great deal of bargaining strength and resulted in planners adopting a critical (and implacably professional) approach to how they interpreted the signals that the development industry sought to transmit:

One might have expected LPAs [Local Planning Authorities] to welcome unsolicited offers of contributions from developers. However, planners in Cambridgeshire were not always happy when unsolicited offers of contributions were made and developers who offered contributions were not infrequently refused planning permission.

(Bunnell, 1995: 91)

Moreover, this strong position was conspicuously signalled back to developers – resonant of play in Quiche – for example, Bunnell (1995: 64) describes how the chief planning officer 'quickly gained a reputation for his aggressiveness in seeking to negotiate contributions from developers. According to Popper, "in negotiating with developers, it's all economics. If they have a lot to gain, we push pretty hard" (Popper, 1990 interview)'.

More recently a new breed of planning academics have sought to investigate the same bargaining processes by which exactions are agreed explicitly using game theory. Central to this project is the work of Samsura and van der Krabben (2009; see also Samsura *et al.*, 2010) who provide an immensely detailed study of the potential ways in which this particular type of planning game might work out. Of particular significance in this work is the focus placed not on the manipulative strategies open to individuals but on the potential for systemically weak players to band together into coalitions to enhance their bargaining strength – the subject of Chapter 8.

Conclusion

Much of the existing research on bargaining and negotiation in environmental planning begins from a recognition shared with game theory that 'Information can be selectively perceived and strategically manipulated. It is often limited and incomplete, misunderstood, contradictory, and further distorted through communication' (Shmueli *et al.*, 2008: 362). Yet, where game theory seeks to hold a light up to these concepts and spell out the intricacies of how bargaining and negotiation might proceed, planning theorists have often glossed over these specifics, despite negotiation and bargaining being a, perhaps *the*, core business of planning practice in virtually every context within which it takes place.

Perhaps the reason for this is that, as most academics working in the field agree, context is inherently important in accounting for the agreements that emerge from specific episodes of bargaining and negotiation. Under the various forms of post-positivist planning theory it would surely be argued that it falls to individual researchers to qualitatively distil the pertinent aspects of what is assumed to be a contextually-specific process and set out how that process might have been better attuned to local circumstances and grass roots, community aspirations.

This overlooks the potential for community representatives, just as much as any other agency, to behave tactically in seeking to secure their preferred ends. Moreover, it takes too little account of the binding principle that makes negotiation and bargaining of such general interest for all planning academics: the idea that planning exists to support or enhance the 'public interest' and so should seek to secure the 'best' – most sustainable, perhaps – result for society at large. We as the public, therefore, not only expect planners to bargain on our behalf but we must also hope that they are effective bargainers. This inevitably 'involves negotiations with the relevant private-sector actors [in which] the emphasis is on the means by which public authorities establish and operate negotiating frameworks in pursuit of their own interests, presumed to be the public interest' (Ennis, 1997: 1938).

Despite some contention that the public interest is no longer a worthwhile concept, particularly in Western societies that, because they are increasingly diverse, are allegedly more fragmented (for a review see Campbell and Marshall, 2002), for many there is still a great deal of value in the notion of planning for the public interest: we all, regardless of age, gender, ethnicity, sexual orientation or other personal politics take a collective interest in the preservation of a sustainable natural environment and a well-functioning public infrastructure. It is from this perspective that this chapter has sought to investigate how we might begin to take negotiation and bargaining more seriously in planning theory and practice. If planning is the guardian of sustainability in an era of climate change, food insecurity and potential energy crises, it must be adequately equipped to work for the public interest and to secure sustainable development that responds effectively to such environmental threats. Accepting that bargaining and negotiation of a tactical, positional nature are the mainstays of this form of planning practice is the first step towards enhancing the profession's capacity to effect this work.

A game-theoretic interpretation of planning not only accepts this, but it argues that *all* players in the planning game have the opportunity to behave tactically and, in many cases, will choose to do so. Appreciating this fact highlights a radical distinction between a game-theoretic investigation of urban and environmental management and that posited by many of the post-positivist theories of planning. For the former, as tactics and strategy, even those resting on duplicity, are potential occupants of the 'black box', a theoretically neutral attitude is taken that allows for their discovery and analysis. For the latter, the phenomenological origins of the method of investigation make it impossible to decipher what is superfluous cheap talk and what is essential testimony. Worse, for the communicative turn the potential for underhand tactics and double-dealing, about which a game-theoretic (and for that matter any treatment following Foucault) position is ambivalent, are understood to be hallmarks of a dysfunctional and ethically undesirable communicative situation.

The implications for practice of these diametrically opposed positions are fundamental. If we move beyond the detachment that game theory shares with Wittgenstein's philosophical method, we can consider the practical questions that policy makers might ask. For example, if we can unravel how strategies lead to environmentally unsustainable or socially deleterious outcomes, can we also redesign practice to systemically strengthen the hand of one or other participant? Might engaging fully with the planning game require tactical behaviour on the part of, say, a planning authority? For the strictest adherents of principled negotiation as part of a communicative theory of planning, such a prescription would be precluded on the grounds that encouraging tactical behaviour of any sort would be consistent with positional bargaining and could result in uneven outcomes that may in turn destabilise the communicative setting: as Shmueli *et al.* (2008: 362, see also Susskind and Ozawa 1984; Susskind and Field 1996) point out when arguing against any form of positional bargaining, 'while win-win (joint gains) outcomes are possible, lose-lose outcomes often threaten participatory planning and planning negotiations'.

The logical conclusion is that, if we eschew any approach to planning practice that results in one or more parties getting less than they might find desirable, we would never disrupt any status quo, even those that deliver unsustainable or unjust outcomes – despite this running counter to the objectives of social emancipation and environmental justice at the core of the communicative planning project. As significantly, given what we know about the features of mainstream practice, nor does the theory of principled negotiation provide a particularly close approximation of the real world of planning practice. For those who believe that positional bargaining is almost inevitable in planning, delaying tactics and signalling represent two of the strategic options open to players of planning games. Another might be to enlist the support of others. Fortunately, game theory offers us an approach to deal with encounters that are marked by group dynamics in the guise of coalition games – the subject of Chapter 8.

Note

1 If $Q = 2q$ then $1 - B = 2 (1 - b)$. Rearranging gives $2b = 1 + B$ so $2b > B$. When Player B sees *beer* they believe it more likely that the signal masks a weak bargainer than the genuine choice of a strong type. Player B will therefore refuse a signal of beer (Binmore, 1992: 465–67).

8 Team games, coalitions and collaboration

Chapters 6 and 7 introduced non-cooperative game theory as a way of exploring the types of planning game in which some degree of competition might characterise the way in which actors relate to one another. Outlining some of the most fundamental concepts in the field, running some famous games and showing how the theory relates to the real world of urban and environmental management has led to the conclusion that a very great deal of planning practice, as with so many other walks of life, is characterised by individual competition. Somewhat depressingly in many instances we have seen that some of this competition is not conducive to realising a planning polity that might deliver a more sustainable future. For example, those games that we play with our natural environment that mirror the Prisoners' dilemma set out in Chapter 6 suggest that unsustainable overexploitation results from all-out competition, in contrast to the cooperative solutions that might yield 'better' results – in the sense of both game-theoretic pay-offs and environmental sustainability – for all concerned. As has been established, the reason for this is that, in games that display formulaic conformity with the Prisoners' dilemma, cooperation can never be a rational choice. Even outside the class of games that strongly incentivise some degree of individual competition, of which the Prisoners' dilemma is an example, degrees of competition are typical, giving rise to the dominance of non-cooperative game theory as the investigative method best equipped to model the games we play in real life.

For some behavioural economists (for example, Camerer, 2003; Gintis *et al.*, 2006; see also Gintis, 2009) a crumb of comfort is found in the idea that experiments in game theory suggest that the neoclassical construction of a self-interested, unerringly competitive *homo economicus* is a fiction. Instead, this group argue that human beings are not innately ruthlessly competitive and point to an array of economic experiments and anthropological studies, such as the empirical results of the Ultimatum game experiments reported in Chapter 6, in which human beings are shown to cooperate as much (sometimes more) than they compete. This has led to what is said to be a validation of the *folk theorem*: the idea that, over a sufficiently large number of successive rounds, even in games that strongly incentivise non-cooperative behaviour, some degree of coordination will develop; this was most famously put by Axelrod (1984) as the 'evolution of cooperation'. The degree to which this form of self-policed fairness is a result of contextually specific social norms/conventions or a trait owed to the biological evolution of the human race is a debate that still rages (cf. Binmore, 2001b; Sugden, 2001). Regardless, many experiments bear out the idea that human beings are generally 'fair' in their dealings with one another. For example Cárdenas and Ostrum (2004: 311) report that 'in experimental games it is frequently observed that the significant fraction of individuals (roughly half) start cooperating in these experiments (Ledyard, 1995). Arguments for explaining this observation range from presuming a lack of learning and understanding of the game to inherited altruistic preferences for humans'.

For sceptics reluctant to trust in the general fair-mindedness of humankind, ensuring cooperation over conflict in the collective action dilemmas that mark so much of planning practice remains a question of policy intervention. Rather than relying on the behaviourists' account that human nature itself will ensure that encounters do not run on the jungle laws of radical individualism, an alternative might be to institute some form of policy mechanism to encourage cooperation where the likely implications of non-cooperative behaviour are deemed unsustainable or undesirable. The collective hopes of most communicative planning theorists have been pinned on realising such a system. But how do we obtain cooperation between the differing sections of the multiplicity of stakeholders that characterises the landscape of planning policy? What do empirical studies teach us about the existing nature of cooperation in planning practice?; do players cooperate before the commencement of a game, particularly with the purpose of strengthening their bargaining position through the acquisition of allies?; what mechanisms might be used to 'guarantee' cooperation?; do players form loose coalitions based upon informal agreements or use formal contracts and covenants?

On these procedural questions existing planning theory tells us surprisingly little. Furthermore, it tells us still less about fundamental, specific issues such as who is likely to partner with whom; how stable are the coalitions that might emerge; how 'fair shares' are agreed between constituents of a coalition; and the effect that the coalition dynamics that we might observe ultimately have on the animation of planning practice. To address these gaps in our understanding of how coalitions form, and with what effect, we can turn to cooperative game theory.

Coalitions in planning practice

Coalitions are so common in much of planning practice that, in some contexts, researchers now assume their existence a priori. This is most clearly the case in the USA where the frequency with which 'growth coalitions' (Molotch, 1976) and 'urban regimes' (Elkin, 1987) have been observed has been interpreted by some as obviating the requirement for researchers to find further instances of their existence (for a review, see Ward, 1997). Much of this work has drawn attention to the stability of extremely heterogeneous coalitions that in many cases have remained intact for decades, frequently with profound implications for the development of a given city (Stone, 1989). The diversity of the actors, including a set of routinely observed 'usual suspects', such as business interests, local politicians, the chamber of commerce and, almost always, planners (see Dear, 1986, 1989; Winter and Brooke, 1993; McGuirk, 1994; Filion, 1996; McCann, 2001), reveals the most question-begging aspect of research in this vein. How have coalitions that are so diverse proven to be so stable and such a pervasive feature of US city politics?

Outside the USA studies have identified similar formations in much of Western Europe (Harding, 2000; John and Cole, 1998; Stoker and Mossberger, 1994; Stoker, 1995), although with the important caveat that the membership of a coalition will be functionally related to the macro-political culture. For example, the coalitions observed in Europe are said to be qualitatively different to those first observed in the USA, largely due to the greater financial independence afforded to local/municipal governments in most European contexts as a result of tax-raising powers residing at a higher spatial scale of government, unlike in the USA where the fiscal powers invested in local government entail a closer relationship between what Molotch (1976; Logan and Molotch, 1987) refers to as 'parochial capital' – locally rooted businesses – and the local state. Such are these contextual differences that some have argued that the formation and constituents of the coalitions found in Western Europe are so significantly different to those first documented in the USA (Davies, 2002, 2003; Wood, 2004, 2005).

Taking this cue, others have sought to document from first principles those coalitions that have emerged in Europe and elsewhere. The result is the identification of 'grant coalitions' (Cochrane *et al.*, 1996: 1331). These assemblages differ from the US formations in that they coalesce around, depending on context, national or federal government criteria for the award of resources, usually to stimulate urban regeneration. Whilst the motivation behind coalition formation might serve to contrast US and European coalitions, continuity can be found in the diversity of their composition. Again, a broad spectrum of public and private agencies – often with no track record of having worked together prior to the availability of grant funding being made dependent upon coalition formation – have been seen to band together, resulting in a formal partnership, often with planning at its core. For example, Williams *et al.* (2000: 298) identify a 'remarkable coalition of interests' in the redevelopment of Manchester following the explosion of an IRA bomb in the city in 1995. More generally the same authors remark:

> To be successful, it is important that a coalition of local interests and established relational webs and networks are willing to work together to prepare and oversee an agreed strategy. In Manchester, there was ample evidence of public–private partnership working, and institutional capacity-building to achieve ambitious schemes, with the city becoming a British role model for such coalition building – 'more successful than most in playing the partnership game' (Peck and Tickell, 1995: 79). Formal and informal networks were, therefore, in place, and city leaders were able to mobilise the knowledge and relational resources that existed, and build upon them to achieve their objective of rebuilding.

In light of these empirical observations (and those of Box 9.1) it might reasonably be expected that the preeminent questions in planning theory would be: how have such broad coalitions emerged and how is the observed stability of such diverse groups to be understood and explained? are they durable?; are they coherent?; does it matter if they are transitory and riven? However, instead of focusing on this peculiar, counter-intuitive aspect of planning practice, most work has started from the implicit assumption – quite removed from the heterogeneity that empirical research would suggest is the norm – that the only sustainable coalitions in planning are broadly homogeneous and bound together by a common belief system.

For example Wolsink (2003: 705) begins from the entirely logical proposition that 'any achievement of spatial planning requires the formation of a coalition' before going on to articulate the widely-held view that, for a planning coalition to be effective, it must always incorporate interests that share a common set of values. In reflecting on this the same author considers the motivation behind why certain coalitions form and adumbrates a schema of coalition types, such as the 'advocacy-coalition framework' (see also, Sabatier and Jenkins-Smith, 1999), in which the impetus behind coalition formation is a mutually held impulse to advocate a particular policy prescription:

> The unit of analysis is the policy subsystem or the entire set of actors within a policy domain in which public and private actors on all levels participate in advocacy coalitions. Each coalition shares a policy-belief system (PBS) and the actors within a coalition cooperate. Competing coalitions that hold different policy beliefs may exist, but generally there is one dominant advocacy coalition and policy is based on a dominant PBS.

Similarly, in a study of a 'Transportation land use coalition' in the San Francisco Bay Area, Innes and Booher (2000: 18) argue that the coalition was effective because it was constrained to 'environmental grass roots organizations, bus riders unions, the disabled and those concerned with environmental justice'. The same authors go on to explain why, in their view, a wider coalition would not have been possible:

> But the reality is, of course, that a social movement has to be limited in scope and diversity of participants because it cannot hold together if it is too diverse. While the Transportation Land Use Coalition is relatively broad, it does not include, for example, small business, homeowners, workers who are commuting by car, or many others who are citizens wanting to participate. Such citizens would probably not join the movement nor necessarily sympathize with its objectives. If they joined, they would water down the objectives.

The theoretical justification for this practice of constraining coalition membership in the practice of collaborative planning is supplied by the concept of a 'discourse coalition' (Hajer, 1993; 1995: see also, Healey, 1993), the objective of which is to articulate, or 'mobilise', a position that then serves as a clarion call, attracting those of a like-minded disposition whilst, presumably, repelling others. The overall impression is of a mechanism designed to identify, assimilate and perpetuate conformity: a form of coalition by consensus that relies on the idea that unity of purpose can be engineered by demanding acceptance of a creed as a necessary precursor to membership of the group. Healey (1999: 39) spells the argument out by reference to a specific example where:

> the evolution of a new discourse and its development into key choices about sites was accompanied by careful and strategic institutional work in coalition-building. New relationships were built up through which the new discourse could be articulated and diffused.

On this account the coalitions that come to engage with professional planning are usually coherent, in the sense that they have a shared set of objectives and a common world view. Faced with such a predictable world, the core activity of the planning profession becomes orchestration, balancing competing objectives and engineering consensus between blocks that are relatively easy to read and understand. Hajer and Zonneveld (2000: 339) succinctly describe the type of orchestration that this type of planning practice might involve:

> much of the essential work of the planner is discursive: listening to people, making an inventory of problems and wishes, scanning preferences, developing concepts that can guide thinking about spatial development, assessing the possibilities of building coalitions among actors and thus in essence persuading actors of various kinds to think about the future developments in one and the same language.

Whilst this conception of planners as orchestrators and matchmakers might be intuitively appealing, where, for whatever reason, like-minded souls are not drawn to one another naturally, the result in practice has been the creation of some extremely biased coalitions, a far cry from the collaborative paradigm. For example, Rydin and Pennington (2000: 156) note that, often, the best efforts of professional planners to encourage widespread participation have simply 'resulted in selective participation by vocal and well-organised interest groups in negotiation with the professional bureaucracy, with the costs of policy failure spread across non-mobilised sections of the community'. Similar observations have been made by many other empirical studies (see Bickerstaff and Walker, 2000; Bickerstaff *et al.*, 2002; Cooke and Kothari, 2001; Flyvbjerg, 1996; Nienhuis *et al.*, 2011; Rydin, 2003; Tewdwr-Jones and Thomas, 1998) giving rise to what Bickerstaff and Walker (2005: 2123) neatly summarise as 'shared visions, unholy alliances'.

The outcome of this discussion is the presentation of two problems for planning theory. First, attempts to understand the contents of the black box of planning practice first identified in Chapter 5 have been frustrated by the fact that there are numerous examples of coalitions in planning practice that are not easily explained away as the outcome of like-minded agents banding together: real planning coalitions often include public and private elements with seemingly conflicting objectives; they frequently straddle statutory scales of government, again sometimes with competing aims; and in many instances they represent a coalescence of interests not *for* a policy or concept (as in Wolnick's use of the advocacy formation discussed above) but *against* a policy, a proposal or, more often than not, a *competing coalition* (see, for example, Sabatier and Jenkins-Smith, 1999). Second, when confronted with a form of practice that does not accord with existing theory's normative preferences, attempts to beautify the contents of the black box have, in many cases, resulted in dysfunctional and skewed partnerships that are in no sense representative of the circumstances said to typify the 'ideal speech situation' that we might hope for. The net result is a situation where theory cannot explain practice, even that which results from the implementation of its own prescriptions. By contrast, game theory allows us to consider the vagaries of coalition formation that empirical accounts suggest might actually occur. So, why do surprising coalitions form and how might we explain those coalitions that dissolve into domination?

Coalition formation in theory and practice

Building a winning team

To model the types of interaction that might comprise a non-cooperative situation we have so far been preoccupied mostly with two-player games. Of course, in reality the nature of the encounters that might characterise planning practice may have many more players. Moreover, as illustrated by Box 8.1, it is often the case that individual agents in the planning game seek to make strategic alliances, sometimes contrary to our intuition of what might be expected, to enhance their bargaining position. Non-cooperative game theory may still be the most appropriate way of understanding how the players, or assemblages of players, conduct themselves once the decision to assimilate into a group has been made, but first we must seek to understand how coalitions form, whether they are stable or not and how these features might explain how 'fair shares' are determined. For this we need cooperative game theory.

Box 8.1: Breaking up is hard to do: curious planning marriages and why they work ...

Planning, like politics, 'makes strange bedfellows' (Gamson, 1961: 373). Examples of such unusual alliances are legion in the planning literature. These range from the perverse alliance of left-leaning academics, community activists, conservation organisations and the right wing press who jointly opposed housing market interventions in the UK (cf. Allen, 2008; Clover, 2007; Finlay and Brown, 2011), to the multiplicity of diverse actors – the businesses, public sector bodies, universities, police and healthcare providers – who at the local level band together with the built environment professionals, architects, surveyors and realtors to form the typical coalitions identified in empirical studies of urban renewal projects (for example, Peck and Ward, 2002; Williams *et al.*, 2000). Nor is the diversity of the coalitions that emerge restricted to the urban setting. Attempts to privatise the environmental management of some of Britain's forests and Areas of Outstanding Natural Beauty in 2011 resulted in opposition not just from directly affected resident groups and environmentalists but also from an organised coalition of interests including businesses, a bizarre assortment of politicians including the former Trotskyite ex-mayor of London, Ken Livingstone, and the wife of his successor, the Conservative Boris Johnson, various celebrities, artists and religious figures, including the Archbishop of Canterbury.

To explain coalition formation, most planning academics assume the requirement for 'trust', something they believe is most likely to arise from the establishment of a mutually shared purpose and a like-minded ethos.

However, what the heterogeneity of the planning coalitions, of which the ones outlined above are indicative, demonstrates is that the capacity to trust others and work together does not always – if ever – require a common belief system. Experiments in game theory show that, whilst some forms of similarity amongst agents might make cooperation more likely, for many of the types of game we play in everyday life the opposite might be true:

different types of heterogeneity may foster collective action, meaning the homogeneity–cooperation relationship does not always hold. Some evidence indicates that groups that are closer to markets, and less homogenous in race or cultural identity can in fact show high levels of trust and cooperative behaviour.

(Cárdenas and Ostrom, 2004: 313)

This is not to say that trust is not important: quite the reverse, but rather that trust can, and does, exist between actors of different political persuasions, social standing, moral outlook, race, gender, et cetera. For the behavioural school (see for example Gintis, 2009) this trait – usually referred to as the 'other-regarding preference' – is peculiar to humankind and serves to explain the multiplicity of micro-coordination games from the everyday 'kindness of strangers' to the general macro-evolution of the species.

An alternative view is the more mainstream economics interpretation that trust is not solely related to the identification of a common goal but also to the idea that each member of a coalition could be trusted to both contribute to the coalition's work and share equitably in its rewards: the sense that mutual trust emerges from circumstances where there is a proportionate relationship between an individual's value to the coalition and their share of what it achieves.

To get to grips with this intellectual project we must first set out some of the principal theoretical concepts and the language, derived from set theory, through which they are articulated. First, we can define the bounded group of actors who might seek to cooperate with one another in a planning game. In keeping with tradition this would be termed the *grand coalition*. Any subdivision of this grand coalition into constituent sets of actors who sought to cooperate with one another would represent a *partition* of the grand coalition; this might also include those elements of the grand coalition who decide that it is in their best interests to work alone, *singleton* coalitions. Finally, for the sake of mathematical integrity, there is the empty or *null* set (usually denoted by the Greek letter, φ), the set with no elements.

To give these abstract ideas clearer articulation, we may consider the simplest format within which cooperation might exist in a game, a three-player interaction in which, besides the null set, there are seven possible coalition arrangements of the players, denoted by braces { } (see Figure 8.1):

Coalition	Elements
Grand coalition	{a, b, c}
Partitions 2 : 1	{a,b} : {c}
	{a, c} : {b}
	{b, c} : {a}
Singletons	{a}
	{b}
	{c}

Figure 8.1 Potential coalition formation under three-player cooperation

But which of these seven possibilities will prevail? In answering this question, the qualitative variables upon which existing theories of coalition formation in environmental planning rely so heavily might be important: for example, *a* may loathe *b* and refuse to work with them, whilst simultaneously enjoying a cordial relationship with *c*, which predisposes them to the cooperative alliance {a, c}. This kind of contextual information is necessary to rendering a full account of a game. However, whilst necessary, it is not sufficient. There may be other systemic features of the game that encourage some coalition formations over others. Indeed, these systemic forces might be so compelling as to overwrite a purely qualitative account premised on an understanding of emotions – such as enmity and empathy – as drivers of, or barriers to, alliances.

To illustrate, we might consider an adaptation of a coalition game of clear significance to environmental planning: McCain's (2009a: 152–53) account of a three-player waste management situation. In this example, players *a*, *b* and *c* could be thought of as three neighbouring planning authorities, each of which has the opportunity to dump their waste on one of the other two. To model this, McCain assigns each player an opening utility of 10 from a scale that, we assume here, is unitary and indivisible – that is, no player can receive fractions of a unit. Each player's utility is diminished by 1 in the event of them

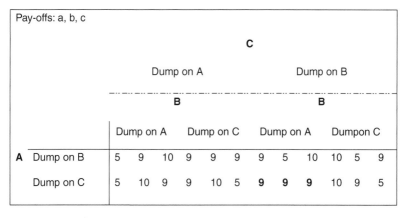

Pay-offs: a, b, c											
			C								
		Dump on A					Dump on B				
		B					B				
		Dump on A		Dump on C			Dump on A		Dump on C		
A Dump on B		5	9	10	9	9	9	9	5	10	10 5 9
Dump on C		5	10	9	9	10	5	**9**	**9**	**9**	10 9 5

Figure 8.2 McCain's waste game
(Source: McCain, 2009a: 152)

being the recipient of one neighbour's waste, or by 5 should they be unfortunate enough to have both neighbours' waste dumped on their territory. As McCain (2009a: 152) points out, this reflects the frequently made implicit assumption that 'even if pollution cannot be reduced ... its worst effects may be prevented by dispersing it as widely as possible'. The possible results of the game given this pre-play structure are set out in Figure 8.2.

The first observation that might follow from Figure 8.2 is that a coalition of two versus one is likely to form, as the grand coalition (highlighted in bold), in which each agrees to an even distribution of waste dumping is unstable: it guarantees each member a pay-off of 9, whereas a coalition of two against one results in the singleton receiving 5, whilst each of the other two can do no worse than they would in the grand coalition (9), but know that one of them – the one who receives no waste – will maintain their starting position (10).

But which two will join together and will this coalition be any more stable than the grand coalition? If we consider a candidate solution where {a, b} receives the pay-off {9, 10} as a result of a pre-play negotiation to gang-up on c, we can see that this arrangement is no more stable than the grand coalition: there is a clear incentive for c to approach a and offer a successor coalition arrangement of the form {a, c} as this enhances c's position from 5 to either 9 or 10 and guarantees that a does no worse than they did from the previous arrangement (9), but offers the opportunity of being waste-free and the corresponding pay-off of 10. Of course, in turn this coalition may be subsequently disrupted by a similar approach, this time from b, now the big loser in the game, to *c*. The result is a temporally unstable series of coalitions characterised by a cycle of disruption in the groupings that prevail: a theoretical prediction that is strongly mirrored by the reality of much planning practice (see Box 8.2).

Box 8.2: When three is not a crowd: coalitions in planning theory and practice

Three-player games are the simplest format for the investigation of coalition formation in cooperative game theory. However, for planning the three-player typology represents an important class, as much of planning practice conforms to precisely this format.

For example, in their cooperative game theory account of brownfield remediation and development Wang *et al.* (2011: 511) begin from the proposition that 'a typical brownfield redevelopment project involves only 3 DMs [decision makers] identified as the landowner, the developer and the government'. In this research the important issue of who is likely to cooperate with whom and which coalition is likely to form as a result introduces the important idea of *essential players* (the subject of further analysis in Box 8.3):

> The landowner may choose to cooperate with either the government or the developer, and all three DMs can form a grand coalition because without the landowner it is impossible for them to complete a redevelopment project on the landowner's site. Consider the coalition of the landowner and the developer. To complete the redevelopment project it will cost the coalition more without participation and financial assistance from the government. Under the coalition of the landowner and the government the landowner can do the clean-up but is unlikely to redevelop the site. If each of the three parties acts separately without any cooperation then normally there is no clean-up nor redevelopment, since the landowner would have no incentive to clean up or redevelop the brownfield without the government's or developer's assistance.

In short, there are only a small number of feasible coalitions that could prevail to fulfil Albrechts's (2006: 1161) demand that 'things must get done!'. Engineering such feasible coalitions is often inhibited in the absence of the necessary incentives.

It is this question that motivates Hideshima and Okada (1996) in their analysis of how coalitions might split the costs of providing public infrastructure in urban renewal projects. The authors argue that 'cooperative game theory gives us a proper way of understanding the rationality of cooperation', before going on to model the stability of coalition scenarios using the same three-player approach as Wang *et al.*, (2011), given alternative cost-sharing solutions. The research concludes that 'fairness' – in the sense that a coalition member should bear costs proportionate to the advantages they receive for being part of the coalition – is an important concept in understanding how coalitions stick together:

> It can be concluded that commonly in the renewal project each party may make claims comparatively proportional to his cost saving advantages in the cost allocation for infrastructure arrangements .... If cooperation drastically varies the benefit value of infrastructure arrangement we should pay attention to this matter in order to keep the grand coalition away from dissociating.
>
> (Hideshima and Okada, 1996: 24)

So the message is clear: for development to occur, three is often the magic number – providing it includes the essential elements and they play fair. If these seem like grand assumptions, perhaps policy makers might be able to encourage the circumstances that make these features of multi-agency cooperation more likely.

The conclusion of this game-theoretic account culminating in Box 8.2 is that we would never deal with the waste management problem, or any of the other myriad examples from planning practice that take a similar form, under circumstances characterised by unstable coalitions. Instead of practical, workable, cooperative solutions, all that would occur would be an incessant whirl of coalitions comprising various assortments of agents who perpetually arrange and then rearrange themselves on an ongoing basis without ever maintaining continuity for a sufficiently long period to arrive at a solution of any kind. No doubt this understanding of coalition instability might partly explain the perpetual upheaval in the landscape of planning coalitions identified in many countries: what Nienhuis *et al.* (2011: 107), in their analysis of planning reform in the Netherlands, refer to as 'more a matter of reshuffling power structures than repairing or balancing them'. Few would care to argue that such a turbulent policy environment would be conducive to framing sufficiently far-sighted solutions to the most pressing issues in urban and environmental management. Yet our empirical understanding would suggest a reality quite different from that which theory predicts. We know from Box 8.1 that many counter-intuitive – in the sense that they do not display the unity of purpose or shared value system that are said to be necessary for stability – coalitions do work in planning. Heterogeneity, coupled with a structure prone to disruption and reorganisation, do not seem to inhibit our capacity to work out solutions, albeit often imperfect and sometimes 'unfair' ones. In short, despite systemic and contextual factors that should lead to disunity and 'strife' (Pløger, 2004), many coalitions in planning are able to sustain themselves, work cooperatively and arrive at workable solutions to the collective action problems that characterise planning practice. So how and why do such planning coalitions survive?

Winning trust or buying friends?

To answer this question we must first broaden our understanding of the concept of equilibrium in a situation where players choose to band together to enhance their standing. In many examples from cooperative game theory a range of values exist for how the resultant pay-off to a coalition might be divided. This range of solutions is captured by the idea of a *core*: the set of pay-off values that would satisfy each member of a coalition. For a stable coalition to exist we might also say that the core must be *superadditive*: each individual member must receive more as a result of being part of the coalition than they could achieve by operating as part of a different coalition or as a singleton. Any possible coalition outside this core set would be an unfeasible solution, as a rational player could always enhance their return from the game by joining a coalition within the core. Taken to its logical conclusion, the outcome of any game that displays this property of superadditivity, and for which one or more core solutions exist, will see the ultimate emergence of a stable grand coalition:

> For a superadditive game in coalition function form, the only rational arrangement is the grand coalition. If the grand coalition is formed nothing can be lost (since the grand coalition must have a value no less than those for any proper coalition into which it can be decomposed) and something will usually be gained. All that remains is to determine how the value of the grand coalition will be divided amongst the decision makers.
>
> (McCain, 2009a: 122)

Its neatness aside, the experience outlined in Boxes 8.1 and 8.2 would suggest that the propitious circumstances necessary for stable formation of a grand coalition are rare. Rather, in a game such as the waste game that we have used to illustrate the types of coalition that might exist in planning practice, the core is said to be null, as there is no range of values that ensures the integrity of any coalition. The set of all possible pay-offs does not display the principle of superadditivity: given any possible coalition, one member could always leave to secure the same or higher pay-off than that coalition would guarantee.

So, how might cooperation emerge from circumstances in which an empty core suggests perpetual upheaval in the assemblage of actors who play out the planning game? Once again, in keeping with the remarks that opened this chapter, two possible answers present themselves that are themselves incumbent upon a fundamental epistemic debate: we can either intervene to stabilise inherently unstable coalitions or we can allow the psychology of participants to stabilise the situation for themselves. Taken to their logical conclusion the alternatives are put clearly by Binmore (2001b: 221):

> I believe that we are unique among social species in having available two separate and distinct equilibrium selection devices at our disposal. The first is to turn the choice of an equilibrium over to a leader … . The second mechanism is to use *fairness* as a coordinating device in the manner still practiced by the hunter-gatherer societies that continue to occupy marginal habitats around the world.

By *fairness*, the author refers to the behavioural economists' idea that human beings, in many instances, choose to act cooperatively out of instinct. Such a position would suggest that well-functioning social systems and solutions to problems such as those that arise in urban and environmental planning can often emerge organically, bound only by a system of self-policing, coupled with a socially-constructed and biologically-inherited sense of common decency. But would such a settlement work? should we trust our players of the waste game to do the fair thing and treat the problem of waste disposal equitably as the behavioural economists might argue or should we institute a system of authority that first encourages and then enforces cooperation through a system of incentives and penalties? In short, would 'doing nothing' work?

A relatively small amount of work has sought to investigate the degree to which informal groups produce better results (in the sense of finding best responses and securing the best possible pay-offs) than individuals acting alone when pitted against one another. Despite the cognitive advantages of having a number of minds devoted to a task ('many hands make light work'), the capacity for groups to assimilate information and arrive at clear strategies may result in them performing less well than individuals in experiments ('too many cooks spoil the broth') (Cox and Hayne, 2006). Although much more work on this subject would be welcome, perhaps the most interesting issue is how groups respond to a dynamic decision-making process, particularly the propensity for groups to subordinate the collective will to that of an authority figure. In reflecting on these issues Kocher and Sutter (2005: 200) arrive at a conclusion with which anyone with an interest in urban and environmental management could empathise: 'the decision maker matters'.

But how does the decision maker emerge from a group dynamic? Is authority the knowing creation and fulfilment of office or do leaders *emerge*, just as cooperation is said to emerge – in a way that game theory might be able to explain?

It takes TU to tango: side payments and reciprocity

To explore these questions we can investigate how a system of reg-ulatory control – similar to that offered by environmental planning and management – might intervene to encourage cooperation, before going on to examine how our acceptance of, and acquiescence to, such a form of authority might also be explained through the same game-theoretic prism.

For game theorists the principal method by which cooperation might be encouraged in a situation where coalition formations are systemically unstable is through transferable utility, often abbreviated to TU: the idea that a system of enforced redistribution from winners to losers in a game might foster stability. For an example of how this system, also sometimes referred to as side payments, might work we can return to the waste game and imagine that a coalition of the form two versus one – as the game is symmetrical, it makes no difference if this is $\{a, b\}$ versus $\{c\}$ or either of the two other possible permutations – is subjected to a system of regulatory redistribution that recompenses c for being the recipient of the other two's waste. Were the ombudsman of this system of regulatory control 'fair', in the sense of seeking an equality of outcome, this side payment would proportionately diminish the utility of a and b and enhance that of c, resulting in an equitable final outcome. For example, if we imagine that the party – say a – that

receives no waste must pay the bearer of two allotments of waste, say
c, a sum of 2 and, finally, that b, the recipient of one allotment
of waste, must pay c a sum of 1, the revised pay-offs would be: {a, b},
{c} = {8, 8}, {8}. The net result would be a disruption of this
two-versus-one coalition structure, and the succession of the 'fairest'
waste allocation mechanism, the grand coalition, in which an ordered
cycle of 'taking turns' to deal with the waste problem can be represented as {a, b, c} = {9, 9, 9}: a superior outcome for all, compared
to any coalition of two versus one with transferable utility.

The implication is that, to arrive at a stable solution we must institute a mechanism that coerces players into a cooperative coalition;
but is this genuine cooperation? Furthermore, whether the set of circumstances that prevails is fair or not is a quite separate question that
will depend upon the character of the system that is upheld and our
individual normative assessment of what constitutes equity. These
questions aside, perhaps a more interesting issue is whether a radically
different set of circumstances would have prevailed had we simply
relied on humankind's alleged instinct for fairness to find a solution
to the game. Put another way, would the set of players {*a*, *b*, *c*} in the
waste game have found another way of cooperating without a system
of regulatory control imposed from above?

Who can you trust? Optimism, pessimism and the emergence of leaders

To consider this question we can reconsider the two-versus-one partition
of the waste game in its initial formulation set out in Figure 8.2. Here,
a candidate successor function to the grand coalition {*a*, *b*, *c*} = {9, 9, 9}
is the partition {*a*, *b*} {*c*} – again it does not matter which two versus
one is considered, as each possible alternative is symmetrical – with
pay-offs {10, 9} {5} or {9, 10} {5}, as we have assumed that units of
utility are indivisible and cannot know which of the coalition part-
ners, *a* or *b*, will receive 10 or 9. If we take, for example, the possible
solution {*a*, *b*} {*c*} = {10, 9} {5}, the question remains, should *b* dissolve the coalition {*a*, *b*} and pair with *c* in the likely event that *c*
should propose such an alliance? So far we have argued that this is
precisely what *b* should do, as that alliance guarantees them the same
outcome as they have in the existing coalition (a pay-off of 9) and
offers the possibility of the best conceivable result (the pay-off of 10,
in this scenario currently enjoyed by *a*). In the event of legally binding
contracts this would be the logical choice for *b*, but would result in
the perpetually oscillating assemblage of coalitions outlined above.

However, what if, as is more usual, the players were left to their own devices to agree *after* the formation of a coalition who should receive 10 and who should receive 9; would *b* still leave *a* and pair up with *c* if that alliance was based solely on trust?

For game theorists the answer to this question would turn on the same qualitative features that we have invoked in previous chapters to understand other scenarios in the planning game, namely *b*'s 'character' and the degree to which they are optimistic or pessimistic, weak or strong-willed. To spell these concepts out, *b* could be said to be pessimistic if they joined only coalitions in which the core of the new coalition represented a guaranteed enhancement of their position. This contrasts with optimism where a successor coalition provides an opportunity, but no guarantee, of advancement (for a technical discussion see Kóczy, 2007).

In a situation such as the waste game of Figure 8.2 in which a two-versus-one arrangement offers a chance, but no guarantee, of a better outcome for a deviator, whether the coalition will be disrupted or not will be determined by the psychology of the players. If *b* is pessimistic, this character trait will see them remain coupled with *a*, unwilling to take a chance that they will be rewarded by defection and a union with *c*. The strength of these 'weak' coalitions might explain the longevity of some of the more unexpected formations that empirical observation tells us are far from unusual in planning practice (see Boxes 8.1 and 8.2).

But under what circumstances might *b* become sufficiently confident to switch?; how might they become more optimistic about their chances of enhancing their position under a successor coalition? The answer to this question might be qualitative: for example the intuition common to so much of planning theory that *b* may feel more comfortable with *c* than *a*, perhaps because they share a value system. No doubt in many cases this might be true in explaining those examples where a common cause seems to unite agents in a planning game. However, it is not the only possible explanation. An alternative interpretation may be that optimistic defection might occur when a player believes that they are better able to dominate one over another potential partner: so, in our waste game, disruption might occur if *b* believes they have a better chance of dominating *c* than *a*.

This raises the related issue of 'strength of will', a concept identified first by Selten (1964; see also McCain, 2008, 2009b; essays in Stroud and Tappolet, 2008) and defined as the degree of inter-temporal consistency that an individual might show. The more committed an actor is to a chosen course of action (or, in game-theoretic terms, a response such as 'defect' or 'cooperate'), particularly when abandonment of an original position is incentivised, the stronger their will is said to be. This concept, with clear echoes of the 'tough' and 'weak' bargainers that played out Quiche in Chapter 7, is of great significance to this discussion as it suggests an alternative manner in which a coalition might remain intact even when the core is null: through the presence of strong-willed individuals who remain committed to a course of action and inspire loyalty in other coalition members – in short, leaders:

> Suppose that the population includes individuals both with strong and weak wills, and that at least some of those with strong wills are honest. How then will coalitions form? First there will be no mutually beneficial coalitions comprising only the weak-willed. Such coalitions would accomplish nothing that would not be accomplished by the non-cooperative equilibrium. The typical coalition, then, will include at least a subset of the strong-willed individuals who adopt threat strategies that encourage the others to keep agreements and correlate their strategies so as to increase the value of the coalition. These strong willed individuals may be known to the others as leaders, but more probably as officious busybodies, nosy parkers or snitches. It may be that the officious busy bodies, nosy parkers and snitches will form a grand coalition and formalize some of their threat strategies as institutions such as property rights and enforcement of contracts.
>
> (McCain, 2009a: 163)

To close the circle it might be argued that it is precisely these strong-willed types who might be said to hold coalitions together, despite the disintegrative pull of a game-theoretic structure that suggests disruption. As Shmueli *et al.* (2008: 361) argue, in planning:

> an agreement to work together can be reached for a number of reasons, not least of which may be intimidation of the powerless by the powerful, a perception of lack of other choices, or a dispirited lack of motivation to pursue other options.

Moreover, it is this self-same group – perhaps best referred to as 'leaders' – who may ultimately go on to forge the social contracts and norms of engagement that explain why coalitions that should logically break down actually stabilise over time. In short, the leaders who emerge from the jungle laws of the planning game become the architects of its rules.

Box 8.3: The 'essentials': are leaders needed to engineer collaboration in planning practice?

The work set out in Box 8.2 introduced the idea of *essential* players: those, sometimes combinations of, agents whose participation in a coalition is a necessary condition of its viability. In the set of planning games that pertain to development and construction (as opposed to regulation and conservation) the theoretical value of such essentials is vital, as there is evidence to suggest that they are ubiquitous in practice.

For example, in his three-player (m, n and k) cooperative game theory analysis of the 'land development game' (LDG) Asami (1985: 237) notes that 'for any land-development game, LDG (m, n, k) there exists at least one essential player'.

However, being an essential player brings with it a degree of power in that a player who knows their essentiality might be able to exploit the fact to extract an overly representative share of the spoils that might accrue to the existence of the coalition to which they belong. This calls into question whether the ostensibly cooperative structures implied by the existence of a stable coalition and heralded as evidence of collaboration are genuinely what we have in mind when we talk about cooperation and mutuality. If the coalition that prevails does so because of the existence of a dominant partner who is able to use threat strategies and domineering tactics, are we witnessing genuine collaboration? Nevertheless, this is precisely what Asami (1985: 237) predicts will arise in our typical three-player land development games with at least one essential player:

> Notice, in this example that d1 and l2 are contained in every maximally profitable coalition. In other words d1 and l2 are indispensible players for a coalition to make a maximal profit. Such players are called *essential* (in the set of maximally profitable coalitions). An essential player can effectively threaten any player that he may leave the coalition unless he has a positive share of profit. Without him, the coalition must lose a profit of k. We can hence expect that an essential player should get a positive share.

Explaining what might superficially seem like collaboration then rather becomes about quite different qualitative variables: threats and punishment.

Conclusion

Explaining the coalitions of interest that emerge and mutate over time in planning practice is complex. Game theory offers a way of understanding vital concepts such as coalition stability and the idea of a core solution, but a full account of why a particular coalition prevails might well entail reference to qualitative variables such as optimism/pessimism, the strength of will of the actors involved and their essentiality to coalition success. These qualitative variables are central to game theory but capturing them within an empirical setting is a project that has roused only limited interest in most game theorists. As Binmore (2007b: 521), reflecting on our collective understanding of cooperative game theory, honestly remarks, 'game theory hasn't gone very far down this road as yet'.

Part of the reason for this acknowledgement is that cooperative theory often unravels into questions that seem better dealt with by the non-cooperative paradigm. For example, how a pay-off is split once a coalition is formed is essentially a bargaining problem such as those of Chapter 7. Furthermore, if we come to think of leaders as the strong-willed types who engineer coalition stability and, subsequently, act as authors of the game's rule book, cooperative theory serves primarily to tell us who the leaders are and how they emerged; once the rule book of Chapter 5 is in place, all encounters have a structure that is best handled by non-cooperative theory. It is these features that led Roth (1991: 212) to remark: 'I anticipate that the distinction between "cooperative" and "non-cooperative" game theory will become much less important.'

For the purposes of this volume, cooperative game theory sheds light on a raft of questions previously neglected by planning theory relating to how coalitions form and, more importantly, why the straightforward groupings we might expect to form in planning practice rarely do so. Moreover, in explaining why coalitions that are systemically unstable sometimes endure, enjoying long and successful lives, it resituates leadership at the centre of collaborative planning: perhaps sometimes, often even, the sense of direction and unity of purpose that planning theorists have argued is a necessary prerequisite to coalition formation is something supplied *after* the event, and on an ongoing basis, by an authority figure. The traditional suspicions that some planning theorists have had of these authoritarian types relates to their potential propensity to use a coalition of interests for their own individual ends (for example, Innes, 1995). And this might certainly be true. Their absence, however, may often secure nothing but instability, uncertainty and inaction. As Binmore (2001b: 222) has noted:

> whether leaders know what they are doing better than their followers or not, they can be very useful to a society as a coordinating device for solving the equilibrium selection problems in games for which the traditional methods are too slow or uncertain.

From this perspective, leaders are simply 'coordinating devices'. We know from game theory that, for any finite game, irrespective of which might be the particular solution in a given instance, there must be more than one Nash equilibrium; from Wittgenstein (and games that use the Harsanyi transformation, such as Follow the leader) we know that, regardless of which one prevails, there are many possible 'states of affairs'. In practice the role of the leader is to select one alternative over others: 'the real reason that authority can work is that a leader's role is simply to point to a perfect equilibrium of the game being played' (Binmore, 2004: 31). If that equilibrium is unfair or deemed unacceptable to a sufficiently large body of the coalition of interests that the leader marshals, a disruption occurs and a new coalition emerges around a different leader.

This conceptual transition from a cooperative to a non-cooperative situation reveals an epistemic distinction between an understanding of planning derived from game theory and those theories of planning that have gone before it. If the emergence of authority turns collaboration into competition, a theory that simply states its disapproval on normative grounds or bemoans decisions that run counter to positivist evidence is ill-equipped to explain the situations with which it is confronted. Whether a positivist or a Habermasian, the ideal speech situation and theoretical constructs such as perfect competition are equally unattainable. Instead, the real life drama, intrigue and generally flawed nature of the characters who play out the planning game can only be understood by a theory that acknowledges our frailty, irrationality and, sometimes, outright confusion.

9 Putting the planning game in context

Even at their most simple, the games we play in planning are complicated. In the 'classical planning game' introduced in Chapter 5 a trip to court was understood as the ultimate end for those examples where conflict over how we produce (and reproduce) the built environment and choose to exploit or conserve nature prove to be irreconcilable. Chapters 6 and 7 sought to investigate the systemic features that might incentivise the types of conflict that lead to that end point, before Chapter 8 contemplated how policy makers could potentially incentivise cooperation over conflict. However, the conclusion of the chapter showed how cooperation and conflict might sometimes be co-constitutive: the threat of conflict might be the answer to why cooperation exists at all. Furthermore, through the threat makers, the essential players in the planning game, we find a route back to Chapter 4 and an explanation of from where the legal code and informal rules by which we play the planning game emanated: a system codified by 'leaders', but checked by what the coalition they 'represent' will tolerate.

Explaining specific examples of how the planning game is played in one context and comparing it to others, therefore, becomes a description of how the dominant characters in each setting have chosen one set of rules over alternatives. Periodic rearrangements result from coalition reformation: perhaps because whichever leader is preeminent at that particular time has chosen a course of action that is unacceptable to a sufficiently large cohort of the coalition to create the conditions for disruption and the original coalition's replacement by a successor. The material differences resulting from reform might be negligible. In fact, one would expect relative continuity, as the explanation for why coalition reformation occurs at all is that a leader's choices that deviate too markedly from the terms that hold the coalition together – what is deemed by the majority to be 'fair' – are punished by disruption and leader deselection. Echoing Michels's (1915) 'Iron Law of Oligarchy', all that remains to be seen is 'how long it takes for the new elite to become indistinguishable from their predecessors' (Binmore, 2001b: 227).

This implied entrenchment and slowly evolving norms forms the basis for the ancient case for a representative form of constitutional democracy (Plato, 2003). Stability is said to arise from a mutual system of guardianship: each player of the game acts both as their own agent and as a self- and other-regulating component of a wider whole or community. Moreover, such observations provide renewed insight into, and confidence in, the notion of a 'public interest', as discussed in Chapter 7: leaders and elites emerge and steer the games that we play in policy spheres such as environmental planning, guided by an equilibrium settlement acceptable to the wider constituency – a settlement that we might now understand to be the reflexively defined idea of a public interest.

In empirical terms, explaining how the system holds together can be messy; actors may behave 'strategically', meaning anything from being unerringly cooperative to even-handed in their duplicity. Game theory would tell us to expect all possibilities. Appreciating that a range of tactics and approaches might be taken to playing a game such as environmental planning does not mean that game theorists are amoral or apolitical. Quite the reverse: many game theorists believe that it is this very appreciation that allows an insight into the social evolution of human kind and offers a political prescription for progress. If, as our engagement with game theory in this volume has shown repeatedly, we acknowledge that the prevailing state of affairs represents just one equilibrium choice from many possible alternative 'states of the world', how might we encourage the 'right' choice?

What game shall we play next?

Ultimately, defining the 'right' choice for many game theorists is a socially progressive polity not dissimilar to the vision of the communicative school of planning theory. For example Gintis (2009) combines game theory, anthropology and biological sciences to establish human beings' innate propensity for cooperation – or 'other-regarding preferences' – and in so doing explains aspects of our social evolution. Similarly, Binmore (2001b, 2004, 2006) makes repeated references to Marx's post-socialist communist societies, characterised by mutual interdependences and a communitarian allocation mechanism, as the ultimate end, should this behaviourist school be correct about humankind's genetic disposition for cooperation around fairness norms. Achieving this end state would imply a completely devolved form of environmental management in which communities made and implemented their own choices – very much redolent of the communicative turn's ultimate vision of fully realised participative democracy.

Such projections on reality echo Freud's (1922) idea that groups that require authoritarian leadership represent a primitive counterpoint to the more highly evolved, self-assembled coalitions redolent of Chapter 8's waste game. Evolutionary game theory with all its insights into biological (for a review, see Hagen and Hammerstein, 2006; see also Maynard Smith, 1982; Maynard Smith and Price, 1973) and social (see Gintis, 2000; 2009) evolution contains no prediction of how long it may take to arrive at an end point where states have withered away and the impulse felt by some to exert control over others has been biologically or socially (or, if the two are considered inter-dependent, both) subdued. In the meantime, however, in our still-evolving state, game theory shows us that collaboration and conflict often go hand in hand and that the coalitions of interest that play out games such as environmental planning often do so by producing the circumstances for leaders, or a controlling elite, to emerge. These leaders then go on to fulfil the role of 'co-ordinating device' – selecting a game equilibrium and marshalling support amongst others to work towards it. Under these conditions the choice of environmental planning game that we ultimately come to play reduces to the distinction between types of leadership under a system of either formal or informal representative democracy.

To illustrate this, Rydin and Pennington (2000: 166) draw a distinction between a 'facilitator state', which 'allows considerable local autonomy to individuals and groups but provides a supportive framework, including the provision of specialised information, arenas for conflict resolution and the capacity to enforce institutional rules' and a 'controller regime', in which, 'by contrast, the state rather than helping communities to develop their own institutions for environmental planning, effectively takes over the task of managing the environment itself'. Our normative preferences aside, deciding which of these two forms of representative democracy is more viable turns on whether our collective capacity to arrive at fair-minded, sustainable decisions is sufficiently evolved to simply be facilitated by a state with little more than a co-ordinating brief. If not, a more authoritarian form of leadership, closer to the controller regime, might be required to coercively guide actors to a sustainable outcome using the levers of incentives, threats and punishments.

Even the most hopeful behaviourists would probably not argue that we are ready for complete, or even lightly regulated, autonomy in how we play games such as those that arise in environmental planning. Much – although not all – of experimental economics shows that, as players become more experienced, their capacity to act strategically also increases. In some instances, like planning, this might be a good thing, if the strategies that emerge turn out to be cooperative and, therefore, perhaps more environmentally sustainable; but often they are a mixture of cooperation and conflict and may involve some degree of strategic duplicity – or cheap talk – such as that modelled in the game Quiche set out in Chapter 7.

The implication is that the idealistic visions expressed by previous forms of planning theory place unrealistic expectations on planning practice. The communicative school's vision of fully stimulated community consciousness and participative working practices grates against the intransigence of existing power relations and the capacity for all players of the planning game to behave strategically. The rationalists who preceded the communicative movement sought recourse to independent evidence of a positivist stripe to achieve optimal solutions and a modernist understanding of progress; but they were also ill-equipped to explain how evidence could be distorted or misinterpreted by those who dominate the planning polity (Lord and Hincks, 2010). In short, we are stuck with messy, complex games played by actors who cannot always be persuaded to play fairly:

> there is no point in designing ideal social systems whose workability depends on first changing human nature. Human nature is as it is, and no amount of wishing that it were different will make it so. We therefore have to resign ourselves to living in a second-best society because first-best societies are not stable.
>
> (Binmore, 2001b: 230)

A central objective of this volume has been to demonstrate how an understanding of planning practice derived from information economics, using game theory as its investigative method, is unencumbered by an urge to move towards a unique theoretical construction of 'perfection'. Games are not perfect in either an epistemic or a moral sense: they may have many Nash equilibria and are very often characterised by double-dealing and underhand tactics. Using game theory as a lens through which to regard planning we can see that these features are not likely to be lessened simply by creating space for new voices and/or new information to be introduced into the planning game. Indeed, the reverse may be true. Instead, we might helpfully return to first principles and acknowledge that players will often behave strategically. In turn this might help us to really make a difference to how the planning game is played.

Box 9.1: Is game theory any use? Planning as 'beauty contest' or auction?

One of the principal functions of urban and environmental planning is the allocation of development rights. In many contexts around the globe, where more than one developer is interested in procuring a single site, planning authorities frequently adjudicate between rival proposals using criteria intended to specify what would be 'best' for the area – with the bargaining and negotiations designed to secure community benefits identified in previous chapters representing a rather imperfect addendum to this fundamental part of the process by which development is permitted.

Economists refer to this form of allocation mechanism as a 'beauty contest' (Kocher and Sutter, 2005); and planning is an extremely good example of a system that works overwhelmingly on the basis of arbitrating between competitors on the grounds of which proposal is most subjectively appealing. The positive aspects of the approach – that it allows professional planners to exercise judgements on issues for which they have been specially trained – has been impugned by both the communicative school of planning theory, suspicious of the capacity of technocratic experts to arrive at 'good' judgements, and the neoclassical critique of planning practice, that the default beauty contest circumvents market forces and places planners in a position of significant market power that is rarely matched by a cognisance amongst the profession of the market impacts that their actions might have. The result is that there is now a widely held suspicion, amongst commentators from widely divergent perspectives, that there is something significantly wrong with planning's use of beauty contests as a way of deciding what development should occur.

An alternative to the beauty contest may be to institute an auction. Game theorists have tended to favour auctions over beauty contests for several reasons. First, a well-designed auction should open up the allocation process and will often arouse the interest of new entrants – those who may not have considered subjecting themselves to the beauty contest. Second, they prevent what many believe to be the negative aspects of bargaining in that they militate against collusion. Finally, auctions remove the non-binding commitments, or 'cheap talk', that characterise the negotiations that accompany beauty contests. In so doing they encourage bidders to reveal their true valuation of the asset under consideration:

> how does one find out the bidders' valuation? There is no point in simply asking the bidders. If asked, each bidder will earnestly insist that his value is the highest. An auction gets around this problem by making bidders back their plans with their money.
>
> (Binmore and Klemperer, 2002: C79–C80)

Perhaps the most famous example of game theory being used by policy makers in this way was in the auctions used in a number of countries – the UK, the Netherlands, Germany, Italy, Austria, Switzerland, Belgium, Greece and Denmark – to allocate third-generation mobile telephone licences during 2000–2001. Each country organised its own system of auction with, sometimes subtle, sometimes more fundamental, differences designed to reflect differing macroeconomic circumstances, political preferences, engineering constraints and geographical location. The results were wildly divergent and serve to illustrate the potential value of using game theory to inform policy design (for a review see Klemperer, 2002).

Proportionately (per capita), the most lucrative auction to any national exchequer was that conducted in the UK and designed by game theorists Binmore and Klemperer (for a review see Binmore and Klemperer, 2002). The simultaneous ascending auction – where multiple items are auctioned at the same time to allow bidders to switch interest between lots – raised £22.5 billion ($33 billion), far in excess of original estimates.

Press speculation at the time, that the auction's design had effectively manipulated bidders' behaviour, 'forcing' them to 'overpay' for licences that would ultimately be passed back to consumers in higher prices, has since been shown to have been unfounded by a thriving mobile telecommunications industry and consistently falling prices for consumers. Shortly after the first auction (in the UK) the logic that auctions are somehow punitive to the private sector was theoretically rebutted by the auction's designers using an analogy that is particularly pertinent to our subject of environmental planning:

> The price of new housing is no lower when the developer has the good fortune to obtain the land below its current market value (e.g. because it was obtained free through inheritance or was bought before planning permission was available) than when the developer has paid the full market value. In either case the price is determined by the housing market at the time the new housing is sold. There is no more sense in handing out free spectrum to the telecom companies than *in failing to charge developers for land in the belief that this will lead to cheaper houses.*
>
> (Binmore and Klemperer, 2002: C77–C78)

I have italicised part of the last sentence because *'failing to charge developers for land'* – at least, failing to encourage developers to pay what they think a site is genuinely worth – is precisely the risk of administering planning as a beauty contest.

The end game

The lasting impression of research such as that summarised in Box 9.1, coupled with the remarks above, is that some may have been too hasty to proclaim the wane of 'government' – understood as Western representative democracy – and its succession by 'governance'. The power of an administration that can use game theory to manipulate corporations' behaviour and maximise the pay-off to the public purse jars against the interpretation of the state as a fundamentally weakened entity that had become popular in the 1990sand thereafter. From this perspective 'governance' simply describes the administrative counterpart to the whir of often-superficial activity – the empty promises and 'cheap talk' of signalling and screening strategies – that game theory accounts for so well. The real business of designing the rule book of incentives and penalties that structure these games has remained the business of governments.

For planning theorists this forces a re-evaluative confrontation with the latterly accepted wisdom, driven by the communicative turn, that a participative or deliberative mode of planning practice, built on an associative model of democracy, is a desirable end in itself and a necessary one, should planning be adapted to the new century.

Considered afresh, the practices that such mechanisms encourage are just more of what we are used to – more cheap talk, more signalling – and suggest the most obvious way in which an information economics approach to understanding planning might ultimately inform its practice. The potential for policy makers to radically alter the way in which the planning game is orchestrated opens up the possibility – as with the auctions of Box 9.1 – to reduce, or even eliminate, the incentives for trading in superfluous or disingenuous information.

However, even ostensibly radical action such as this would not alter the fact that many other aspects of the planning game would fundamentally remain a language game: debate would still rage on what would be an appropriate or fair allocation mechanism and what objectives should be enshrined in its design. This in turn would take us back to the strategies and tactics that, whilst they might no longer have purchase in the actual process by which development rights are assigned, would still inform the debates that surrounded that process. To get to grips with how these communication strategies play out in the planning game, we can pursue a game-theoretic analysis such as those outlined in Chapters 6, 7 and 8 of this volume. Methodologically, however, this presents a huge intellectual challenge.

Game theory provides us with the insight that each linguistic encounter in the planning game is systemically analogous to one of Wittgenstein's language games: we determine our own linguistic rules by the action of using language; similarly, the rules of the planning game are a reflection of how we play that game. This connection between the analytical philosophy of Wittgenstein and the method we have used to unpack the human interactions that typify planning practice is not simply a semantic one built on the consonance between 'language games' and 'game theory'; it is a deeper epistemological relationship, as Binmore (2006: 92) points out in drawing a connection between our linguistic development and our capacity to interact in games:

> I argue that our capacity to solve coordination problems by appealing to fairness criteria is part of what separates us from other animals. It therefore evolved before we were human, and certainly before language had evolved to a stage at which it would have been possible to conduct a 'negotiation', as we understand that term in modern times ... we had to have some way of coordinating with each other to create the condition under which true language could evolve.

This fundamental connection between game theory and language represents the leading edge of the discipline and simultaneously illustrates the central challenge to planning theorists. New work in Game Theoretic Semantics (see Pietarinen, 2007; Jaeger, 2009; see also Saarinen, 1979; Hintikka and Kulas, 1983) provides the opportunity to develop an understanding of how meaning is developed through social interaction and ultimately how natural speech might be rendered into a perspicuous concept script: a project begun by Frege (see Kenny, 2000) and advanced by North Whitehead and Russell (1927) and Wittgenstein (1922) almost a century ago, but which in more recent times has been developed into an increasingly elaborate hybrid of linguistics and game theory.

Despite the interest that this work has excited in scholars of the philosophy of language, linguistics and economics (for a review and the development of a 'deliberative game theory' see Landa and Meirowitz, 2009; see also Van Damme, 1994), there is a danger that its academic currency will be limited by the fact that, in disciplines such as planning theory for example, there is seemingly a suspicion of intellectual projects that are communicated, either wholly or in part, through the languages of formal logic and mathematics. It is this methodological division that largely explains the historical antipathy felt by planning theorists towards economics – characterised by Evans (2003: 196) as two groups of people 'shouting very loudly' at each other.

The challenge for planning theorists is to overcome this mistrust or unwillingness to engage with disciplines such as game theory that marry quantitative and qualitative methods. This may require a renewed effort to breach the inured stand-off between positivism and critical theory in the social sciences and reconsider genuinely how distant language and formal logic/mathematics are from one another:

> Mathematical proof, certainly in its axiomatic form, developed in Classical Greece, probably due to the widespread practices of disputation and dialectical reasoning, which were central to the public democratic institutions and cultural practices of the day (the word 'dialectic' is derived from the verb meaning 'to discuss'). Szabo and others locate the source of deductive mathematics and logic in dialectical argument, disputation and conversation.
>
> (Ernest, 1994: 4)

A failure to move beyond a mutually held mistrust on the part of both those who favour qualitative or quantitative methods prevents a full engagement with academic traditions, such as Wittgenstein's analytic philosophy and information economics, that demand both. The cost of adhering to one or other form of planning theory – either that wedded to Comtian positivism or post-positivist sociology – is to acknowledge that only a partial and limited understanding of the contents of the 'black box' of planning practice can be accomplished; on those parts that we cannot reach we must remain mute: 'what we cannot speak about we must pass over in silence' (Wittgenstein, 1922: TLP7).

If, as a fundamentally practical discipline, part of the role of planning theory is to provide guidance and direction to practitioners, such an admission would constitute an acknowledgement of defeat; the world of practice would be beyond the capabilities of theory to either, first, conceptualise or, second, suggest wholly workable alternatives.

This brings us to the final question: how might we actually provide for a game-theoretic analysis that could genuinely inform new ways of designing planning practice? As an analytical project, the investigative method that game theory represents has, like Wittgenstein's linguistic philosophy, no preconceived ideas regarding what would be legitimate or, perhaps more importantly, illegitimate investigative methods. Much will depend upon the content of the specific game to be analysed. Where the planning game is one with clearly defined quantifiable impacts, it may be possible to develop a pay-off matrix similar to those used in the specification of the games outlined in this volume. However, it should be noted that, whilst cardinal integers have been used in setting out examples of famous games throughout, this has been to help make the games used for illustrative purposes accessible and easy to follow. In many cases, the structure of the game need not have specific values assigned to pay-offs but rather needs only to have a discernible structure such as that in the formal articulation of the formal Prisoners' dilemma (see Chapter 6 this volume, Figure 6.2). More importantly, as has been shown repeatedly in this volume, quantitative and qualitative explanations for why specific outcomes prevail are almost always complementary in game theory. Therefore it is essential that we are able to marry an account of 'pay-offs', however defined, with a qualitative appreciation that sometimes behaviour deviates from what might be rational on the basis of neoclassical economic logic.

In this volume, by parsing work at what might now be seen to be the porous border between information economics and game theory, linguistics, logic, the philosophy of language and psychology, the objective has been to show what might be achieved if some of the work that has married these academic traditions could be applied to environmental planning and management. For example, might it be possible for policy makers to learn from other arenas, such as those summarised in Box 9.1, to design new game theory-inspired forms of planning practice? Could alternative allocation mechanisms be used to maximise the value to the public purse of assets, the fate of which are often currently the subject of informal, clandestine negotiation? Answering questions such as these implies a research agenda that might include the empirical application of game theory, either *in situ*, or through experiments, to investigate how we might develop new versions of the planning game that encourage sustainable over unsustainable uses of the natural environment and the design and redesign of cities that can adapt to the demands of ageing populations, food and energy insecurity and the transport implications of peak oil. The urgency of these issues is matched only by their complexity. It is therefore vital that planning theory matures into a conceptually robust, yet practically supportive role. Information economics and its analytical toolkit, game theory, provide the potential for a fulfilment of both these objectives.

References

Adams, D. and Tiesdell, S. (2010) Planners as market actors: rethinking state-market relations in land and property. *Planning, Theory and Practice*, 11 (2), 187–207.

Agger, A. and Löfgren, K. (2008) Democratic assessment of collaborative planning processes. *Planning Theory*, 7 (2), 145–64.

Albrechts, L. (2006) Shifts in strategic spatial planning? Some evidence from Europe and Australia. *Environment and Planning A*, 38, 1149–70.

Alexander, E. R. (1992) A transaction cost theory of planning. *Journal of the American Planning Association*, 58, 190–200.

——(1997) A mile or a millimeter? Measuring the 'planning theory–practice gap'. *Environment and Planning B: Planning and Design*, 24 (1) 3–6.

——(1998) Doing the impossible: notes for a general theory of planning. *Environment and Planning B: Planning and Design*, 25, 667–80.

——(2001) A transaction-cost theory of land use planning and development control; toward the institutional analysis of public planning. *Town Planning Review*, 72 (1), 45–75.

Allen, C. (2008) *Housing market renewal and social class formation*. Routledge: Oxford.

Allmendinger, P. (1998) Planning practice and the post-modern debate. *International Planning Studies*, 3 (2), 227–48.

——(2001) *Planning in postmodern times*. Routledge: London.

——(2002a) Towards a post-positivist typology of planning theory. *Planning Theory*, 1 (1), 77–99.

——(2002b) The post-positivist landscape of planning theory. In P. Allmendinger and M. Tewdwr-Jones (2002) *Planning futures: new directions in planning theory*, 1–28. Routledge: London.

Allmendinger, P. and Tewdwr-Jones, M. (1997) Mind the gap: planning theory–practice and the translation of knowledge into action; a comment on Alexander (1997). *Environment and Planning B*, 24, 802–6.

——(2002) The communicative turn in urban planning: unravelling paradigmatic, imperialistic and moralistic dimensions. *Space and Polity*, 6 (1), 5–24.

Ambrose, P. (1994) *Urban process and power*. Routledge: London.

Arce, A. and Long, N. (1992) The dynamics of knowledge: interfaces between bureaucrats and peasants. In N. Long and A. Arce (eds) *Battlefields of knowledge: the interlocking of theory and practice in social research and development*, 211–46. Routledge: London.

Asami, Y. (1985) A game-theoretic approach to the division of profits from economic land development. *Regional Science and Urban Economics*, 18 (2), 233–46.

——(1993) Inappropriateness of lot-evaluation functions used in land readjustment projects. *Comprehensive Urban Studies*, 49, 67–79 (in Japanese).

Axelrod, T. (1984) *The evolution of cooperation*. Basic Books: New York City, NY.

Ayer, A. J. (1946) *Language, truth and logic*. Dover Press: New York City, NY.

Aylett, A. (2010) Conflict, collaboration and climate change: participatory democracy and urban environmental struggles in Durban, South Africa. *International Journal of Urban and Regional Research*, 34 (3), 478–95.

Baccaro, L. (2006) Civil society meets the state: towards associational democracy. *Socio-Economic Review*, 4, 185–208.

Bacow, L. S. and Wheeler, M. (1984) *Environmental dispute resolution*. Plenum Press: New York City, NY.

Barker, K. (2003) *Review of housing supply: securing our future housing needs – Interim report – Analysis*. HMSO: London.

——(2004) *Review of housing supply – Delivering stability: steering our future housing needs, final report – Recommendations*. HMSO: London.

Barlow, J. and Chambers, D. (1992) Planning agreements and social housing quotas. *Town and Country Planning*, May 1992, 136–42.

Batty, M. (2007) *Cities and complexity. Understanding cities with cellular automata, agent-based models and fractals*. MIT Press: Cambridge, MA.

Batty, M. and Longley, P. A. (1987) Urban shapes as fractals. *Area*, 19 (3), 215–21.

Batty, M. and Xie, Y. C. (1999) Self-organized criticality and urban development. *Discrete Dynamics in Nature and Society*, 3 (2–3), 109–24.

Batty, S. E. (1977) Game theoretic approaches to urban planning and design. *Environment and Planning B*, 4 (2), 211–39.

Beauregard, R. A. (1989) Between modernity and postmodernity: the ambiguous position of US planning. *Environment and Planning D: Society and Space*, 7, 381–95.

Bengs, C. (2005) Planning theory for the naïve? *European Journal of Spatial Development*. Available at: http://www.nordregio.se/EJSD. Accessed 21 April 2011.

Berkman, H. G. (1965) The game theory of land use determination. *Land Economics*, 41 (1), 11–19.

Bernanke, B. and Gertler, M. (1995) Inside the black box: the credit channel of monetary policy transmission. *Journal of Economic Perspectives*, 9 (4), 27–48.

Bianchi, M. and Moulin, H. (1991) Strategic interaction in economics. The game theoretic alternative. In N. de Marchi and M. Blaug (eds) *Appraising economic theories*, 179–96. Edward Elgar: Cheltenham.

176   *References*

Bickerstaff, K. and Walker, G. (2000) Participatory local governance and transport planning. *Environment and Planning A*, 33, 431–51.

——(2005) Shared visions, unholy alliances: power governance and deliberative processes in local transport planning. *Urban Studies*, 42 (12), 2123–44.

Bickerstaff, K., Tolley, R. and Walker, G. (2002) Transport planning and participation: the rhetoric and realities of public involvement. *Journal of Transport Geography*, 10, 61–73.

Binmore, K. (1992) *Fun and games*. D. C. Heath and Company: Lexington, MA.

——(2001a) Evolutionary social theory: reply to Robert Sugden. *The Economic Journal*, 111, F244–48.

——(2001b) The breakdown of social contracts. In Steven N. Durlauf and H. Peyton Young (eds) *Social dynamics*, 213–33. Brookings Institution: Washington, DC/MIT Press: Cambridge, MA.

——(2004) Reciprocity and the social contract. *Politics, Philosophy and Economics*, 3 (1), 5–35.

——(2005) *Natural justice*. Oxford University Press: Oxford.

——(2006) Why do people cooperate? *Politics, Philosophy and Economics*, 5 (1), 81–96.

——(2007a) *Game theory. A very short introduction*. Oxford University Press: Oxford.

——(2007b) *Playing for real: a text on game theory*. Oxford University Press: Oxford.

——(2010) Game theory and institutions. *Journal of Comparative Economics*, 38 (3), 245–52.

Binmore, K. and Klemperer, P. (2002) The biggest auction ever: the scale of the 3G telecom licences. *The Economic Journal*, 112, C74–96.

Bobot, L. (2008) Teaching negotiation for town planners in France. *Journal of European Real Estate Research*, 1 (2), 183–200.

Boghossian, P. (2006) *Fear of knowledge. Against relativism and constructivism*. Oxford University Press: Oxford.

Boyne, G. A. (1996) Competition and local government: a public choice perspective. *Urban Studies*, 33 (4–5), 703–21.

Bramley, G. (1999) Housing market adjustment and land supply constraints. *Environment and Planning A*, 37, 1169–88.

——(2007) The sudden rediscovery of housing supply as a key policy challenge. *Housing Studies*, 22, 221–41.

Brams, S. J. (1975) *Game theory and politics*. Macmillan: London.

Brand, R. and Gaffikin, F. (2007) Collaborative planning in an uncollaborative world. *Planning Theory*, 6, 282–313.

Breda-Vázquez, I. and Oliveira, C. (2008) Coalition-building in Portuguese spatial planning: is there a Southern European context? *European Planning Studies*, 16 (6), 761–84.

Brenner, N. (1999) Globalisation as reterritorialisation: the rescaling of urban governance in the European Union. *Urban Studies*, 36 (3), 431–51.

——(2004) *New state spaces: urban governance and the rescaling of statehood*. Oxford University Press: Oxford.

Bresnahan, T. F. (1989) Empirical studies of industries with market power. In R. Schmalensee and R. Willig (eds) *Handbook of industrial organization*. North Holland: Amsterdam.

Bresnahan, T. F. and Reiss, P. C. (1991) Empirical models of discrete games. *Journal of Econometrics*, 48, 57–81.

Bridges, D. (1998) Research for sale: moral market or moral maze? *British Educational Research Journal*, 24, 593–607.

Brown, K. and Rosendo, S. (2000) Environmentalists, rubber tappers and empowerment: the politics and economics of extractive reserves. *Development and Change*, 31, 201–27.

Brunsdon, C. and Fotheringham, A. S. (1996) Geographically weighted regression: a method for exploring spatial nonstationarity. *Geographical Analysis*, 28 (4), 281–98.

Bruton, M. and Nicholson, D. (1987) *Local planning in practice*. Stanley Thornes: Cheltenham.

Buitelaar, E. (2004) A transaction cost analysis of the land development process. *Urban Studies*, 41 (13), 2539–53.

Bunnell, G. (1995) Planning gain in theory and practice – negotiation of agreements in Cambridgeshire. *Progress in Planning*, 44, 1–113.

Burkardt, N., Lamb, B. L. and Taylor, J. G. (1998) Desire to bargain and negotiation success: lessons about the need to negotiate from six hydropower disputes. *Environmental Management*, 22 (6), 877–86.

Byrne, D. (2003) Complexity theory and planning theory: a necessary encounter. *Planning Theory*, 2 (3), 171–78.

Callies, D. L. and Grant, M. (1991) Paying for growth and planning gain: an Anglo-American comparison of development conditions, impact fees and development agreements. *Urban Lawyer*, 221.

Camerer, C. (2003) *Behavioural game theory: experiments in strategic interaction*. Princeton University Press: Princeton, NJ.

Campbell, H. (2003) Interface: reforming planning systems. *Planning Theory and Practice*, 4 (3), 347–48.

Campbell, H. and Marshall, R. (2002) Utilitarianism's bad breath? A reevaluation of the public interest justification for planning. *Planning Theory*, 1 (2), 163–86.

Cárdenas, J-C. and Ostrom, E. (2004) What do people bring into the game? Experiments in the field about cooperation in the commons. *Agricultural Systems*, 82, 307–26.

Carnap, R. (1959) The elimination of metaphysics through the logical analysis of language. In A. J. Ayer, *Logical positivism*, 60–81. Free Press, Glencoe, IL.

Carraro, C., Marchiori, C. and Sgobbi, A. (2005) Applications of negotiation theory to water issues. World Bank Research Working Paper 3641. World Bank: New York City: NY.

Castells, M. (1992) The world has changed, can planning change? *Landscape and Urban Planning*, 22, 73–78.

Castree, N. and MacMillan, T. (2004) Old news: representation and academic novelty. *Environment and Planning A*, 36, 469–80.

Cheshire, P. and Sheppard, S. (1989) British planning policy and access to housing: some empirical estimates. *Urban Studies*, 26, 469–85.

—(2005) The introduction of price signals into land use planning decision making: proposal. *Urban Studies*, 42 (4), 647–63.

Chettiparamb, A. (2006) Metaphors in complexity theory and planning. *Planning Theory*, 3 (1), 71–91.

Chiu, C. P. and Lai, S. K. (2009) An experimental comparison of negotiation strategies for siting NIMBY facilities. *Environment and Planning B: Planning and Design*, 36, 956–67.

Cho, I-K. and Kreps, D. M. (1987) Signaling games and stable equilibria. *The Quarterly Journal of Economics*, CII (2), 179–221.

Clarke, R., Lawrence, A. and Foster, S. (1996) *Groundwater: a threatened resource*. United Nations Environment Programme: Nairobi, Kenya.

Claydon, J. (1985) Negotiating in planning. *The Planner*, 76 (41), 11–13.

—(1996) Negotiations in planning. In C. Greed (ed.) *Implementing town planning: the role of town planning in the development process*, 110–20. Longman: Harlow.

Claydon, J. and Smith, B. (1997) Negotiating planning gains through the development control system. *Urban Studies*, 34 (12), 2003–22.

Clover, C. (2007) Kelly does more harm than the Luftwaffe. *Daily Telegraph*, 12th April, 2007. Available at: http://www.telegraph.co.uk/comment/personal-view/3639141/Kelly-does-more-harm-than-the-Luftwaffe.html. Accessed 19th June 2011.

Coase, R. (1937) The nature of the firm. *Economica*, 4 (16), 386–405.

Cochrane, A., Peck, J. and Tickell, A. (1996) Manchester plays games: exploring the local politics of globalization. *Urban Studies*, 33 (8), 1319–36.

Coliva, A. (2010) Was Wittgenstein an epistemic relativist? *Philosophical Investigations*, 33 (1), 1–23.

Colman, A. M. (1995) *Game theory and its applications*. Routledge: London.

Connelly, S. and Richardson, T. (2004) Exclusion: the necessary difference between ideal and practical consensus. *Journal of Environmental Planning and Management*, 47 (1), 3–17.

Cooke, B. and Kothari, U. (eds) (2001) *Participation: the new tyranny?* Zed Books: London.

Cox, J. C. and Hayne, S. C. (2006) Barking up the right tree: are small groups rational agents? *Experimental Economics*, 9 (3), 209–22.

Crawford, V. P. and Sobel, J. (1982) Strategic information transmission. *Econometrica*, 50 (6), 1431–51.

Davies, H. T. O. and Nutley, S. M. (1999) The rise and rise of evidence in health care. *Public Money and Management*, 19, 9–16.

Davies, H. T. O., Nutley, S. M. and Smith, P. C. (eds) (2000) *What works? Evidence-based policy and practice in public services*. Policy Press: Bristol.

Davies, J. S. (2002) Urban regime theory: a normative-empirical critique. *Journal of Urban Affairs*, 24 (1), 1–17.

—(2003) Partnerships versus regimes: why regime theory cannot explain urban coalitions in the UK. *Journal of Urban Affairs*, 25 (3), 253–69.

Davoudi, S. (2006a) Evidence-based planning. Rhetoric and reality. *disP*, 42, 14–24.

——(2006b) The evidence–policy interface in strategic waste planning for urban environments: the 'technical' and the 'social' dimensions. *Environment and Planning C: Government and Policy*, 24, 681–700.

DCLG (Department for Communities and Local Government) (2006) *Delivering affordable housing.* HMSO: London.

——(2011) *Localism and decentralisation bill.* HMSO: London.

de Carlo, L. (2002) A proposal to use mediation and night correspondents to curb urban violence in Cergy, France. *Negotiation Journal*, 18 (2): 163–75.

——(2006) The French high-speed Méditerranée train decision process: a large-scale public decision case study. *Conflict Resolution Quarterly*, 24 (1), 3–30.

de Roo, G. and Silva, A. (eds) (2010) *A planner's encounter with complexity.* Ashgate: Farnham.

Dear, M. J. (1986) Postmodernism and planning. *Environment and Planning D: Society and Space*, 4, 367–84.

——(1989) Survey 16: privatization and the rhetoric of planning practice. *Environment and Planning D: Society and Space*, 7, 449–62.

Deas, I. and Ward, K. (1999) The song has ended but the melody lingers: regional development agencies and the lessons of the urban development experiment. *Local Economy*, 14 (2), 114–32.

——(2000) From the new localism to the new regionalism? The implications of RDAs for regional local relations. *Political Geography*, 19 (3), 55–75.

Dehaene, M. (2002) Survey and the assimilation of a modernist narrative in urbanism. *The Journal of Architecture*, 7 (1), 33–55.

Dennett, D. C. (1987) *The intentional stance.* MIT Press: Cambridge, MA.

Dixit, A. and Skeath, S. (2004) *Games of strategy.* W. W. Norton & Co.: New York City: NY.

Dixon, L. S. (1999) Common property aspects of ground-water use and drainage generation. In A. Dinar and D. Zilberman (eds) *The economics and management of water and drainage in agriculture*, 677–97. Kluwer: Boston.

Dobbs, L. and Moore, C. (2002) Engaging communities in area based regeneration: the role of participatory evaluation. *Policy Studies*, 23, 157–71.

Douglas, J. D. (2010) Understanding everyday life. In J. D. Douglas (ed.) *Everyday life*, 3–28. Transaction Publishing: New Brunswick, NJ.

Drummond, W. J. and French, S. P. (2008) The future of GIS in planning. *Journal of the American Planning Association*, 74 (2), 161–74.

Ehrman, R. (1990) *Nimbyism: The disease and the cure.* Centre for Policy Studies: London.

El Ansari, W., Phillips, C. J. and Hammick, M. (2001) Collaboration and partnerships: developing the evidence base. *Health and Social Care in the Community*, 9, 215–27.

Elkin, S. L. (1987) *City and regime in the American republic.* University of Chicago Press: Chicago: IL.

Elson, M. J. (1986) *Green belts: conflict mediation in the urban fringe.* Heinemann: London.

Elwood, S. (2002) Neighbourhood revitalization through 'collaboration': assessing the implications of neoliberal urban policy at the grassroots. *Geojournal*, 58, 121–30.

——(2004) Partnerships and participation: reconfiguring urban governance in different state contexts. *Urban Geography*, 25 (8), 755–70.

Ennis, F. (1996) Planning obligations and developers. *Town Planning Review*, 67 (2), 145–60.

——(1997) Infrastructure provision, the negotiating process and the planner's role. *Urban Studies*, 34 (12), 1935–54.

Ernest, P. (1994) Conversation as a metaphor for mathematics and learning. In *Proceedings of the British Society for research into learning mathematics day conference, Manchester Metropolitan University*, 58–63. BSRLM: Nottingham.

Evans, A. W. (1988) *No room, no room!* Occasional Paper No. 79. Institute of Economic Affairs: London.

——(1991) Rabbit hutches on postage stamps: planning, development and political economy. *Urban Studies*, 28, 853–70.

——(2003) Shouting very loudly: economics, planning and politics. *Town Planning Review*, 74, 195–212.

Evans, B. (1993) Why we no longer need a planning profession. *Planning Practice and Research*, 8 (1), 9–15.

——(1995) *Experts and environmental planning*. Avebury: Aldershot.

Faludi, A. (1973) *Planning theory*. Pergamon: Oxford.

——(1986) *Critical rationalism and planning methodology*. Pion: London.

——(1987) *A decision centred view of environmental planning*. Pergamon: Oxford.

——(2002) Positioning European spatial planning. *European Planning Studies*, 10 (7), 897–909.

Faludi, A. and Hamnett, S. (1975) *The study of comparative planning*. Centre for Environmental Studies, CES CP, vol. 13. Delft University of Technology: Luxembourg.

Faludi, A. and Waterhout, B. (2006a) Introducing evidence-based planning. *disP*, 42, 4–13.

——(2006b) Debating evidence-based planning. *disP*, 42, 71–72.

Farrell, J. and Rabin, M. (1996) Cheap talk. *Journal of Economic Perspectives*, 10 (3), 103–18.

Few, R. (2002) Researching actor power: analyzing mechanisms of interaction and negotiations over space. *Area*, 34 (1), 29–38.

Filion, P. (1996) Metropolitan planning objectives and implementation constraints. Planning in a post-fordist and post-modern age. *Environment and Planning A*, 28 (9), 1637–60.

——(1999) Rupture or continuity: modern and postmodern planning in Toronto. *International Journal of Urban and Regional Research*, 23 (3): 421–45.

Finlay, W. and Brown, J. (2011) *Housing scandal! Pathfinder: a post-mortem*. SAVE Britain's Heritage. Available at: http://www.savebritainsheritage.org/docs/articles/Jb%20intro.pdf. Accessed 29 June 2011.

Fisher, R. and Shapiro, D. (2005) *Beyond reason: using emotions as you negotiate.* Viking Books: New York City, NY.

Fisher, R., Ury, W. and Patton, B. (1991) *Getting to yes,* 2nd Edition. Random House: London.

Fischler, R. (2000) Communicative planning theory: a Foucauldian assessment. *Journal of Planning Education and Research,* 19, 358–68.

Flyvbjerg, B. (1996) The dark side of planning: rationality and 'realrationalität'. In S. Mandelbaum, L. Mazza and R. Burchell (eds) *Explorations in planning theory,* 383–94. Center for Urban Policy Research, Rutgers University: New Brunswick, NJ.

——(1998a) *Rationality and power.* University of Chicago Press: Chicago, IL.

——(1998b) Habermas and Foucault: thinkers for civil society? *The British Journal of Sociology,* 49 (2), 210–33.

——(2002) Bringing power to planning research: one researcher's praxis story. *Journal of Planning Education and Research,* 21, 353–66.

Flyvbjerg, B. and Richardson, T. (2002) Planning and Foucault: in search of the dark side of planning theory. In P. Allmendinger and M. Tewdwr-Jones (eds) *Planning futures: new directions for planning theory,* 44–62. Routledge: London.

Fodor, J. A. (1980) Methodological solipsism considered as a research strategy in cognitive psychology. *The Behavioural and Brain Sciences,* 3, 63–109.

Forester, J. (1980) Critical theory and planning practice. *Journal of the American Planning Association,* 46 (3), 275–86.

——(1982) Planning in the face of power. *Journal of the American Planning Association,* 48 (1), 67–80.

——(1987) Planning in the face of conflict: negotiation and mediation strategies in local land use regulation. *Journal of the American Planning Association,* 53, 303–14.

——(1989) *Planning in the face of power.* University of California Press: Berkeley, CA.

——(1993) *Critical theory, public policy and planning practice.* State University of New York Press: Albany, NY.

——(1996) Beyond dialogue to transformative learning: how deliberative rituals encourage political judgment in community planning processes. In S. Esquith (ed.) *Democratic dialogues: theories and practices,* 141–68. University of Poznan: Poznan.

——(1999a) *The Deliberative practitioner: encouraging participatory planning processes.* MIT Press: Cambridge, MA.

——(1999b) Reflections on the future understanding of planning practice. *International Planning Studies,* 4, 175–94.

——(2003) On fieldwork in a Habermasian way: critical ethnography and the extra-ordinary charter of ordinary processional work. In Mats Alvesson and Hugh Willmott (eds) *Studying management critically,* 46–65. Sage: London.

——(2006) Exploring urban practice in a democratising society: opportunities, techniques and challenges. *Development Southern Africa,* 23 (5), 569–86.

Fotion, N. (1995) Logical Positivism. In T. Honderich (ed.) *The Oxford companion to philosophy,* 507–8. Oxford University Press: Oxford.

Freud, S. (1922) *Group psychology and the analysis of ego.* Translated by James Strachey. W. W. Norton & Company: New York City, NY.

——(1930) *Civilisation and its discontents.* Penguin: London.

Fudenberg, D. and Tirole, J. (1991) *Game theory.* MIT Press: Cambridge, MA.

Gamson, W. A. (1961) A theory of coalition formation. *American Sociological Review,* 26 (3), 373–82.

Geach, P. T. (ed.) (1988) *Wittgenstein's lectures on philosophy of psychology 1946–7. Notes by P. T. Geach, K. J. Shah and A. C. Jackson.* Harvester Press: London.

Geddes, P. (1905) *Civics: as applied sociology.* The Echo Library: Teddington.

——(1915) *Cities in evolution.* Williams and Norgate: London.

Giddens, A. (1984) *The constitution of society. Outline of the theory of structuration.* Polity Press: Cambridge.

——(1994) *Beyond Left and Right.* Polity Press: Cambridge.

——(1998a) Globalization: the runaway world. Keynote address, Prix Latsis Universitaires. Available at: http://www.fondationlatsis.org/plpdf/guest_speakers/Guest_1998.pdf. Accessed, 26 May 2011.

——(1998b) *The third way: the renewal of social democracy.* Polity Press: Cambridge.

——(2002) *Runaway world. How globalisation is reshaping our lives.* Profile Books: London.

Gintis, H. (2000) *Game theory evolving: a problem centred introduction to modelling strategic interaction.* Princeton University Press: Princeton, NJ.

——(2009) *The bounds of reason: game theory and the unification of the behavioural sciences.* Princeton University Press: Princeton, NJ.

Gintis, H., Bowles, S., Boyd, R. and Fehr, E. (eds) (2006) *Moral sentiments and material interests: the foundations of cooperation in economic life.* MIT Press: Cambridge, MA.

Glasson, B. and Booth, P. (1992) Negotiation and delay in the development control process. Case studies in Yorkshire and Humberside. *Town Planning Review,* 63 (1), 63–78.

Glimcher, P. W. (2004) *Decisions, uncertainty and the brain. The science of neuroeconomics.* MIT Press: Cambridge, MA.

Glimcher, P. W., Fehr, E., Camerer, C., Rangel, A. and Poldark, R. A. (2008) *Neuroeconomics. Decision making and the brain.* Academic Press: London.

Goodchild, B., Booth, C. and Henneberry, J. (1996) Impact fees. A review of alternatives and their implications for planning practice in Britain. *Town Planning Review,* 67 (2), 161–81.

Govindon, S. and Wilson, R. (2008) *Decision-theoretic forward induction.* Research Paper No. 1986. Stanford Graduate School of Business: Stanford, CA.

Grüne-Yanoff, T. and Schweinzer, P (2008) The roles of stories in applying game theory. *Journal of Economic Methodology,* 15 (2), 131–146.

Gunder, M. and Hillier, J. (2009) *Planning in ten words or less.* Ashgate: Farnham.

Güth, W. and Tietz, R. (1990) Ultimatum bargaining behaviour: A survey and comparison of experimental results. *Journal of Economic Psychology,* 11, 417–49.

Habermas, J. (1975) *Legitimation crisis.* Translated by Thomas McCarthy. Heinemann: London.

———(1984) *The theory of communicative action; volume 1: reason and the rationalization of society.* Translated by T. McCarthy. Polity Press: Cambridge.

———(1987) *The philosophical discourse of modernity.* MIT Press: Cambridge, MA.

Hacker, P. M. S. (1995a) Wittgenstein. In T. Honderich (ed.) *The Oxford companion to philosophy.* Oxford University Press: Oxford.

———(1995b) Private language problem. In T. Honderich (ed.) *The Oxford companion to philosophy.* Oxford University Press: Oxford.

Hagen, E. H. and Hammerstein, P. (2006) Game theory and human evolution: a critique of some recent interpretations of experimental games. *Theoretical Population Biology,* 69, 339–48.

Hajer, M. A. (1993) Discourse coalitions and the institutionalization of practice: the case of acid rain in Great Britain. In F. Fischer and J. Forester (eds) *The argumentative turn in policy analysis and planning,* 43–76. Duke University Press: Durham, NC.

———(1995) *The politics of environmental discourse. Ecological modernization and the politics of the policy process.* Oxford University Press: Oxford.

Hajer, M. and Zonneveld, W. (2000) Spatial planning in the network society – rethinking the principles of planning in the Netherlands. *European Planning Studies,* 8 (3), 337–55.

Hall, P. and Tewdwr-Jones, M. (2010) *Urban and regional planning,* 5th Edition. Routledge: Oxford.

Hamelink, C. J. (2008) Urban conflict and communication. *The International Communication Gazette,* 70 (3–4), 291–301.

Hanley, N. (2001) Cost-benefit analysis and environmental policy making. *Environment and Planning C: Government and Policy,* 19, 103–18.

Hardin, G. (1968) The tragedy of the commons. *Science,* 162 (3859), 1243–48.

Harding, A. (2000) Regime formation in Edinburgh and Manchester. In G. Stoker (ed.) *The new politics of British local governance.* Macmillan: London.

Hargreaves-Heap, S. P. and Varoufakis, Y. (1995) *Game theory: A critical introduction.* Routledge: London.

Harper, T. L. and Stein, S. M. (1995) Out of the post-modern abyss: preserving the rationale for liberal planning. *Journal of Planning Education and Research,* 14 (4), 233–44.

Harris, N. (2002) Collaborative planning: from critical foundations to practice forms. In P. Allmendinger and M. Tewdwr-Jones (eds) *Planning futures: new directions for planning theory,* 21–43. Routledge: London.

Harris, S. (2002) Modernising governance: the impact on policy and research communities in the United Kingdom. *International Studies in Sociology of Education,* 12, 319–34.

Harsanyi, J. C. (1967) Games with incomplete information played by 'Bayesian' players. Part I, the basic model. *Management Science,* 14 (3), 159–82.

———(1968a) Games with incomplete information played by 'Bayesian' players. Part II, Bayesian equilibrium points. *Management Science,* 14 (5), 320–34.

——(1968b) Games with incomplete information played by 'Bayesian' players. Part III, the basic probability distribution of the game. *Management Science*, (14) 7, 486–502.

Harvey, D. (2005) *A brief history of neoliberalism*. Oxford University Press: Oxford.

Hausman, D. M. and McPherson, M. S. (1996) *Economic analysis and moral philosophy*. Cambridge University Press: Cambridge.

Healey, P. (1990) Policy processes in planning? *Policy and Politics*, 18 (1), 91–103.

——(1991) Debates in planning thought. In H. Thomas and P. Healey (eds) *Dilemmas of planning practice: ethics, legitimacy and the validation of knowledge*, 11–33. Avebury: Aldershot.

——(1992a) A planner's day: knowledge and action in communicative practice. *Journal of the American Planning Association*, 58, 9–20.

——(1992b) Planning through debate. *Town Planning Review*, 63 (2), 143–62.

——(1992c) An institutional model of the development process. *Journal of Property Research*, 9, 33–44.

——(1993) The communicative work of development plans. *Environment and Planning B: Planning and Design*, 20, 83–104.

——(1997) *Collaborative planning. Shaping places in fragmented societies*. Macmillan: London.

——(1999) Sites, jobs and portfolios: economic development discourses in the planning system. *Urban Studies*, 36 (1), 27–42.

——(2000) Planning theory and urban and regional dynamics: a comment on Yiftachel and Huxley. *International Journal of Urban and Regional Research*, 24, 917–21.

——(2003) Collaborative planning in perspective. *Planning Theory*, 2 (2), 101–23.

——(2007a) The new institutionalism and the transformative goals of planning. In N. Verma (ed) *Institutions and planning*, 61–89. Elsevier: Oxford.

——(2007b) The 'collaborative planning' project in an institutionalist and relational perspective: a note. *Critical Policy Analysis*, 1 (1), 123–30.

——(2009) The pragmatic tradition in planning thought. *Journal of Planning Education and Research*, 28, 277–92.

Healey, P. and Barrett, S. M. (1990) Structure and agency in land and property development processes: some ideas for research. *Urban Studies*, 27 (1), 89–104.

Healey, P., McDougall, G. and Thomas, M. (eds) (1991) *Planning theory: prospects for the 1990s*. Pergamon: Oxford.

Healey, P., Purdue, M. and Ennis, F. (1993) *Gains from planning?* Joseph Rowntree Foundation: York.

Healey, P., Davis, J., Elson, M. and Wood, M. (1982), *The implementation of development plans*. Department of the Environment: London.

Healy, A. (2002) Commentary: evidence-based policy – the latest form of inertia and control. *Planning Theory and Practice*, 3, 97–98.

Heap, D. and Ward, J. (1980) Planning bargaining: the pros and cons or how much more can the system stand? *Journal of Planning and Environmental Law*, 631–37.

Hechter, M. (1992) The insufficiency of game theory for the resolution of real-world collective action problems. *Rationality and Society*, 4, 33–40.

Hideshima, E. and Okada, N. (1996) A game theoretic approach to cost allocation for infrastructure arrangement in an urban renewal project. *Interdisciplinary Information Sciences*, 2 (1), 11–25.

Hideshima, E., Okada, N., Yoshikawa, K. and Tskamoto, A. (1995) A game theoretic approach to multi-agent infrastructure development for urban renewal. JSCE *The Review of Infrastructure Planning*, 11, 295–302 (in Japanese).

Hillier, J. (1993) To boldly go where no planners have ever … . *Environment and Planning D: Society and Space*, 11, 89–113.

——(1998) Beyond confused noise: ideas towards communicative procedural justice. *Journal of Planning Education and Research*, 18, 14–24.

——(2000) Going round the back? Complex networks and informal action in local planning processes. *Environment and Planning A*, 32, 1–20.

Hintikka, J. and Kulas, J. (1983) *The game of language*. D. Reidel Publishing: Dordrecht, the Netherlands.

HM Treasury (2001) *Productivity in the UK: the regional dimension*. London: HM Treasury.

Hoch, C. (1984) Doing good and being right: the pragmatic connection in planning theory. *American Planning Association Journal*, 4, 335–45.

——(1992) The paradox of power in planning practice. *Journal of Planning Education and Research*, 12, 206–15.

——(1995) *What planners do*. Planners Press: Chicago, IL.

——(1996) A pragmatic inquiry about planning and power. In J. Seymour, L. Mandelbaum and R. Burchell (eds) *Explorations in planning theory*, 30–44. Center for Urban Policy Research: New Brunswick, NJ.

——(1997) Planning theorists taking an interpretive turn need not travel on the political economy highway. *Planning Theory*, 17, 13–64.

Hoch, C. and Cibulskis, A. (1987) Planning threatened: a preliminary report of planners and political conflict. *Journal of Planning Education and Research*, 6 (2), 99–107.

Hoernig, H. and Seasons, M. (2004) Monitoring of indicators in local and regional planning practice: concepts and issues. *Planning Practice and Research*, 19, 81–99.

Holgersen, S. and Haarstad, H. (2009) Class, community and communicative planning: urban redevelopment at King's Cross, London. *Antipode*, 41 (2), 348–70.

Holmwood, J. (2006) Economics, sociology and the 'professional complex'. *American Journal of Economics and Sociology*, 65 (1), 127–60.

Hooper, A. J. (1992) The construction of theory: a comment. *Journal of Property Research*, 9, 45–48.

Horgan, J. (1995) From complexity to perplexity. *Scientific American*, 272, 74–79.

Hudalah, D. and Woltjer, J. (2007) Spatial planning system in transitional Indonesia. *International Planning Studies*, 12 (3) 291–303.

Humphries, B. (2003) What else counts as evidence in evidence-based social work? *Social Work Education*, 22, 81–91.

Husserl, E. (1970) *The crisis of European sciences and transcendental phenomenology*. Translated by David Carr. Northwestern University Press: Evanston, IL.

Huxley, M. (2000) The limits to communicative planning. *Journal of Planning Education and Research*, 19, 369–77.

Huxley, M. and Yiftachel, O. (1998) New paradigm or old myopia? Unsettling the 'communicative turn' in planning theory. *Journal of Planning Education and Research*, 19, 333–42.

Imrie, R. and Raco, M. (1999) How new is the new local governance? Lessons from the United Kingdom. *Transactions of the Institute of British Geographers*, 24 (1), 45–63.

Inch, A. (2009) Planning at the crossroads again. Re-evaluating street level regulation of the contradiction in New Labour's planning reforms. *Planning, Practice and Research*, 24 (1), 83–101.

Innes, J. (1992) Group processes and the social production of growth management: Florida, Vermont and New Jersey. *Journal of the American Planning Association*, 58, 440–53.

——(1995) Planning theory's emerging paradigm: communicative action and interactive practice. *Journal of Planning Education and Research*, 14 (3), 183–90.

——(1998) Information in communicative planning theory. *Journal of the American Planning Association*, 64 (1), 52–63.

——(2004) Consensus building – clarifications for the critics. *Planning Theory*, 3 (1), 5–20.

Innes, J. and Booher, D. (1999) Consensus building and complex adaptive systems: a framework for evaluating collaborative planning. *Journal of the American Planning Association*, 65 (4), 412–23.

——(2000) *Public participation in planning: new strategies for the 21st century*. Working Paper 2000–2007. Institute of Urban and Regional Development, University of California at Berkley: Berkley, CA. Available at http://escholarship.org/uc/item/3r34r38h;jsessionid=65A5C37799855B4E2778D7D21661024E. Accessed 17 November 2010.

Innes, J. and Gruber, J. (2001) *Bay area transportation decision making in the wake of ISTEA: planning styles in conflict at the Metropolitan Transportation Commission*. University of California Transportation Center: Berkeley, CA.

Innes, J. E. and Booher, D. E. (2010) *Planning with complexity. An introduction to collaborative rationality for public policy*. Routledge: Oxford.

Innes, J., Gruber, J., Thompson, R. and Neuman, M. (1994) *Co-ordinating growth and environmental management through consensus-building*. University of California Press: Berkeley, CA.

Jaeger, G. (2009) Applications of game theory in linguistics. *Language and Linguistics Compass*, 2 (3), 406–21.

John, P. and Cole, A. (1998) Urban regimes and local governance in Britain and France: policy adaptation and coordination in Leeds and Lille. *Urban Affairs Review*, 33 (3), 382–404.

Jonas, A. E. G. and Bridge, G. (2003) Governing nature: the re-regulation of resources, land–use planning and nature conservation. *Social Science Quarterly*, 84 (4), 958–62.

Jowell, J. (1977) The limits of law in urban planning. *Current Legal Problems*, 30, 63–83.

Karacapilidis, N., Papadias, D. and Thomas Gordon, H. V. (1997) Collaborative environmental planning with GeoMed. *European Journal of Operational Research*, 102, 335–46.

Keil, R. and Ronneberger, K. (2000) The globalization of Frankfurt am Main: core, periphery, and social conflict. In P. Marcuse and R. van Kempen (eds) *Globalizing cities: a new spatial order?*, 228–48. Blackwell: Oxford.

Kennedy, G. (1982) *Everything is negotiable*. Business Books: London.

——(1988) *Kennedy on negotiations*. Gower: London.

——(1992) *The perfect negotiator*. Random House: London.

Kennedy, G., Benson, J. and McMillan, J. (1980) *Managing negotiations*. Business Books: London.

Kenny, A. (2000) *Frege: an introduction to the founder of modern analytic philosophy*. Wiley-Blackwell: London.

Kipfer, S. and Keil, R. (2002) Toronto Inc? Planning the competitive city in the New Toronto. *Antipode*, 34 (2), 227–64.

Kirchsteiger, G. (1994) The role of envy in ultimatum games. *Journal of Economic Behaviour and Organization*, 25 (3), 373–89.

Kitchen, T. and Whitney, D. (2004) Achieving more effective public engagement with the English planning system. *Planning Practice and Research*, 19 (4), 393–413.

Klemperer, P. (2002) How (not) to run auctions: the European 3G telecom auctions. *European Economic Review*, 46, 829–45.

Kocher, M. G. and Sutter, M. (2005) The decision maker matters: individual versus group behaviour in experimental beauty contest games. *The Economic Journal*, 115, 200–223.

Kóczy, L. Á. (2007) A recursive core for partition function form games. *Theory and Decisions*, 63, 41–51.

Kriesberg, L. and S. J. Thorson (eds) (1991) *Timing and the de-escalation of international conflicts*. Syracuse University Press: Syracuse, NY.

Kunzmann, K. (2006) The Europeanization of spatial planning. In N. Adams, J. Alden and N. Harris (eds) *Regional development and spatial planning in an enlarged Europe*, 43–64. Ashgate: Aldershot.

Laffont, J.-J. (1997) Game theory and empirical economics: The case of auction data. *European Economic Review*, 41 (1), 1–35.

Lai, L. W. C. (1994) The economics of land-use zoning, a literature review and analysis of the work of Coase. *Town Planning Review*, 65 (1), 77–98.

——(2010) A model of planning by contract: implementing comprehensive state planning, freedom of contract, public participation and fidelity. *Town Planning Review*, 81 (6), 647–73.

Lai, L. W. C. and Lorne, F. T. (2006) Planning by negotiation for sustainable development. *Economic Affairs*, 26 (1), 54–58.

Landa, D. and Meirowitz, A. (2009) Game theory, information and deliberative democracy. *American Journal of Political Science*, 53 (2), 427–44.

Lasswell, H. D. (1951) The policy orientation. In D. Lerner and H. D. Lasswell (eds) *The policy sciences*, 3–15. Stanford University Press: Palo Alto, CA.

Lauria, M. and Whelan, B. (1995) Planning theory and political economy. *Planning Theory*, 15, 8–33.

Lax, D. A. and Sebenius, J. K. (1986) *The manager as negotiator*. The Free Press: New York City, NY.

Laycock, G. (2000) From central research to local practice: identifying and addressing repeat victimisation. *Public Money and Management*, 20, 17–22.

Leach, W. D. and Sabatier, P. A. (2005) Are trust and social capital the keys to success? Watershed partnerships in California and Washington. In P. A. Sabatier, W. Focht, M. Lubell, Z. Trachtenberg, A. Vedlitz and M. Matlock (eds) *Swimming upstream. Collaborative approaches to watershed management*, 233–59. MIT Press: Boston, MA.

Ledyard, J. O. (1995) Public goods: a survey of experimental research. In J. Kagel and A. Roth (eds) *Handbook of experimental economics*, 111–94. Princeton University Press, Princeton, NJ.

Levitt, S. D. and Dubner, S. J. (2007) *Freakonomics*. Penguin: London.

——(2010) *Superfreakonomics*. Penguin: London.

Lewis, R. (ed) (1992) *Rethinking the environment*. Adam Smith Institute: London.

Lindblom, C. (1959) The science of 'muddling through'. *Public Administration Review*, 19, 79–88.

Loáiciga, H. (2004) Analytic game-theoretic approach to ground-water extraction. *Journal of Hydrology*, 297, 22–33.

Loáiciga, H. A. and Leipnik, R. B. (2000) Closed-form solution to coastal aquifer management. *Journal of Water Resources Planning and Management*, 126 (1), 30–35.

Logan, J. R. and Molotch, H. (1987) *Urban fortunes*. University of California Press: Berkeley, CA.

Lord, A. D. and Hincks, S. (2010) Making plans: the role of evidence in England's reformed spatial planning system. *Planning Practice and Research*, 25 (4), 477–96.

Loughlin, M. (1981) Planning gain: law, policy and practice. *Oxford Journal of Legal Studies*, 1 (1), 61–97.

McCain, R. A. (2008) Cooperative games and cooperative organizations. *Journal of Socio-Economics*, 37 (6), 2155–67.

——(2009a) *Game theory and public policy*. Edward Elgar: Cheltenham.

——(2009b) Commitment and weakness of will in game theory and neoclassical economics. *The Journal of Socio-Economics*, 38, 549–56.

McCann, E. (2001) Collaborative visioning or urban planning as therapy? The politics of public-private policy making. *Professional Geographer*, 53 (2), 207–18.

McCarty, N. and Meirowitz, A. (2007) *Political game theory: an introduction*. Cambridge University Press: Cambridge.

McDermott, P. (1998) Positioning planning in a market economy. *Environment and Planning A*, 30, 631–46.

McGinn, M. (1997) *Wittgenstein and the Philosophical Investigations*. Routledge: London.

McGuirk, P. (1994) Economic restructuring and the realignment of the urban planning system: the case of Dublin. *Urban Studies*, 31 (2), 287–308.

——(2001) Situating communicative planning theory: context power and knowledge. *Environment and Planning A*, 33, 195–217.

——(2005) Neoliberalist planning? Re-thinking and re-casting Sydney's metropolitan planning. *Geographical Research*, 43 (1), 59–70.

McGuirk, P. and Dowling, R. (2009) Master-planned residential developments: beyond iconic spaces of neoliberalism? *Asia Pacific Viewpoint*, 50 (2), 120–34.

McLoughlin, J. B. (1969) *Urban and regional planning: a systems approach*. Faber and Faber: London.

Majoor, S. (2008) Progressive planning ideals in a neo-liberal context, the case of Ørestad, Copenhagen. *International Planning Studies*, 13 (2), 101–17.

Malbert, B. (1998) *Urban planning participation: linking practice and theory*. Chalmers University: Gothenburg.

Mandarano, L. A. (2008) Evaluating collaborative environmental planning outputs and outcomes: restoring and protecting habitat and the New York-New Jersey Harbor Estuary Programme. *Journal of Planning Education and Research*, 27, 456–68.

Mandelbaum, S. (1996) The talk of the community. In S. Mandelbaum, L. Mazza and R. Burchell (eds) *Explorations in planning theory*, xi–xix. Center for Urban Policy Research: New Brunswick, NJ.

Manson, S. and O'Sullivan, D. (2006) Complexity theory in the study of space and place. *Environment and Planning A*, 38 (4), 677–92.

Mäntysalo, R. (1999) Learning from the UK: towards market-oriented land-use planning in Finland. *Housing, Theory and Society*, 16 (4), 179–91.

——(2002) Dilemmas in critical planning theory. *Town Planning Review*, 73 (4), 417–36.

Margerum, R. (2002) Evaluating collaborative planning: implications from an empirical analysis of growth analysis. *American Planning Association Journal*, 68 (2), 179–93.

Marmot, M. G. (2004) Evidence-based policy or policy based evidence? *British Medical Journal*, 328, 906–7.

Martin, S. and Sanderson, I. (1999) Evaluating public policy experiments: measuring outcomes, monitoring progress or managing pilots? *Evaluation*, 5, 245–58.

Maskin, E. S. (1999) *Recent developments in game theory*. Edward Elgar: Cheltenham.

Maynard Smith, J. (1982) *Evolution and theory of games*. Cambridge University Press, Cambridge.

Maynard Smith, J. and Price, G. R. (1973) The logic of animal conflict. *Nature*, 246, 15–18.

190   *References*

Meen, G. (2005) On the economics of the Barker review of housing supply. *Housing Studies*, 20, 949–71.

Merleau-Ponty, M. (1962) *Phenomenology of Perception*. Translated by Colin Smith. Humanities Press: New York City, NY.

Meyerson, M. and Banfield, E. C. (1955) *Politics, planning and the public interest*. Free Press: New York City, NY.

Michels, R. (1915) *Political parties; a sociological study of the oligarchical tendencies of modern democracy*. Translated by Eden Paul and Cedar Paul, 2008. Kessinger Publishing: London.

Milgrom, P. (2004) *Putting auction theory to work*. Cambridge University Press: Cambridge.

Molotch, H. (1976) The city as growth machine. *American Journal of Sociology*, 82, 309–22.

Monk, R. (1991) *Wittgenstein: the duty of genius*. Penguin: London.

Moote, M. A., McClaran, M. P. and Chickering, D. K. (1997) Theory in practice: applying participatory democracy theory to public land planning. *Environmental Management*, 21 (6), 877–89.

Muller, J. (1992) From survey to strategy: twentieth century developments in western planning method. *Planning Perspectives*, 7 (2), 125–55.

Murtagh, B. (1998) Community, conflict and rural planning in Northern Ireland. *Journal of Rural Studies*, 14 (2), 221–31.

Nadin, V. (2006) *Spatial plans in practice: the role and scope of spatial planning*. CLG: London.

——(2007) The emergence of the spatial planning approach in England. *Planning Practice and Research*, 22, 43–62.

Nash, J. F. (1951) Non-cooperative games. *Annals of Mathematics*, 54 (2), 286–95.

Nedović-Budić, Z. (2001) Adjustment of planning practice to the new Eastern and Central European context. *Journal of The American Planning Association*, 67 (1), 38–52.

Neuman, M. (2000) Communicate this! Does consensus lead to advocacy and pluralism? *Journal of Planning Education and Research*, 19, 343–50.

Newman, J. (2001) *Modernising governance: New Labour, policy and society*. Sage: London.

Newman, K. and Ashton, P. (2004) Neoliberal urban policy and the new paths of neighbourhood change in the American inner city. *Environment and Planning A*, 36, 1151–72.

NHPAU (2008) *Meeting the housing requirements of an aspiring and growing nation: taking the medium and long-term view. Advice to the Minister about the housing supply range to be tested by Regional Planning Authorities*. National Housing and Planning Advice Unit: Fareham.

Nienhuis, I., van Dijk, T. and de Roo, G. (2011) Let's collaborate! But who's really collaborating? Individual interests as a leitmotiv for urban renewal and regeneration strategies. *Planning Theory and Practice*, 12 (01), 95–109.

Nientied, P. (1998) The question of town and regional planning in Albania. *Habitat International*, 22, 41–47.

Niskanen, W. A. (1971) *Bureaucracy and representative democracy*. Aldine: Chicago.

North-Whitehead, A. and Russell, B. (1927) *Principia mathematica*, volumes 1–3, 2nd Edition. Cambridge University Press: Cambridge.

Norris, P. (1999) *Critical citizens. Global support for democratic governance*. Oxford University Press: Oxford.

North, D. C. (1990) *Institutions, institutional change and economic performance*. Cambridge University Press: Cambridge.

——(2003) *The role of institutions in economic development*. Gunanr Myrdal Lecture. United Nations: Geneva, Switzerland. Available at: http://books. google.co.uk/books?hl=en&lr=&id=1ns8w24r3dAC&oi=fnd&pg=PP4& dq=%22problem+with+institutional+economics%22&ots=RI5LiRrq5R& sig=B-w1HF7_smT9-GWp1lwNqen4GyE#. Accessed 25 May 2011.

Nutley, S. M. and Davies, H. T. O. (2000) Making a reality of evidence-based practice: some lessons from the diffusion of innovations. *Public Money and Management*, 20, 35–42.

Nutley, S. M., Davies, H. T. O. and Tilley, N. (2000) Getting research into practice. *Public Money and Management*, 20, 3–6.

Nutley, S., Davies, H. and Walter, I. (2002) *Evidence-based policy and practice: cross sector lessons from the UK*, Working Paper 9. ESRC UK Centre for Evidence-based Policy and Practice, ESRC: Swindon.

ODPM (Office of the Deputy Prime Minister) (1998) *Modernising planning: a progress report*. HMSO: London.

——(2005) *Planning policy statement 1: delivering sustainable development*. HMSO: London.

Olsson, A. R. (2009) Relational rewards and communicative planning: understanding actor motivation. *Planning Theory*, 8, 263–81.

Ordeshook, P. C. (1986) *Game theory and political theory*. Cambridge University Press: Cambridge.

Osborn, T. (1989) Planning and the developer. *The Planner*, 75 (29), 28–31.

Ostrom, E. (1990) *Governing the commons: the evolution of institutions for collective action*. Cambridge University Press: New York City, NY.

——(1999) Coping with tragedies of the commons. *Annual Review of Political Science*, 2, 493–535.

——(2000) Collective action and the evolution of social norms. *Journal of Economic Perspectives*, 14, 137–58.

Outhwaite, W. (2009) *Habermas*, 2nd Edition. Polity Press: Cambridge.

Painter, C. and Clarence, E. (2001) UK local action zones and changing urban governance. *Urban Studies*, 38, 1215–32.

Parsons, W. (2002) From muddling through to muddling up – evidence-based policy making and the modernisation of British government. *Public Policy and Administration*, 17, 43–60.

Pawson, R. (2002a) Evidence-based policy: in search of a method. *Evaluation*, 8, 157–81.

——(2002b) Evidence-based policy: the promise of a 'realist synthesis'. *Evaluation*, 8, 340–58.

——(2006) Evidence-based policy: a realist perspective. Sage: London.

Peck, J. and Tickell, A. (1995) Business goes local: dissecting the 'business agenda' in Manchester. International Journal of Urban and Regional Research, 19 (1), 55–78.

——(2002) Neoliberalizing space. Antipode, 34 (3), 380–404.

Peck, J. and Ward, K. (2002) City of revolution. Restructuring Manchester. Manchester University Press: Manchester.

Peltonen, L. and Sairinen, R. (2010) Integrating impact assessment and conflict management in urban planning: experiences from Finland. Environmental Impact Assessment Review, 30, 328–37.

Pennington, M. (1996) Conservation and the countryside: by quango or market? Studies on the environment no. 6. Institute of Economic Affairs: London.

——(2000) Planning and the political market: public choice and the politics of government failure. Athlone: London.

——(2002) A Hayekian liberal critique of collaborative planning. In P. Allmendinger and M. Tewdwr-Jones (eds) Planning futures: new directions in planning theory, 187–205. Routledge: London.

Perri 6, (2002) Can policy making be evidence-based? MCC: Building Knowledge for Integrated Care, 10, 3–8.

Petersen, T. (1994) On the promise of game theory in sociology. Contemporary Sociology, 23 (4), 498–502.

Pietarinen, A. V. (2007) Game theory and linguistic meaning. Elsevier: San Diego, CA.

Pirrie, A. (2001) Evidence-based practice in education: The best medicine? British Journal of Educational Studies, 49, 124–36.

Pitcher, G. (1968) Preface. In G. Pitcher (ed) Wittgenstein: the Philosophical Investigations, vii-x. Macmillan: London.

Plato (2003) The Republic. Translated by D. Lee and H. D. P. Lee. Penguin: London.

Pløger, J. (2004) Strife: urban planning and agonism. Planning Theory, 3, 71–92.

Poulton, M. C. (1991) The case for a positive theory of planning. Part 1: what is wrong with planning theory? Environment and Planning B, Planning and Design, 18, 225–32.

Powell, M. and Moon, G. (2001) Health action zones: the third way of a new area based policy? Health and Social Care in the Community, 9, 43–50.

Prior, A. (2005) UK planning reform, a regulationist interpretation. Planning Theory and Practice, 6 (4), 465–84.

Purcell, M. (2009) Resisting neoliberalization: communicative planning or counter hegemonic movements? Planning Theory, 8 (2), 140–65.

Raquel, S., Szidarovsky, F., Coppola, Jr., E. and Abraham, R. (2007) Application of game theory for a groundwater conflict in Mexico. Journal of Environmental Management, 84, 560–71.

Rasmusen, E. (2007) Games and information. Blackwell: Oxford.

Reade, E. (1987) British town and country planning. Open University Press: Milton Keynes.

Reeder, H. P. (1979) Language and the phenomenological reduction: A reply to a Wittgensteinian objection. Man and World, 12, 35–46.

Rhodes, R. A. W. (1994) The hollowing out of the state: the changing nature of the public service in Britain. *The Political Quarterly*, 65 (2), 138–51.

——(1997) *Understanding governance*. Open University Press: Milton Keynes.

Richardson, T. (1996) Foucauldian discourse: power and truth in urban and regional policy making. *European Planning Studies*, 4 (3), 279–92.

Riley, J. G. (1975) Competitive signalling. *Journal of Economic Theory*, 10 (2), 174–86.

Riley, R. (1997) Central area activities in a post-communist city: Lódž, Poland. *Urban Studies*, 34, 453–70.

Rorty, R. (1979) *Philosophy and the mirror of nature*. Princeton University Press: Princeton, NJ.

——(1986) Foucault and epistemology. In D. Hoy (ed) *Foucault: a critical reader*, 41–49. Blackwell: Oxford.

Roth, A. E. (1991) Game theory as part of empirical economics. *The Economic Journal*, 101 (404), 107–14.

Rothschild, M. and Stiglitz, J. E. (1976) Equilibrium in competitive insurance markets: an essay on the economics of imperfect information. *Quarterly Journal of Economics*, 90 (4), 629–49.

Roughgarden, J. (2009) *The genial gene. Deconstructing Darwinian selfishness.* University of California Press: Berkeley, CA.

Rousseau, J. -J. (1755) *Discourse on the origin of inequality.* Translated by Franklin Philip, 1994. Oxford University Press: Oxford.

Russell, B. (1950) *Unpopular essays*. George Allen and Unwin: London.

——(1972) *The philosophy of logical atomism*. Open Court: Peru, IL.

Rydin, Y. (2003) *Conflict, consensus and rationality in environmental planning: An institutional discourse approach.* Oxford University Press: Oxford.

Rydin, Y. and Pennington, M. (2000) Public participation and local environmental planning: the collective action problem and the potential of social capital. *Local Environment*, 5 (2), 153–69.

Saarinen, E. (1979) *Game-theoretical semantics*. D. Reidel Publishing: Dordrecht: the Netherlands.

Sabatier, P. A. (1986) What can we learn from implementation studies? In F. X. Kaufmann, G. Majone, V. Ostrom and W. Wirth (eds) *Guidance, control and evaluation in the public sector*, 313–25. Walter de Gruyter: Berlin.

Sabatier, P. A. and Jenkins-Smith, H. C. (1999) The advocacy coalition framework: an assessment. In P. A. Sabatier (ed) *Theories of the policy process*, 117–66. Westview Press: Boulder, CO.

Sager, T. (1994) *Communicative planning theory*. Ashgate: Aldershot.

——(2005) Communicative planners as naïve mandarins of the neo-liberal state? *European Journal of Spatial Development*. Available at: http://www.nordregio.se/ejsd/debate051208.pdf. Accessed 27 January 2011.

——(2006) The logic of critical communicative planning: transaction cost alteration. *Planning Theory*, 5 (3), 223–54.

——(2009) Responsibilities of theorists: the case of communicative planning theory. *Progress in Planning*, 72 (1), 1–51.

Samsura, A. and van der Krabben, E. (2009) *Funding transport infrastructure developments through value capturing: a game theoretical analysis.* Paper presented to Positioning planning in the global crises: international conference on urban and regional planning to celebrate 50th anniversary of planning education in Indonesia, 12th–13th November, 2009. Institute of Technology of Bandung: Bandung, Indonesia.

Samsura, A., van der Krabben, E. and van Deemen, A. M. A. (2010) A game theory approach to the analysis of land and property development processes. *Land Use Policy,* 27 (2), 564–78.

Samuelson, P. A. and Nordhaus, W. D. (1995) *Economics,* 15th Edition. McGraw-Hill, New York City, NY.

Sandercock, L. (1998) *Towards Cosmopolis.* Wiley: London.

Sandercock, L. (ed) (1998) *Making the invisible visible: a multicultural planning history.* University of California Press: Berkeley, CA.

——(2000) When strangers become neighbours: managing cities of difference. *Planning Theory and Practice,* 1 (1), 13–30.

Sanderson, I. (2000) Evaluation in complex policy systems. *Evaluation,* 6, 433–54.

——(2003) Is it 'what works' that matters? Evaluation and evidence-based policy-making. *Research Papers in Education,* 18, 331–45.

Saxer, S. R. (1997) Local autonomy or regionalism? Sharing the benefits and burdens of suburban commercial development. *Indiana Law Review,* 30, 659–92.

——(2000) Planning gain, exactions and impact fees: a comparative study of planning law in England, Wales and the United States. *The Urban Lawyer,* 32, (1), 21–71.

Schön, D. A. (1973) *Beyond the stable state: public and private learning in a changing society.* Penguin Books: Harmondsworth.

——(1983) *The reflective practitioner.* Basic Books: New York City, NY.

Searle, G. and Cardew, R. (2000) Planning, economic development and the spatial outcomes of market liberalisation. *Urban Policy and Research,* 18 (3), 355–76.

Selten, R. (1964) Valuation of n-person games. In M. Dresher, L. S. Shapley and A. W. Tucker (eds) *Advances in game theory.* Annals of Mathematics Study, no. 52, 577–626. Princeton University Press: Princeton.

Sen, A. (1970) *Collective choice and social welfare.* Holden-Day: San Francisco, CA.

Shaban, R. A. (1987) Testing between competing models of sharecropping. *Journal of Political Economy,* 62 (3), 893–920.

Sheldon, H. and Claydon, J. (1991) *Negotiations in planning. Local authority/developer negotiations.* Working Papers 15, 16 and 17. Department of Town and Country Planning, Bristol Polytechnic: Bristol.

Shibata, K. (2008) Neoliberalism, risk and spatial governance in the developmental state: Japanese planning in the global economy. *Critical Planning,* 15, 92–118.

Shields, D. J., Tolwinski, B. and Kent, B. M. (1999) Models for conflict resolution in ecosystem management. *Socio-economic Planning Sciences,* 33, 61–84.

Shmueli, D. F., Kaufman, S. and Ozawa, C. (2008) Mining negotiation theory for planning insights. *Journal of Planning Education and Research,* 27, 359–64.

Shove, C. and Anderson, R. (1997) Russian city planning, democratic reform, and privatization: emerging trends. *Journal of Planning Education and Research*, 16, 212–21.

Shubik, M. (1971) The dollar auction game: a paradox in noncooperative behavior and escalation. *Journal of Conflict Resolution*, 15, 109–11.

Simons, H., Kushiner, S., Jones, K. and James, D. (2003) From evidence-based practice to practice-based evidence: The idea of situated generalisation. *Research Papers in Education*, 18, 347–64.

Smith, N. (1996) *The new urban frontier: gentrification and the revanchist city*. Routledge: London.

Snidal, D. (1985) The game theory of international politics. *World Politics*, 38 (1), 25–57.

Solesbury, W. (2001) *Evidence-based policy: whence it came and where it's going*. Working Paper 1, ESRC Centre for Evidence-based Policy and Practice. ESRC: Swindon.

——(2002) The ascendancy of evidence. *Planning Theory and Practice*, 3 (1), 90–96.

Southern, A. (2001) What matters is what works? The management of regeneration. *Local Economy*, 16, 261–74.

Spence, A. M. (1973) Job market signalling. *Quarterly Journal of Economics*, 87 (3), 355–77.

——(1974) *Market signalling: informational transfer in hiring and related screening processes*. Harvard University Press: Cambridge, MA.

St. Augustine (1961) *Confessions*. Penguin: London.

Stein, A. A. (1990) *Why nations cooperate: circumstance and choice in international relations*. Cornell University Press: Ithaca, NY.

Stein, S. M. and Harper, T. L. (2003) Power, trust and planning. *Journal of Planning Education and Research*, 23, 125–39.

Stern, D. G. (2004) *Wittgenstein's Philosophical Investigations: an introduction*. Cambridge University Press: Cambridge.

Stewart, P. (2001) Complexity theories, social theory and the question of social complexity. *Philosophy of the Social Sciences*, 31, 323–60.

Stiglitz, J. E. (1974) Incentives and risk sharing in sharecropping. *Review of Economic Studies*, 41 (2), 219–55.

——(1975) The theory of screening, education and the distribution of income. *American Economic Review*, 65 (3), 283–300.

——(1985) Credit markets and the control of capital. *Journal of Money, Credit and Banking*, 17 (2), 133–52.

——(2000) The contributions of the economics of information to twentieth century economics. *Quarterly Journal of Economics*, 115 (4), 1441–78.

Stoker, G. (1995) Regime theory in urban politics. In D. Judge, G. Stoker and H. Wolman (eds) *Theories of urban politics*, 54–71. Sage: London.

——(1999) The modernisers' guide to local government. In G. Hassan and C. Warhurst (eds) *A Different future: The modernisers' guide to Scotland*. Big Issue Books: Glasgow.

——(2010) Exploring the convention of experimentation in political science: micro-foundational insights and policy relevance. *Political Studies*, 58, 300–319.

Stoker, G. and Mossberger, K. (1994) Urban regime theory in comparative perspective. *Environment and Planning C: Government and Policy*, 12, 195–212.

Stone, C. N. (1989) *Regime politics: governing Atlanta, 1946–1988.* University Press of Kansas, Lawrence, KA.

Stroud, S. and Tappolet, C. (eds) (2008) *Weakness of will and practical irrationality.* Oxford University Press: Oxford.

Sugden, R. (2001) Ken Binmore's evolutionary social theory. *The Economic Journal*, 111, F213–43.

Supalla, R., Klaus, B., Yeboah, O. and Bruins, R. (2002) A game theory approach to deciding who will supply instream flow water. *Journal of the American Water Resources Association*, 38 (4), 959–66.

SURF (Centre for Sustainable Urban and Regional Futures) (2003) *Evaluating urban futures: enhancing quality and improving effectiveness.* Centre for Sustainable Urban and Regional Futures, University of Salford: Salford.

Susskind, L. and Cruikshank, J. (1987) *Breaking the impasse.* Basic Books, New York City, NY.

Susskind, L. and Ozawa, C. (1984) Mediated negotiation in the public sector: the planner as mediator. *Journal of Planning Education and Research*, 4 (1), 5–15.

Susskind, L. and Field, P. (1996) *Dealing with an angry public: the mutual gains approach to solving public disputes.* The Free Press: New York City, NY.

Tait, M. and Campbell, H. (2000) The politics of communication between planning officers and politicians: the exercise of power through discourse. *Environment and Planning A*, 32, 489–506.

Taylor, N. (1980) Planning theory and the philosophy of planning. *Urban Studies*, 17, 159–68.

Tewdwr-Jones, M. (2004) Spatial planning: principles, practice and culture. *Journal of Planning and Environment Law*, 57 (5), 560–69.

Tewdwr-Jones, M. and Allmendinger, P. (1998) Deconstructing communicative rationality: a critique of Habermasian collaborative planning. *Environment and Planning A*, 30, 1975–89.

Tewdwr-Jones, M. and Thomas, H. (1998) Collaborative action in local plan-making: planners' perception of 'planning through debate'. *Environment and Planning B: Planning and Design*, 25, 127–44.

Tewdwr-Jones, M. and Allmendinger, P. (2002) Conclusion. Communicative planning, collaborative planning and the post-positivist planning theory landscape. In P. Allmendinger and M. Tewdwr-Jones (2002) *Planning futures: new directions in planning theory*, 206–16. Routledge: London.

Thomas, M. J. (1979) The procedural planning theory of A. Faludi. *Planning Outlook*, 22 (2), 72–76.

Tiesdell, S. and Oc, T. (1991) The London Docklands Development Corporation 1981–91: a perspective on the management of urban regeneration. *Town Planning Review*, 62 (3), 311–30.

Tirole, J. (1988) *The theory of industrial organization.* MIT Press: Cambridge, MA.

Tullock, G. (1992) Games and preference. *Rationality and Society*, 4, 24–32.

Umenoto, K. (2001) Walking in another's shoes: epistemological challenges in participatory planning. *Journal of Planning Education and Research*, 21, 17–31.

Urban Task Force (2005) *Towards a strong urban renaissance*. Urban Task Force: London.

Van Damme, E. (1994) Evolutionary game theory. *European Economic Review*, 38, 847–58.

Van Driesche, J. and Lane, M. (2002) Conservation through conversation: collaborative planning for reuse of a former military property in Souk County, Wisconsin, USA. *Planning Theory and Practice*, 3 (2): 133–54.

van Gestel, T. and Faludi, A. (2005) Towards a European territorial cohesion assessment network. *Town Planning Review*, 76 (1), 81–92.

Varian, H. (1996) *Intermediate microeconomics*, 4th Edition. W. W. Norton & Company, New York City, NY.

Von Neumann, J. and Morgenstern, O. (1944) *Theory of games and economic behaviour*. Princeton University Press: Princeton, NJ.

Voogd, H. and Woltjer, J. (1999) The communicative ideology in spatial planning: some critical reflections based on the Dutch experience. *Environment and Planning B: Planning and Design*, 26, 835–54.

Wang, L., Fang, L. and Hipel, K. W. (2011) Negotiation over costs and benefits in brownfield redevelopment. *Group Decision and Negotiation*, 20 (4), 509–24.

Ward, H. (1996) Game theory and the politics of global warming: the state of play and beyond. *Political Studies*, XLIV, 850–871.

Ward, K. G. (1997) Coalitions in urban regeneration: a regime approach. *Environment and Planning A*, 29, 1493–1506.

Webster, C. J. (1998) Public choice, Pigouvian and Coasian planning theory. *Urban Studies*, 35 (1), 53–75.

Weibull, J. W. (1997) *Evolutionary game theory*. MIT Press: Cambridge, MA.

Weiss, A. (1995) Human capital vs. signalling explanations of wages. *Journal of Economic Perspectives*, 9 (4) 133–54.

Williams, G., Batho, S. and Russell, L. (2000) Responding to urban crisis: the emergency planning response to the bombing of Manchester City Centre. *Cities*, 17 (4), 293–304.

Winter, I. and Brooke, T. (1993) Urban planning and the entrepreneurial state: the view from Victoria, Australia. *Environment and Planning C: Government and Policy*, 11 (3), 263–78.

Wittgenstein, L. (1922) *Tractatus logico-philosophicus*. Translated by D. Pears and B. F. McGuiness. Routledge: London.

——(1953) *Philosophical investigations*. Translated by G. E. M. Anscombe and R. Rhees. Blackwell: Oxford.

——(1958) *The blue and brown books: preliminary studies for the Philosophical Investigations*. Blackwell: Oxford.

——(1980) Remarks on the philosophy of psychology. In G. E. M. Anscombe and G. H. von Wright (eds) *Remarks on the philosophy of psychology*. Blackwell: Oxford.

Wolsink, M. (2003) Reshaping the Dutch planning system: a learning process. *Environment and Planning A*, 35 (4), 705–23.

Woltjer, J. (2000) *Consensus planning: the relevance of communicative planning theory in Dutch infrastructure networks*. Ashgate: Aldershot.

Wong, C., Baker, M. and Kidd, S. (2006) Monitoring spatial strategies: the case of local development documents in England. *Environment and Planning C: Government and Policy*, 24, 533–52.

Wood, A. M. (2004) Domesticating urban theory? US concepts, British cities and the limits of cross-national applications. *Urban Studies*, 41 (11), 2103–18.

——(2005) Comparative urban politics and the question of scale. *Space and Polity*, 9 (3), 201–15.

Wu, F. L. (1997) Urban restructuring in China's emerging market economy: towards a framework for analysis. *International Journal of Urban and Regional Research*, 21, 640–63.

——(1999) The 'game' of landed-property production and capital circulation in China's transitional economy with reference to Shanghai. *Environment and Planning A*, 31, 1757–71.

Yiftachel, O. and Huxley, M. (2000) Debating dominance and relevance: notes on the 'communicative turn' in planning theory. *International Journal of Urban and Regional Research*, 24 (4), 907–13.

Yonay, Y. P. (1998) *The struggle over the soul of economics: institutionalist and neoclassical economists in America between the wars*. Princeton University Press: Princeton, NJ.

Young, K., Ashby, D., Boaz, A. and Grayson, L. (2002) Social sciences and the evidence-based policy movement. *Social Policy and Society*, 1, 215–24.

Zingales, L. (1994) The value of the voting right: a study of the Milan stock exchange experience. *Review of Financial Studies*, 7 (1), 125–48.

Index

Allmendinger, P. 20, 21, 25, 28, 40, 74
Analytical philosophy 41, 67, 170
Axelrod 95–7, 142

Bayesian updating 100–3, 129–131
Beauty contests 167–9
'black box' 4, 80–5, 147, 172
Binmore, K. : language 170; moral philosophy 64; fairness 66

Carnap, R. 22, 47
Chicken 119–123
Cho and Kreps. 124–140
Collaborative and communicative planning 22–8, 38, 49, 57, 73–80, 145

Delaying tactics 108, 118–123

Essential players 152–3, 160, 163
Evolution 142, 148–9

Faludi, A. 11–12, 14, 22, 53, 76
Flyvbjerg, B. 26, 28, 37, 40, 51, 53
Follow-the-Leader 98–104
Forester. 14, 20–3, 25, 31, 34, 38, 49, 115, 118
Foucauldian planning theory 37, 46–7, 51, 88
Frege, G. 45, 171
Freud, S. 165

Game Theoretical semantics 171
Game Theory: auctions 60–3, 72, 167–9; coalition formation 72,

77–80, 108, 141–162; discourse universe 100–1, 106, 126; extensive 94; strategic form 65; introduction to 63–67; Game Theory Olympiad 95; non-cooperative versus cooperative game theory 72–75; water management 93–94
Geddes, P. 10–11, 22
Giddens, A. 24, 26, 74
Grab the Dollar 118
Growth coalition thesis 143

Habermas, J. 9–10, 23, 27–37
Harsanyi, K. 100, and Harsanyi Transformation 100, 123, 162
Healey, P. 14, 22–5, 29–30, 38, 57, 73, 80
Huxley, M. 29–30

Impact fees 104–6, 135–7
Information economics: introduction to 1–5; and planning theory 58–60; applications of 62–4
Innes, J. 20, 27, 33, 35, 145
Institutional economics 57–8, 67

Leadership 157–160

Matching Pennies 90
McCain, R. 154, 159; and Waste Game 150–2
McGinn, M. 42, 44, 48–50
Merleau-Ponty, M. 43

Nash, J. 65; Nash Bargaining
   Solution 110–12, 115, 127–9;
   equilibrium 65–6, 82, 91, 94, 166
Negotiation 1, 59–62, 108, 114–17;
   in contrast to bargaining 117–120
Neoclassical economics 55–59;
   critique thereof 66–7, 99, 107–8,
   141, 172
Neoliberalism 20, 56, 58, 76–9, 86, 88

Ordinary language philosophy 39,
   41–5, 64, 135

Phenomenology 18, 21, 32–7, 40–9,
   51, 139
Planning gain 135–7
Plato 10, 164
Principled/positional strategies 114–17
Prisoners' Dilemma 82–3, 91, 94–6,
   141, 172; 'tit for tat' 96–7

Quiche-Beer Game 124–37

Rasmusen, E. 86, 98, 101–2, 119,
   134
Rational-Comprehensive planning 1,
   10–14, 18, 21–2; critique thereof
   33–7, 50, 80, 116, 166
Risk 89, 94, 109–12
Russell, B. 39, 45, 54, 171

Screening strategies 4, 60, 169
Signalling strategies 4, 30, 60, 94,
   120, 122–7, 134, 140, 169, 170;
   and cheap talk, 62, 135, 139, 166,
   168–9
Spatial planning 76–80
Stag Hunt Game 64–6, 72
Stiglitz, J. 59, 60, 62
Systems theory 11, 37, 116

Tewdwr-Jones, M. 10, 21, 24, 29, 76
'Theory–Practice Gap' 3, 21, 40
tragedy of the commons 92–4

Ultimatum Game 107–8, 142
Urban regime theory 143

Vienna Circle 47

War of Attrition 118
Wittgenstein, L. : later versus earlier
   philosophy 3–4; the 'Brown
   book' 42; language games 41, 50,
   84, 101, 135, 170; relativism 51;
   Philosophical Investigations 42–53;
   private language 43–4, 48, 52;
   Tractatus Logico-Philosophicus 3–4,
   39, 41–2

Zero-sum games 90, 115